Barbara Cartlidge and Electrum Gallery
A Passion for Jewellery

Barbara Cartlidge and Electrum Gallery
A Passion for Jewellery

Beatriz Chadour-Sampson
Janice Hosegood

arnoldsche ART PUBLISHERS

Contents

Foreword

‘The excellence of every art’, wrote Sir Joshua Reynolds in words that are carved over the main entrance to the Victoria and Albert Museum, ‘must consist in the complete accomplishment of its purpose’. For Barbara Cartlidge, ‘the fundamental purpose of jewellery lies in its spiritual and emotional content’. The three jewels from the late 1960s which represent her in the V&A radiate the passion of her making: stones of numinous depth mounted in silver settings charged with vigorous geometry. Around an agate pendant runs a repeated pattern of silver triangles topped with circles, an echo of the border around the text of the invitation to her first solo exhibition at Heal’s in 1960.

From Barbara’s jewellery, and that of the brilliant generation of jewellers working in the 1960s, sprang the Electrum Gallery in 1971. It became a towering achievement recognised internationally as one of the handful of pre-eminent galleries, a major creative force for the understanding of new work. The V&A bought designs by Susanna Heron and Roger Morris in 1976, jewels by Diego Piazza and Hermann Schafran in 1978, a set of tower rings by Wendy Ramshaw in 1981, an steel bangle by David Watkins from the tenth anniversary exhibition later that year, and a steel necklace by Tone Vigeland in 1984. In 1991 it acquired a brooch by Yasuki Hiramatsu, and, from the 20th anniversary exhibition in the same year, work by Friedrich Becker, Hermann Jünger, Elisabeth Holder and Mary Lee Hu.

Barbara’s writing has been as authoritative as her exhibitions. The modern section of *The Ring: From Antiquity to the Twentieth Century* and her magisterial *Twentieth-Century Jewelry* remain indispensable. For the latter, she was indefatigable in compiling over 200 biographies cross-referenced with 1176 exhibitions. We remember her delight when she nailed down another elusive date of birth.

Refugees from Germany enriched British culture immeasurably. Barbara stands with the writers, musicians, artists and academics whose vision became one of the transforming elements in post-War Britain. As jeweller, gallery director, curator, and author, Barbara is celebrated as a prime mover for nearly 50 years in what she described as the ‘brotherhood of jewellers who make modern and thought-provoking jewellery all over the world’.

Richard Edgcumbe and Clare Phillips
Victoria and Albert Museum

Introduction and Acknowledgements

The journey leading to this publication of the Barbara Cartlidge and Electrum Gallery story began at her Hampstead home and more precisely in her beloved home office. Throughout the years Barbara protected her purple painted work space like a hawk, letting few visitors cross the threshold of her inner sanctum. In the last decade, however, she began to invite family members and trusted friends to view her significant jewellery collection. Eventually due to physical difficulties, she was no longer able to climb the stairway leading to her spacious retreat and gradually needed more and more assistance in sorting out her paperwork. This task led to Barbara's daughter-in-law, Sarah Forni-Cartlidge, spending hundreds of hours shifting through Barbara's paraphernalia and personal effects – everything from 10-year-old grocery lists, lifestyle magazines and adverts of all sorts, which were intermingled with historically important correspondence from world renowned artist-jewellers. These letters and faxes reflected her world and the people she had worked with for over 50 years where she exchanged her thoughts and perceptions on contemporary jewellery – her life's passion. It was quickly discovered that Barbara did not throw anything away, perhaps due to her experiences during World War Two with daily rationing and the fact she had to abandon most of her adored personal possessions when she was forced to flee Nazi Germany and her Berlin family home in September 1938.

Sarah's time spent in this office became an archeological dig into Barbara's past and life history. It became evident to us, from what was being discovered, that Barbara's life was a rich and incredible story that needed to be told. Fortunately, over the years Sarah had purchased several pieces of jewellery from Electrum Gallery and thus met Janice Hosegood, the extremely capable and knowledgeable manager of Electrum Gallery for 22 years. Little did she know at the time that these visits to Electrum Gallery would lead to a more premeditated meeting with Janice at Café Rouge in Hampstead, London, which resulted in the birth of this book.

Initially, Janice and Sarah collaborated on a treasure hunt to determine the names of the jewellery designers whose works had found their way into Barbara's sizable collection. At this time, Barbara was showing signs of dementia so the task of identifying her jewellery pieces had to be undergone without the benefit of her expertise. Janice's own Electrum Gallery history and her wide knowledge of contemporary jewellery became invaluable during the many months of investigation. The wealth of archival material uncovered soon revealed that a book on the gallery and Barbara's life could be a subject of great interest to people who were fascinated with 20th-century jewellery history. Janice then arranged a meeting to introduce us to Dr Beatriz Chadour-Sampson, an international jewellery historian, author and lecturer who might contribute her expertise. Again as luck would have it, Beatriz had also met Barbara many years earlier in Cologne in 1985 at the Museum für Angewandte Kunst. Thankfully, Janice and Beatriz were willing to jump on board to continue the background research into Barbara's life history which included the less well known jewellery she made in the l960s and 1970s as well as the significance of Electrum Gallery. The added skill of Beatriz's fluency in the German language also brought valuable insight into understanding Barbara's early family history in Germany.

We also wish to acknowledge the following persons and institutions who have all played a significant role in this publication bringing Barbara's jewellery history to light and to the page: Dirk Allgaier of Arnoldsche Art Publishers for his foresight and advice regarding the publication and The Worshipful Company of Goldsmiths, of which Barbara is a liveryman, in particular to David Mills, Harriet Scott and Dick Melly, the recently retired Clerk, for their support in launching this book. We are indebted to Dr Richard Edgcumbe and Clare Phillips of the Victoria and Albert Museum for their commitment to having Barbara's avant-garde jewellery displayed in the William and Judith Bollinger Jewellery Gallery and writing the foreword to this book. Thanks to Dr Fritz Falk, retired Director of Schmuckmuseum in Pforzheim, Dr Elizabeth Goring of the National Museums of Scotland, and Rosemary Ransome Wallis, Curator of The Goldsmiths' Company Collection for their thoughtful contributions, along with Ann Westin on behalf of Torun Bülow-Hübe. Special gratitude goes to Sophie Lee for her painstaking proofing and editing. In addition, we wish to recognise Claus Bury, one of Barbara's favourite 'sons' who had a special relationship with Barbara over the years and was therefore able to assist with investigating Barbara's archival material along with other individuals who provided gainful background history into understanding Barbara's contributions to the contemporary jewellery world.

And finally we wish to thank all the artist-jewellers who exhibited at Electrum Gallery, and the selected few who have generously contributed their thoughts and reflections about the gallery and Barbara's vanguard contributions toward recognising contemporary jewellery as an art form.

We hope this book will be an inspiration and a delight to anyone who holds a shared passion for contemporary jewellery.

Sarah Forni-Cartlidge and Tony Cartlidge
September 2016

Barbara Cartlidge
Life and Work

Barbara Cartlidge
Life and Work

Beatriz Chadour-Sampson

Berlin in the 1920s

Barbara Cartlidge has led a remarkable life. Born Emma Feistmann in Berlin in 1922, events would eventually lead her to London where her creative talents and entrepreneurial spirit came to fruition. Electrum Gallery, which she founded in 1971, made London an international platform for contemporary jewellery. The success of the gallery, which was to continue for 36 years, was only possible through Barbara's foresight and dedication, shaped by her early experiences of life in pre-war Germany. Along with the influences of her liberal family and education, they would provide the foundation for her lifelong love of the arts and her strong sense of political commitment.

Barbara – a name she adopted in the late 1950s – spent her childhood and adolescence in the culturally vibrant city of Berlin during a tumultuous period in German political and cultural history. After the nation's humiliating defeat in the First World War, Germany suffered huge economic deprivation caused by the oppressive terms imposed by the 1919 Versailles peace treaty, which forced the country to pay reparation to other countries for war damage and loss. The new Weimar Republic, which replaced the old German imperial government in 1919 after the short-lived German Revolution, oversaw a period of mass unemployment and high inflation. Barbara mentions in one of her many interviews how the family was affected, how the basics of everyday life became unaffordable and paying bills a struggle.

By 1920 Berlin was the third largest city in the world, modern and cosmopolitan in outlook, but economically and politically unstable. This was largely due to the breakneck speed at which the city expanded during the early years of the Republic and the resulting disparity between the impoverished lives of factory workers and labourers and a growing class made prosperous from industry. The volatile environment encouraged the development of Communist movements protesting against social and economic injustices and would eventually lead to the emergence of Hitler's National Socialist German Workers' Party, which intended to draw workers away from Communism and into a militant nationalism.

Against this unsettled background it seems extraordinary that Berlin thrived as a centre of culture and of intellectual thought. In the 1920s it was renowned for its glitz and glamour. It was a city that never slept, boasting cabaret theatres, dance halls hosting jazz music newly imported from the United States, cinemas screening new avant-garde films and hedonistic bars and restaurants. Writers, artists and musicians from all over the world chose to settle in Berlin and experience its uninhibited and inspirational climate. In the arts there was a spirit of renewal and revolution against mainstream values as practitioners turned away from the Establishment in their search for new values. The left-wing November Group was one of the most radical creative movements, named after the start of the 1918–19 German Revolution. It consisted of politically-engaged Expressionist

Dust jacket for Kurt Tucholsky's *Deutschland, Deutschland über alles*, designed by John Heartfield, 1929

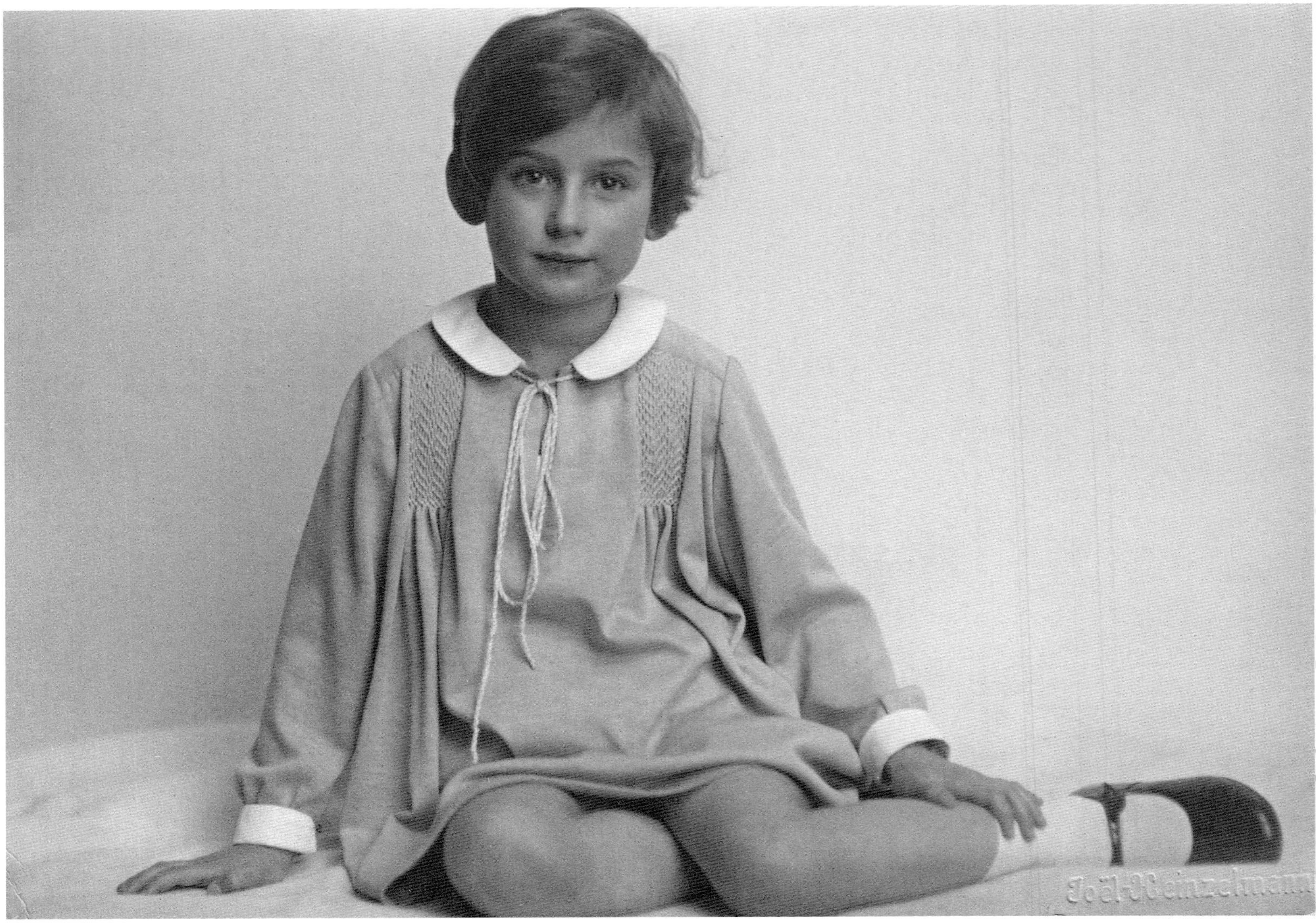

Emma ('Bobbi') Feistmann, 1925

artists, architects, musicians, playwrights and filmmakers – many of whom had experienced the horrors of World War I – who signed a declaration against bourgeois values and encouraged political action. They included the artists Otto Dix, George Grosz, Hannah Höch and John Heartfield. In later years Barbara would become friends with Heartfield, whom she greatly admired for his courage and commitment against Nazi propaganda.

Throughout the 1920s and into the 1930s Berlin continued to be a hub for new cultural movements with a political conscience, reflecting the tensions brought about by stark social contrasts. Chief among these were Dadaism, with its sympathies for the Communist aims of Russian Bolsheviks; the Neue Sachlichkeit (New Objectivity) art movement that expressed social criticism through depictions of everyday life and Cubism and Surrealism, movements which offered new ways of representing reality in art. Many artists and poets found a voice in the literary and art magazine *Der Sturm*, active in Berlin between 1910 and 1932. Its founder, Herwarth Walden, owned a gallery of the same name in which he promoted the revolutionary developments in contemporary German art. Among his protégés were, unusually for the time, a group of female avant-garde artists known as the 'Sturmfrauen' (Storm women). He recognised the increasingly significant role women now played in the arts.

The dynamism of Berlin during Barbara's early formative years, and the roles her family were to play within it, would leave a lasting impression on her. Her passions for the arts and for political activism were defined by the city of her birth.

A Liberal Jewish Family

The Feistmann family did not settle in Berlin until 1910 but originated in the South German (now Bavarian) town of Fürth, near Nuremberg. Little is known about Barbara's paternal grandfather Josef (Joseph) Feistmann but in family records he is described as a tall, handsome man and rather patriarchal. His wife Emma (neé Berlin) is portrayed as loving and good natured. Josef came from a well-situated and affluent family, whose prosperity derived from the production of roasted chicory, an additive or substitute for coffee, which was considered a luxury in the 19th century. Through an advantageous marriage, Josef's forebear Aron Feistmann (1812–80) had inherited the Julius Joel Cohn factory, founded in 1826, and turned it around to become a prosperous industrial enterprise.

In 1872 Josef became a partner and manager of this highly successful business. Fats were required in the production process and the factory prided itself on following strict Jewish rules and producing kosher chicory. The Jüdisches Museum Franken in Fürth holds some of the factory records and in the firm's heyday the scent of roasted chicory dominated the town. Fürth was well-known for its Jewish community which dated back to the 15th century and whose population increased steadily after Jews were deported from Vienna in 1716. By the time the Feistmann family settled there, the residing Jews were leading an increasingly emancipated life. The family appears to have been liberal-minded rather than orthodox and fully assimilated into the community.

In an interview, Barbara described her maternal grandfather Eugen Merzbacher as a devout Jewish gentleman and it is from this side of the family that we see the roots of Barbara's interest in social welfare. A renowned collector of coins, medals and antiques, Eugen lived with his wife Rosa (neé Jaffé) and their family in Munich, in the elegant Residenzstrasse immediately opposite the Residenz, the Bavarian Royal Palace. The Merzbachers held a privileged position in Munich – Eugen counted Italian royalty among his friends – and enjoyed considerable wealth. Their eldest daughter Elisabeth (1881–1966) became so concerned about the physical and spiritual well-being of the less fortunate children of Eastern European Jews that she invited them to her parental home for food and education.

Her parents were initially dismayed by her actions, fearing social repercussions, but later helped Elisabeth found the Merzbacher'sche Privatkindergarten, a private school. Her sister Luise, Barbara's mother, had been trained as a kindergarten teacher and supported this endeavour. As Barbara would demonstrate in her own life, welfare work and helping those in social or financial need was in the family genes.

The Merzbacher family tree contained an impressive number of people holding high public office in the 17th and 18th centuries, a considerable feat for a family of Jewish descent. Later generations took pride in the fact that these included a renowned Rabbi, Mordecai den Avraham Jaffé (about 1530–1612). He famously wrote the ten-part book *Levush Malchut* (Robes of Royalty) which outlined Jewish law and, for the first time in print, recounted the customs of the Eastern European Jews, the Ashkenazim. One ancestor from the Merzbacher line can be seen to foreshadow another of Barbara's passions. The Markgraf of Ansbach-Bayreuth granted Nathan Abraham Oberndoerffer, born 1762, and his wife Kele special permission as Jews to settle in Ansbach. Nathan was in the banking profession and was a retailer for silver and other metals, watches, precious gemstones and pearls. He had ties to the Court and became a very wealthy and influential member of his community. Jewellery was already playing a part in Barbara's history.

Barbara's immediate family played a huge role in shaping her character and guiding her interests. Josef Feistmann's eldest son, Barbara's father, was Wilhelm Eugen Feistmann (1875–1930), known as Willy, who worked alongside his father in the chicory factory at Fürth. Family records portray Willy as an honourable man and a democrat with an enthusiasm for politics. He travelled throughout Bavaria as a salesman for the business, but it gave him little satisfaction. Barbara later described Willy as a frustrated academic who had been obliged to take over the family business after his father's death. He continued rather unwillingly without success, and within a short space of time the factory was no longer profitable. Eventually it was handed over to new ownership and Willy decided to seek a new career.

Eugen and Rosa Merzbacher, 1900

Luise, Emma ('Bobbi') and Willy Feistmann, Berlin, 1930

In 1910 Willy moved to Berlin with his wife Luise (neé Merzbacher, 1886–1977), whom he married in 1907, and his two sons Rudolf (known as Rudi), born 28 January 1908 and Eugen, born 21 September 1909. He was able to join the business of Luise's uncle, a well-respected timber merchant named Schaje Jaffé, which specialised in railway sleepers and supplying fine woods for furniture makers, and owned saw mills in the Ruhr area, the major industrial heartland of Germany. There Willy found great fulfilment in his work, with a particular interest in carpentry. With their improved prosperity the Feistmanns could afford a large flat in Berlin and added to the family. Helene (known as Leni) was born on 10 March 1915, followed seven years later by their youngest child Emma (now Barbara, known as Bobbi after the South German word *bobbele*, meaning baby) on 2nd September 1922. In Barbara's memories he was a disciplinarian Prussian at heart, but warm and humorous. Men in the Feistmann family were known to be tall, but he exceeded them all. Tragically and unexpectedly, Willy died in 1930 aged 55 from a heart attack while on his way to work, leaving his wife to provide for the family. Their sons Rudolf and Eugen were already young men, but their two young daughters were her main concern.

Nothing could prepare Luise for the unfolding political turmoil in 1930s Germany. The family considered themselves Jewish but were not orthodox in their faith and Barbara recalls the childhood excitement of celebrating Christmas. As so often in liberal Jewish families of the time, it was the actions of the Third Reich that awakened their consciousness of their Jewish heritage. As Barbara has often said: 'I did not know I was Jewish until the Nazis came'.

Luise and Willy Feistmann on their wedding day, Munich, April 1907

Willy Feistmann with his son Rudolf ('Rudi'), Fürth, 1909

A Family in Exile

After the National Socialist Party came to power in Germany in 1933, the Feistmann family, like so many other Jewish families at the time, suffered the trauma of persecution and enforced separation and exile. Few documents from this aspect of the Nazi era in Berlin have survived and the personal accounts of those who lived through the horrors remain the chief source for this period. Archive material recounting the experiences of the Feistmann family tells extraordinary stories of courage and conviction in the face of fear.

Barbara's brothers Rudi and Eugen were young students when their father died in 1930, politically minded, idealistic in their views and Communist in outlook, much to the family's dismay. Their mindset was not uncommon for the generation that grew out of Germany's defeat in the First World War and revolted against the disastrous consequences of the Versailles Peace Treaty. Rudi studied law and became an active member of the Communist Party in 1929. He was a well-known opponent of the National Socialists who were anti-Marxist. When Rudi decided to leave home and live in a working class area, his father would only welcome him home for Sunday lunches.

Within the Feistmann family, Rudi was the worst affected by the unfolding political events. Trained as a journalist, his work for the German Communist Party brought him to the unwelcome attention of the Nazi party. In February 1933, the Communists were blamed by the Nazis for an arson attack on the Parliamentary building in Berlin, and for plotting against the German government. After this development, and the recent appointment of Adolf Hitler as German Chancellor in January 1933, Rudi knew he had to leave the country immediately. In a later birthday letter to Barbara, written when she was in Copenhagen in 1938, Rudi adds as a postscript: 'Do you know that it is exactly five years and five months that we have not seen each other. I left Berlin on 8th April 1933. At the time I

Rudolf ('Rudi') Feistmann in Mexico, c.1945

Eugen Feistmann in Berlin, 1933

could not explain to you why I was leaving. You wanted to go downstairs and play with your hoops, and said to me just as I was about to leave, 'let me go down'. These are times long past. You were then not even 11 years old, and now you are 16.' Barbara was devoted to her elder brother.

Only hours after Rudi had left the family flat in Berlin the Gestapo came to arrest him. For Helene, Barbara's older sister, the event was traumatic. She understood the dangers and consequences of her brother's sudden departure. There was a genuine fear on Helene's part that the Nazis would hurt her family if they were unable to find him. She was aware that Rudi had already been brutally attacked by members of the Nazi party just before his father had died and again in March 1933 by the Sturmabteilung (the paramilitary wing of the Nazis). Towards the end of 1934 the Gestapo returned to search the flat and threatened to send the family to a concentration camp. This incident coincided with the arrest of Barbara's younger brother, Eugen, for being a member of the left-wing Socialist student's union. Once again it was the Jewish members of the union that were assigned blame for an undisclosed incident at the University.

Rudi escaped to Paris where he published under the pseudonym Rudolf Fürth (after his birthplace). He wrote articles for a number of exile institutions, became a specialist in geopolitics, fascist policies and German military theories, and was the co-publisher of books highlighting Hitler's atrocities in Germany. He wrote articles for *Die Weltbühne* and was chief editor of the Communist Party newspaper *Unsere Zeit*. Rudi stayed in Paris until June 1940, by which time Germany had invaded France and Paris had surrendered. In August 1940 he was sent together with a group of anti-fascist members of the literary and intellectual elite to Le Vernet internment camp in the Pyrenees, in unoccupied France. They lived in appalling conditions in huts they had to build themselves and many died. In 1941 they were moved by the French to another camp called Les Milles near Marseille, in Vichy France, to be handed over to the Germans in exchange for French prisoners of war. Barbara recounts, in her interview for the British Library, that the family received news from the Red Cross that he had left the camp for a 'destination unknown' and that her mother went into mourning, fearing his chances of survival were almost impossible. Six weeks later a postcard written by Rudi arrived from the St Thomas Virgin Islands in the Caribbean, a British Protectorate, reading simply 'landed here with nothing other than shirt and trousers, please send money.'

For Barbara, the full story of how Rudi and many other famous authors and artists such as Franz Werfel, Heinrich Mann, Jean Arp, Marcel Duchamp, Marc Chagall and Max Ernst managed to flee Marseille and obtain visas to safe havens only much later came to light. She happened to see a screening of the 1997 BBC documentary *The Artist's Schindler* and discovered what had happened at Les Milles. In August 1940, an unassuming young American historian and journalist called Varian Fry (1907–67), who was appalled by Hitler's treatment of German Jews, came to Marseille to rescue about 200 intellectual prisoners he knew were endangered. By the end of the war he had rescued over 2000 anti-Nazi and Jewish refugees by falsifying their papers and helping them pass into Spain and then to neutral Portugal. Under a scheme financially backed by Eleanor Roosevelt, he helped those who were unable to enter the United States, due to their Communist sympathies, to reach other safe havens like Mexico. Because of the dangers of Fry's covert activities in France, and critical publications about US immigration policies towards those fleeing the Nazis, Fry remained an unsung hero for many decades. Rudi would most certainly not have known about him.

Rudi remained politically active in exile. He was a member of the political movement Bewegung Freies Deutschland in Mexiko; in 1942–3 he was editor of the newspaper *Freies Deutschland* and in 1945 wrote *Criminales de Guerra*. His activism would have fatal consequences following his return to Germany in 1947. In East Germany he became a member of the Socialist Unity Party and chief editor of the newspaper *Neues Deutschland,* but it was his decision in 1948 to attend the funeral in Prague of his friend and fellow refugee in Mexico, the anti-Nazi journalist Egon Erwin Kisch, that sealed his fate. In May 1950 Rudi was arrested for being Jewish and falsely accused of being in possession of letters written by Noel Field, an American diplomat and communist who had been interrogated in 1949 in Hungary for espionage. The orders appear to have come directly from Stalin's government in Moscow. The Soviets were wary of association with Western European sympathisers for Communism and Rudi had already expressed disenchantment with Soviet politics. On 4 June 1950, at the age of 42, he was found dead in his flat. The official version was that he had died from 'meat poisoning'. Others believed that he had committed suicide out of desperation that his comrades had betrayed him and fear of the interrogations that were to follow. For his great courage and commitment to his political beliefs Rudi had paid the ultimate price.

Barbara's younger brother Eugen was politically motivated throughout his life but did not pursue a political career. In Berlin he studied medicine and was considered a brilliant student, working under the renowned surgeon Dr Ferdinand Sauerbruch, the first surgeon to attempt open heart and lung surgery. It was a privilege for Eugen to work with him, and it may also have been the reason why he was one of the last remaining Jewish students who were granted special permission to acquire their State exam, despite his run-in with the Gestapo in 1934. Eventually, however, in September 1936, Eugen was forced to flee to Bern, Switzerland, where he continued his studies. This must have been distressing for Barbara as she was very fond of her brother. She keenly awaited him after school and, when time allowed, he would pick her up and they would go for a spin on his motorcycle. She was not in Berlin when he left and this may explain why she was so disappointed at not receiving post from him during that period. The surviving correspondence shows that in later years they made up for lost time, and reflects their closeness.

Eugen's sudden departure had become urgent due to his liaison with a non-Jewish woman, Anne Marie Lutterbeck. This was considered an offence to the German state who described it as 'Rassenschande' (racial defilement), and punishable by death. Ironically, Eugen was blonde and blue-eyed, and even posed for a sculptor as an 'Aryan' in the early 1930s. In Switzerland Eugen married Anne Marie and they had a son, Peter. Much to the amazement and regret of his mother, he took the decision to change his surname to Lutterbeck, and when he emigrated to the United States in 1940 he used the English form of Eugen: Eugene, or simply 'Gene'. He settled in Chicago with his family and became a well-respected radiologist and cancer specialist, before succumbing to the disease himself, aged 64, on 30 July 1973. His many obituaries praise his outstanding contribution to medicine and humanitarian causes. Among the awards bestowed on him during his lifetime was the Bundesverdienstkreuz (Cross of Merit of the Federal Republic of Germany), awarded in 1962, and in 1973 the German Medical Society of Chicago made him Honorary President for Life. He was dedicated to the exchange of students between Germany and the United States, maintaining links with his home country.

Eugen, Luisa, Emma ('Bobbi') and Helene ('Leni') Feistmann, Berlin, 10 November 1935

Of all the Feistmann children, the eldest daughter Helene, or Leni, was emotionally the most scarred by the events in Germany and suffered anxiety attacks and heart problems throughout her life. Her first job, as an apprentice in a solicitor's office in Berlin, only lasted 18 months. In June 1933 it came to an abrupt end for political reasons relating to her employer. Afterwards, her attempts to study dress design, encouraged by her mother, were continuously marred. Even though Leni found a school which allowed a small percentage of Jewish students, the officials did not permit Jews to present their degree work at shows. By January 1937 her mother decided it would be better for Leni to move to England with the hope she could train as a dressmaker. She settled in London but work was hard to come by.

Helene travelled to East Berlin in 1950 to attend Rudi's funeral and decided to remain in East Germany. On 1 November 1951 she made enquiries about the true cause of Rudi's death but the case remained unresolved. In 1954 she married the exiled German Jewish author Arno Reinfrank (1934–2001), with whom she returned to England the following year, but the marriage would end in an amicable divorce. Ursula Adam, the author of a forthcoming book about Helene, met her in 1967 when researching the Free German League of Culture in Great Britain, a social and political institution to which she belonged, which represented anti-Nazi Germans during the war. They became good friends and Adam inherited Leni's invaluable archive, apart from the documents kept today by the Gesellschaft für Exilforschung e.V. in Berlin. By sheer coincidence the authors of this book and Ursula Adam came into contact and we are thankful to her for sharing information and insight about Barbara's sister. The title of Adam's book is based on a quote by Leni: *Helene Feistmann 'Ich blieb eine Deutsche'* (I remained a German). Leni was neither happy in England, nor truly assimilated, like her sister Barbara would be. As well as the seven-year age gap, the sisters could not have had more contrasting temperaments and outlook on life. Leni continually toyed with the idea of moving back to Germany, but her wish was never realised and she died in London on 9 April 2011.

The family never broke their ties with Germany. Willy, Luise, Rudi and Helene were laid to rest in a family grave in the Waldfriedhof Heerstrasse in Berlin, a cemetery for interdenominational Berlin citizens. A quote from a letter from Luise Feistmann to one of her grandsons, Thomas Feistmann (son of Rudi), dated 30 May 1965, sums up the family story: 'We were always conscientious and good Jews, but primarily we considered ourselves as Germans'. The Feistmann brothers and sisters led contrasting lives in different parts of the world, but they never forgot their cultural heritage and their family roots.

Early Creativity at the Landschulheim Caputh

Barbara's experiences of the 1930s were a world away from her siblings. *A Forgotten Paradise* is the subtitle of a book on an exceptional 1930s boarding school for Jewish children near Berlin, the Jüdisches Landschulheim Caputh. It was here that Barbara experienced a life-defining two years between the ages of 13 and 15, from April 1936 to April 1938. After both sons Rudi and Eugen had left Germany, Barbara's mother Luise became concerned about the future of her daughters. Barbara was young and precocious, so Luise decided to send her to the school at Caputh. It had a huge impact on her interests and outlook on life. When asked about her childhood in Germany, Barbara always spoke with great joy about the time she spent at this school, calling it a 'fantastic golden childhood' in one of her many interviews. The personal recollections of many pupils and teaching staff who survived the Second World War shared her enthusiasm.

The school was situated in the fishing village of Caputh near Potsdam, the capital of the region of Brandenburg and not far from Berlin. With its idyllic landscape, forests and beautiful lakes, the area was a much favoured summer retreat from city life for wealthy Berliners. Joseph Goebbels, Hitler's Minister of Propaganda, who was actively inciting anti-semitism and later supported the mass extermination of Jews, was one such resident during the 1930s.

Part of the school was originally the lakeside summer house of Jewish physicist Albert Einstein, built in 1929 in the Bauhaus style. Hitler's Nazi party came to power while Einstein was on a trip to the United States and he was advised not to return. He subsequently rented out the villa for the use of the neighbouring children's school. In happier times, when Einstein resided in Caputh, he was friendly with the staff and allowed the pupils to use his sailing boat. Einstein described the landscape and environment as a paradise. In an awkward incident, and quite unwillingly, Barbara met Einstein after she had climbed over the fence into his garden and stolen an apple from his orchard. One of the teachers caught her in the act and made her knock on Einstein's door to apologise for her misbehaviour. He smiled and forgave her.

The Jüdisches Landschulheim Caputh was well-known for teaching the Pestalozzi method of education. The Swiss educational reformer Johann Heinrich Pestalozzi (1746–1827) was one of the founders of modern educational theory. He believed in training the whole child, that pupils should develop the powers of the head, heart and soul. According to his teachings, the interests and needs of the pupil were paramount. The education should be child-centred, rather than teacher-centred. Barbara once remarked how the latter suited her so well. She admitted that she had been an obstructive child and that her mother's decision was the right one.

The Landschulheim was founded in 1931 by Gertrud Feiertag (1890–1946), nicknamed Aunt Trude by the pupils. With the financial support of her brother, Feiertag bought a villa in Caputh as a summer school for disadvantaged children. She opened with nine pupils and two teachers. In the ensuing years of political turmoil there was an increasing demand to find safe havens for children

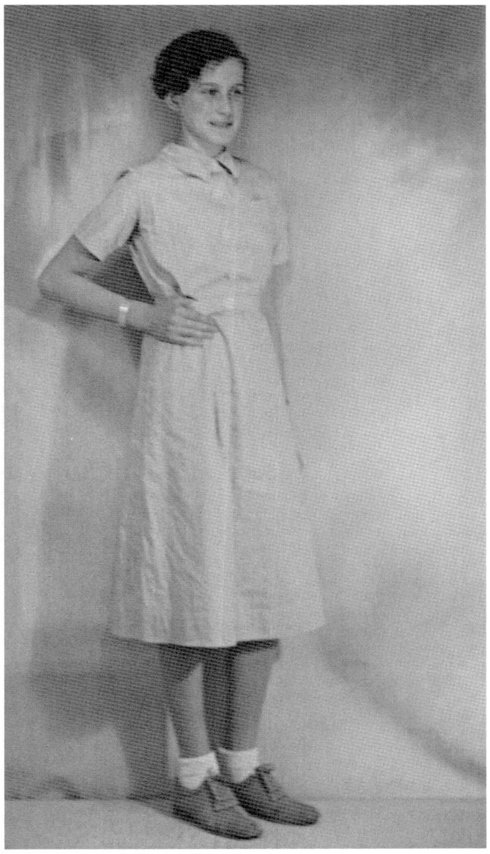

Emma ('Bobbi') Feistmann,
September 1936

from Jewish families who had been previously assimilated into their communities but were now restricted to schools for Jewish pupils only. The same applied to Jewish teachers who were no longer permitted to work at German schools after the Nazi party came to power. For many teachers the school at Caputh provided new opportunities to continue their profession. One of these was Fridolin Friedmann (1897–1976) who became head of the school in 1932 and Barbara recounts how influential he had been to her.

Through the 1930s the school expanded to take in about 150 pupils from the ages of four to sixteen, and rooms were rented in surrounding villas to accommodate them all. This aspect of independence held great appeal for Barbara. The pupils were neither restricted nor controlled; they learnt to be free and independent thinkers, at the same time learning what was right and wrong. Boys and girls were taught together, which was unusual at the time. Languages formed a major part of the curriculum: English, French, Spanish and, notably, Hebrew. The significance of such a broad education, also encompassing Jewish religious customs and history, was not immediately evident to the pupils but was later seen to be an intentional preparation for the possibility of exile from Germany. It gave them the foundation to integrate into other countries throughout Europe and in Palestine and the United States of America.

Social commitment and engagement was very much advocated by Gertrud Feiertag, as was strengthening the body through physical exercise. Barbara remembered enjoying skating and rowing. Little did she know that the physical exercises were part of a programme to subtly teach the children how to survive danger. Creativity and crafts, such as working with paper, wood, metal and ceramics were also much encouraged. As one pupil recalls, they were taught about recent German artists, such as Paula-Modersohn-Becker and her circle, as well as more widely known European painters. There was an emphasis on literature, poetry, theatre and classical music. Poems by Rainer Maria Rilke featured as much as plays by William Shakespeare. Their education was German, yet international; the pupils were being equipped for the challenges that lay ahead. As Barbara would later recall in an interview, the school's maxim was 'it does not matter what you do not know, as long as you know, when you need something, where to find it'. How the teachers managed to cover all these fields is remarkable considering school books were not available for them. As well as intellectual nourishment they were given a greater understanding of nature and the environment, the location of the school being ideal for such classes.

Yet the idyll was not immune to the dangerous political climate. Villagers became increasingly opposed to the Jewish school in their midst. They would throw stones through the windows, say offensive things and frighten the children. The worst was to come on the night of 10 November 1938. Barbara was very fortunate to be spared the horrifying final hours of the school when Nazi paramilitaries and civilians arrived, destroyed its contents and demanded that the children and staff leave immediately. This was a direct consequence of what is often called the Reichskristallnacht (The Night of Broken Glass) on 9–10 November 1938, a pogrom against all Jews. On the morning of 10 November, due to local aggression in Caputh, the teachers led the children through the woods and back to Berlin in the hope of keeping them safe.

After the forced closure of her school, Gertrud Feiertag's life's work seemed to be in ruins, but her desire to help children persisted. She moved to Berlin and assisted orphaned children to safety by finding ways to send them abroad. Even when her own life was in danger, she refused to leave. Feiertag was adamant that as long as there was still one child that required her help, she would stay. It was not long before she was deported to the concentration camp in Theresienstadt and then to Auschwitz on 17 May 1943, where she met her death in the gas chambers. Fridolin Friedman was also committed to the fate of children in need but had a more fortunate outcome. He accompanied many of the children of the 'Kindertransport', rescue efforts to evacuate Jewish children to safer countries such as Britain, but stayed in Germany until 1939. After the war he worked in reception

Music class in the dining room of the
Jüdisches Landschulheim Caputh, 1936

centres for children affected by the Holocaust. Sophie Friedländer (1905–2006) and Hilde Jarecki (1911–95), both teachers in Caputh who settled in England and later wrote of their experiences, dedicated their lives to exiled children and prepared them for the hardships of life. The school in Caputh reopened after the war as an educational institution and exists today as a youth centre. It was briefly named after the young Jewish diarist Anne Frank, but in 1988 was renamed after its inspiring and courageous founder, Gertrud Feiertag.

Barbara was fifteen when she left Caputh in April 1938 and only a few months later her life would change drastically. Not only had her creative talents been nurtured in this extraordinary place, but also, in hindsight, her skills for survival.

Fleeing Germany

The seeds of Barbara's remarkable escape from Berlin were sown at the Landschulheim in Caputh, in the villa where Barbara lived with a group of school children and teachers. This was situated a few streets away from the main school building and Barbara had a small attic room to herself. It contained a bookshelf where she kept her diaries and where she safely hid from view forbidden song texts and private letters from friends and family who were living abroad. The most politically dangerous of these were from her brother Rudi, by then a well-known journalist and Communist, who was living in Paris.

In the autumn of 1937, Barbara discovered with horror that all her papers, including her beloved diary, had mysteriously disappeared. At first she suspected a boyish prank and gave it no further thought, especially since no one owned up to the deed and none of her secrets were divulged. Then in early 1938 Barbara received a letter from Obersturmgruppenführer Paul Elke (the exact spelling of his name escaped her mind in later recollections). He wrote cryptically that he had come into possession of a diary and some papers which belonged to her. He felt sympathetic towards her, and would very much like to meet her in person. He gave her instructions to meet him outside the railway station at Lichterfelde on the following Sunday and followed his signature with 'Heil Hitler'. The letter arrived too late for the proposed meeting, giving an alarmed Barbara an excuse to politely decline his offer and to ask if he could return the diary and papers by post. She decided not to inform anyone at the school about the incident.

Some time elapsed, then in March she received a picture postcard from Vienna inscribed 'I am here with my Führer, wish you could be here too, it's a beautiful city. As soon as I return to Berlin, I will

Bobbi's railway ticket from Berlin to Copenhagen, 3 September 1938

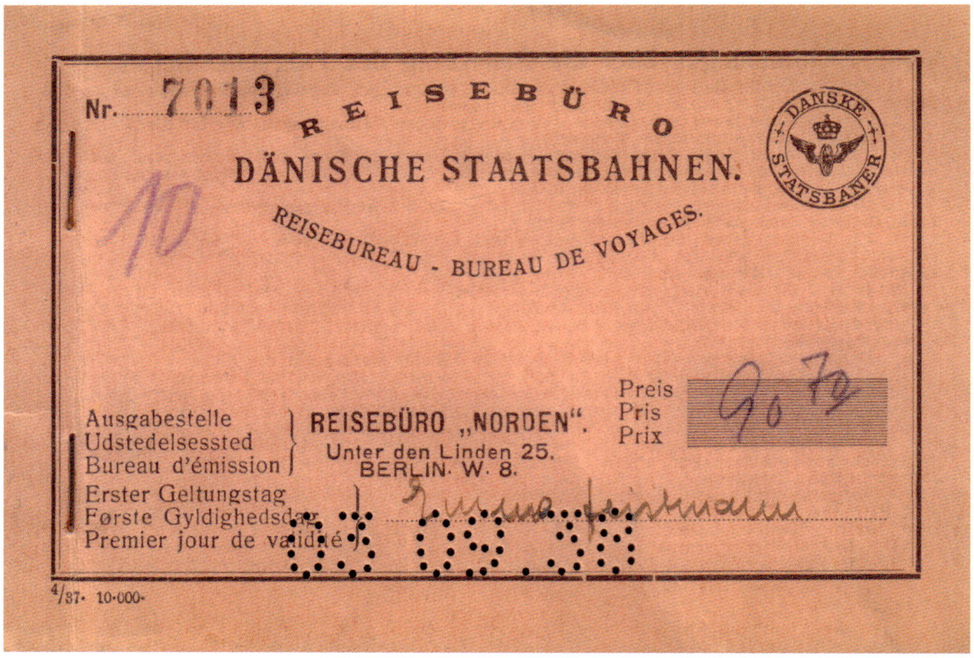

send you the papers, Heil Hitler, Paul Elke'. A postcard from Prague followed, with a similar message, eventually followed by a package containing her diary with a note apologizing for the delay. Neither the letters nor the illegal song texts had been returned. In this more personal note, ending with 'Herzliche Grüße' (Kindest regards) and without 'Heil Hitler', he asks why she would not meet him. Barbara felt secure enough to reply that she was from a Jewish family and did not share his political persuasion and thanked him for the return of the diary. It was not long before she received his reply, saying 'I fully understand, please forgive me', and asking for two favours. One was to take a walk in a particular location (the address escaped Barbara's memory) at a given time, so that he could see what she looked like. He gave her his promise that he would neither approach nor speak to her. The other favour was to leave Germany as quickly as possible and send him a postcard stating that she was safe. Barbara complied with his first request but saw no one.

Not long after this occurrence Barbara left the Landschulheim. When she returned to Berlin to live with her mother Luise, she did not to mention the episode to her. However, on Saturday 3 September 1938, the day after Barbara's sixteenth birthday, she answered a telephone call early in the morning in the family flat at 39 Emserstrasse, in Berlin-Wilmersdorf. A man's voice simply stated that the Gestapo were on their way, and that she must leave immediately. Barbara never found out who their informant was, but assumed it may have been Elke. She woke her mother immediately but her story was dismissed as a youthful fantasy. At 8am there was a knock on the door and four men from the Gestapo entered with instructions to wait at their flat for further orders.

Luise invited them into the kitchen and made them some coffee. After a while she asked if it would be possible for her 'child' to go out to do some shopping. They agreed and Barbara was hurriedly dressed in a short skirt and socks to make her look younger and sent to the family solicitor to explain the situation. The solicitor took her to the British consulate in a last-minute attempt to obtain a visa to go to England, as her mother already had one to visit her daughter, Helene. The consulate refused the application, so the solicitor then purchased two train tickets from Berlin to Copenhagen. Denmark was the only country at the time that would allow entrance without a visa and residence for three months. Unluckily, Barbara's passport was out of date and required an extension validated with an official government stamp. The solicitor was able to attach the extension but the stamp was an impossibility. Drawing on her artistic skills, and with the instinct for survival, Barbara carved the official motif of eagle and swastika into a potato to forge the required endorsement.

When she returned to the flat the men from the Gestapo were still sitting in the kitchen. Thinking quickly, Luise explained that they had been planning to go away for the weekend, and asked if this would still be possible. Astonishingly, they agreed as they had no other instructions to the contrary. The women quickly packed as much as they could carry into enormous suitcases. Barbara remembers taking her 'indispensable skis' and her prized typewriter, given to her the day before, but valuable paintings and antiques were left behind, as well as her beloved Mickey Mouse paraphernalia. Leaving the Gestapo in the flat, they took a taxi to the station and left Germany forever. The train took them via the coastal resort of Warnemünde, part of Rostock, to Copenhagen, where they arrived the following day, 4 September. Barbara remembers how her mother cried when they left Berlin but for Barbara it was the beginning of an adventure.

Barbara was never able to trace the elusive Paul Elke, however she kept her second promise to him, and sent a postcard from Copenhagen to say that she was safe.

Alone in Copenhagen

A series of letters, dating from 10 September to 24 November 1938, survive in the family archive that bear witness to Barbara's courage and adventurous nature. They give an almost daily account of Barbara's trials and tribulations during her three-month stay in Copenhagen, where she anxiously awaited a visa to join her family in England. Due to strict regulations, Barbara's mother Luise had to leave her sixteen-year-old daughter unaccompanied in the big city. The Danish border officials showed no sign of compassion. One can only imagine the fear and heartache such a situation must have caused, especially after the trauma of their sudden flight from Berlin.

Barbara's letters reflect a mature sensitivity to Luise's concerns about how a young girl without life experiences would cope with daily life and making major decisions on her own in difficult political and financial circumstances. Barbara was fully aware of the situation and, in general, made great effort to reassure her mother that she was capable of acting responsibly. The letters were predominantly written in German, their mother tongue, and it is amazing that they survived the upheavals of the period.

On arrival in Copenhagen on 4 September, Luise Feistmann was obliged to leave Denmark immediately and continue her journey to England. Before the Gestapo arrived at their Berlin flat, Luise had already obtained a visa to visit her elder daughter, Helene, who had been living in London since January 1937. With this documentation Luise was unable to obtain a permit to stay in Copenhagen, but entrance to Britain was secure, although she would be entirely dependent on Helene until residence and work permits were issued. For Barbara, however, there was an underlying worry that she would be sent back to Germany as permission to stay was only granted for three months. Arrangements had to be made to move on, otherwise the alternative was deportation.

The earliest of Barbara's letters were addressed to the 'Mousen' (the mice) and variations on this theme, referring to her mother and sister. Her passion for mice was a family trait and this form of endearment is found throughout the letters. Barbara signs some 'Mickey Mouse' rather than her name. Her fascination for Walt Disney's cartoon character started during her childhood; he first appeared in 1928 when she was six years old. In another letter from this period Barbara calls her sister 'Steppenmaus' (a mouse from the Steppes). Otherwise Barbara's mother is often addressed as 'Mumpi'.

Despite expressing some concern about her mother's permit, Barbara writes on 10 September that 'Mickey no. 3' is doing well and that she hopes the visa will not come through too soon, as she is enjoying herself greatly, eating too much and taking advantage of many invitations. She is delighted to have received plenty of post from the family and most of all from her beloved brother Rudi in Paris. Barbara describes her visit to Tivoli, the famous amusement park in Copenhagen, and excitedly describes the guards of the Royal Palace with their huge bearskin hats. She also mentions Rudi's suggestion for the family to come to Paris if all else failed: 'this would be MUCH nicer than London!!!!!!!!!!'.

On 15 September Barbara gives a full account of the people she has seen and her visits to Copenhagen's museums, churches and beautiful harbour. Perhaps encouraged by Luise, Barbara is continuing to sketch, but she now favours head portraits over fashion drawings or posters. She reports proudly on her frugality, spending money only on travel and postage. She even offers to return some of the money that she has been sent knowing that both mother and sister are in more need of it than her. It is also the first time that Barbara expresses concern about not having heard anything about her visa. It seems the initial excitement of being in Copenhagen is beginning to wear off. She was closely following the political situation in Germany and asks if her mother had heard Hitler's speech, writing 'how will this all end?'

Emma ('Bobbi') Feistmann with Mickey Mouse book, 1935

Financial difficulties featured increasingly. On 21 September Barbara mentions that she had asked for 150 Krone from a Mr Hansen, so that she could pay her accommodation at the guest house. Mr Hansen was employed in the timber business and had been a friend of her father's and was asked by Luise to keep an eye on her daughter. He seems also to have been responsible for releasing Feistmann family funds from an earlier transaction in Danzig and Barbara's mother was anxiously awaiting it. Showing foresight and a sense of responsibility, Barbara had asked Mr Hansen for a little more money in case of an emergency. He was very friendly and took her along on business trips so that she could see more of the sights of Denmark, which she greatly enjoyed. After describing the costs of daily life in Copenhagen she writes about her love of photography and that it was her only luxury. By this period Barbara was obviously concerned if her mother's residence permit to stay in England had come through, and if her sister Leni had found work.

Barbara is more positive on 23 September. She explains that her rent is being paid fortnightly to save 12 Krone per week, with the promise of a refund if the visa comes through early. Barbara suggests that her mother comes to Copenhagen for a holiday and assumes the city is cheaper to live in than London. Luise must have given her an account of the dire situation she was in and although Barbara is clearly disappointed in her letter of 24 September that her mother cannot travel, she sympathises with her predicament and, perhaps as consolation, writes that life can be better without money. She herself is being invited everywhere and everyone is so generous. She is now speaking more English than German. She rhapsodises about Mr Hansen, his elegance, his family fortune, their fine dining in restaurants and his children, a daughter of nineteen and son of seventeen. She confesses the desire to have a special dress and nice shoes either in blue or brown with heels, rather than flat ones with rubber soles. She quotes Rudi from his letters and states how she would prefer to be in Paris.

On the 3 October Barbara begins to show frustration about her situation. 'How long should I wait here?' she asks. Her mother has suggested further education to keep her mind occupied but Barbara replies it is extremely difficult to find any courses, and that they are too expensive. For the first time the correspondence reflects Barbara's unhappiness. She asks why it would not be possible for her to go to the United States from Paris, and that she had a great longing to see her brother Rudi. She does not wish to stay over the winter in Copenhagen and Rudi has said he could organise a residence permit and visa for France. Barbara is clearly at a low point and longs to be with her family. She demands an immediate reply, asks after her other brother Eugen who rarely writes, continually enquires about Leni and enquires what has happened with the flat in Berlin.

By her letters of 5 and 6 October Barbara is showing signs of desperation, although confirms she is doing well. She complains about boredom and the fear of lost time, not knowing what to do with her herself beyond reading, playing patience and going for walks. Finances are beginning to weigh heavily on her mind. She is clearly despondent that Luise is not replying about going to Paris and cannot understand why. She calculates in detail if it would be cheaper to stay with Rudi in Paris, and frets that it would be impossible for a third person to be dependent on Helene's earnings in London. Alarmingly, she shows doubts about ever obtaining a visa for England. To find further schooling in Copenhagen is difficult and expensive. She scathingly writes that the only suitable school caters for girls who have wealthy parents and who do not know what to do with their lives before getting married; 'this I most certainly do not want' she underlines in her letter. Luise has obviously advised her to seek some work to earn some money and keep her from mischief but she maintains the language barrier is a hindrance. Luise also encourages her daughter to pursue her drawing but Barbara complains about the cost of postage and refuses to send any more drawings to England. Above all, Paris keeps resurfacing. She hazards that her mother probably considers her too young to cope in such a large city, but promises to be very sensible and begs for permission. 'England is not going to happen, only the devil knows why' she declares in exasperation.

By 20 October Barbara's spirits had rallied. Luise, knowing how to galvanise her daughter, had clearly given her advice to be more active and Barbara had befriended a young girl training to be a painter. Her outlook regarding the visa to England was more positive. Increasingly, however, she was worried about financing her stay. By this stage her mother was regularly sending her money but Barbara was living in straightened circumstances. In a letter of 2 November she is contemplating the idea of a live-in job with little enthusiasm – her free spirit showing through here – and is terribly concerned about her precarious position. 'What should I do, if I do not get the visa? In a month will I be thrown out? Should we not try for the French visa, otherwise where should I go? In Denmark they are extremely severe with residences permits and they are preparing to reduce numbers of foreigners down to 1000. I will try and find out about all possibilities.' The letter is signed 'affectionately kisses from your deeply saddened Mickey Mousli'.

This state of uncertainty continued for several weeks until a letter of 11 November revealed an alarming change in circumstances. Barbara describes her visit to the State Police in Copenhagen and her efforts to learn what would happen once the three month stay ran out. Barbara was told in unpleasant terms that she would definitely be sent back to Germany on 4 December. If the Germans would not allow her to enter, the Danish police would secretly take her over the border by night. After that she would be of no concern to the Danish government. Barbara writes to her mother 'What should I do? kiss, Bobbi.'

A long letter of 14 November shows how, in desperation, Barbara had taken matters into her own hands. She mentions a boyfriend called Poul Eriksen who has offered to help, and a Jewish solicitor, Dr Enoch, who has advised marriage if other solutions failed. She would then gain Danish citizenship and could even enter Britain without a visa. She asks Luise once more if she could write to Rudi in Paris and enquire about a French visa, or would she give her permission to marry? Poul had agreed to a marriage, but she revealingly writes 'I would find that very funny'. A second letter that day states that Dr Enoch was going to contact someone at the British Consulate, and Mr Hansen, horrified by the information she had been given, was going to the State Police on her behalf. Obviously a lot was going through Barbara's mind and how her mother would react to the idea of marriage. She writes, 'You will probably wish to know what kind of a boy Poul is, 24 years old, a student of medicine from Laale, and his father is a priest, yet Poul is not religious. I do hope that I can stay here a little longer even without getting married. From a moral point of view you need not worry, he is a very decent fellow'. When hearing that mother had had her application for a passport turned down, Barbara was dismayed and asked 'does this mean you cannot go onto America? I wait with great suspense and wonder what will happen in the coming month. Poul would like me to stay here forever, but that is out of the question'.

By the 20 November Barbara was more confident that she would get permission to enter England, bolstered by magazines and newspapers sent by Luise to prepare her daughter for the move. On 24 November she states that Mr Hansen has arranged to go to the police and Barbara feels all will be well and apologises for all the worry she has caused to the family. There has been some discussion for Barbara and her mother to go on to the United States from England. The final letters confirming the arrival of her visa appear to be missing, but we know that she finally left Copenhagen on 4 December – exactly three months after arriving – to be reunited with her mother and sister in England.

Many years later, in an interview arranged by the Imperial War Museum in London, Barbara talked very positively of this episode in her life and all the difficulties seemed to have been brushed away. She remembered how she tearfully left Poul, her 'great love' (with whom she continued to correspond), and the city of Copenhagen. When she arrived in the English port of Harwich she felt she could not speak English and was not looking forward to London. Little did she know that this was the city where she would find domestic and professional fulfilment for the rest of her life.

Life as a Refugee in London

Barbara's journey from Copenhagen to England was not a happy one. Arriving on 6 December 1938, the trip took over a week and she had been 'unbelievably' seasick. A few of her beloved toys, her typewriter and her treasured skis came along with her. On arrival at Harwich she realised her English was insufficient for general conversation and she had to use a phrase book to find her way around the station and onto the train to London. However, in a later interview she stated 'she had experienced a sense of relief'. She later said of Copenhagen, which no doubt also applied to England: 'I could breathe freely, no fear of getting snatched on any sort of pretext and dumped in a concentration camp or worse. There were anti-war films to see, which were forbidden in Germany, books to read that were banned by the Nazis'.

At first, the reunion with her family must have been wonderful, but reality soon set in as she took an intense dislike to London. Barbara described the city simply as 'horrible, horrible London'. One year to the day after Barbara fled Germany, on 3 September 1939, Britain declared war on her home country. In an interview, when Barbara was asked how she felt about this moment, she responded: 'Very glad, but very frightened. Remember, with my experiences throughout my childhood in Germany, I knew that it would happen long before people in Britain did, but I also knew the ruthless strength and power of Nazi Germany. Along with many others, I was convinced that this island would be overrun by them in absolutely no time. The British were not prepared for war, like the Germans, and I could not imagine anybody would be able to defeat them, yet obviously hoped it might be possible'. She described how the situation for foreigners from Europe was changing in Britain and not always for the better. They were obliged to go in front of a tribunal, where they were interrogated by magistrates who had the powers to decide whether a person was a threat or even dangerous to Britain.

For refugees who were not in possession of the appropriate paperwork life was extremely burdensome. Barbara urgently needed to renew her German passport and according to existing documents in the archive she made several attempts without success. On 20 July 1939 the German Embassy turned down an application and over a year later a compliment slip dated 7 November 1940 from 'The Swiss Legation, Special Division' stated that they did not issue German passports. By June 1940 the refugees were sorted into three categories and some were sent to internment camps, either in Britain or far away in Canada or Australia. Barbara, Helene and her mother were fortunate and classified as 'Friendly Enemy Aliens'. This meant they could remain in London but were obliged to stay within a 30-mile radius of the city, either to live, study or work. Due to the lack of a passport, many refugees were issued with an Alien's Registration Book, as were Barbara, Luise and, most probably, Helene.With this document they were obliged to report any move, job or change of address to the local police station.

In her early days in London, Barbara chaffed against the loss of independence she had enjoyed in Copenhagen as she now shared her accommodation with both mother and sister. The young Barbara did not see eye to eye with their outlook on life, and she stubbornly refused to learn English. Her shrewd thought was that if she lacked knowledge of the language her mother might send her back to Copenhagen, which she had grown to love, and to her boyfriend Poul, or if that failed, then maybe Paris to join Rudi. In these early days she had little contact with British people and found that they assumed all refugees were Jewish. Barbara later remonstrated: 'I don't feel personally very Jewish, I don't believe in the religion nor see Jews as a race, and, particularly during the war, I was quite concerned that people would understand that the Nazis did not only persecute Jews, but also people of other races and religions or political views. Many of my fellow refugees and friends were not Jewish, but decent Germans who had opposed the regime. So I always took great pains to explain all this, and in many ways, I still do …' However, it was by meeting these kindred spirits that her attitude to England changed and she began to feel more settled.

By 1939, two organisations had been founded in London to help refugees from Germany establish new roots, learn to assimilate and have a more positive outlook on life. A simple exchange between refugees who shared similar experiences was often a great help. One of these organisations was the Free German Youth, who met at 12 Belsize Park. In August 1939, the British Youth Peace Assembly hosted an international youth event at Hoddesdon, in Hertfordshire, and invited the Free German Youth to attend. In need of a logo, Barbara's spontaneous creativity came to the rescue, and from various coloured cotton fabrics she designed their emblem: a blue flag with yellow star and the initials FDJ (Freie Deutsche Jugend). In later years Barbara saw the original flag on display in the Central Museum of Revolution, in Moscow. Many refugees were assembled at Hoddeson, chiefly from Austria, the Czech Republic, Poland and Spain, and Barbara remembers their camaraderie around the camp fires, enjoying guitar music and sharing songs from all over Europe. The Free German Youth organised outings and concerts and their aim was to publicize to the British people that there was a strong anti-fascist movement in Britain. These were hard times for the young refugees, but, as in Barbara's case, they helped each other find a meaning in life and were fortunate to have survived. After the war, in 1946, the Free German Youth movement was dissolved in London, but continued as a Communist youth organisation in East Germany. Their increasing disillusionment with the way Communism developed there would later contribute to the fall of the Berlin wall in 1989 and the collapse of its Communist dictatorship.

Barbara was also actively involved in the Free German League of Culture, founded in London towards the end of 1938. She found great satisfaction and stimulation in meeting well-known authors, actors, artists, musicians and scientists who had shared her experiences. She would spend most of her days in the League's clubhouse in Upper Park Road, Hampstead, which was opened in January 1940. There, refugees would be given a meal and sometimes even a roof over their heads, especially during air raids. Cultural activities such as theatre, concerts and exhibitions were a welcome distraction from the dangers they faced. In 1940, when the British started sending refugees, especially Germans,

Free German Youth flag flying at the International Youth Camp, Hoddesdon, Hertfordshire, designed and made by Emma ('Bobbi') Feistmann, August 1939

Emma ('Bobbi') Feistmann preparing
the *Allies Inside Germany* exhibition, 1941

to internment camps, the organisation sent food and clothes and campaigned for their release. The League worked together with refugee associations representing other nationals, such as the Austrians and Czechs. They organised charity events to raise funds for those in dire need. One of the most successful events was an exhibition in the summer of 1942 called *Allies Inside Germany*. It later toured various British cities under a different title: *We accuse – Ten Years of Hitler Fascism*. Barbara was active in setting up the exhibition and remembers working with the artist John Heartfield, a former member of the radical November Group in 1920s Berlin, who contributed many illustrations with powerful messages. As she said, 'we all knew each other and got involved'; the refugees wanted to tell their story. Barbara was actively writing for and editing the newsletters of both organisations. For a teenager it must have been incredible to be involved in these events and to meet famous artists such as Oskar Kokoschka.

Survival on a daily basis in London must have been quite a struggle for the family, and especially for Barbara's mother. From a business deal in Danzig negotiated by her late husband (and assisted by the helpful Mr Hansen in Copenhagen), Luise was able to salvage a fair sum of money. Barbara also recalled that her mother had brought practical items with her from Berlin, such as sheets, and a few gold coins. These were possibly coins inherited from her grandfather, the numismatist Eugen Merzbacher. However, these funds were limited and the official refusal of Luise's application for a residence permit restricted her ability to work. Even if regulations had been relaxed, the outbreak of World War II brought further complications as German refugees found it very difficult to get employment. Barbara described her first job interview at a newspaper: first she was greeted warmly, but after fifteen minutes and detecting her German accent, the interviewer confessed 'Sorry, I could not possibly employ you'. Finally, Luise was able to get a job as a sales assistant in Selfridges department store, and later found secretarial work. For Helene it was equally challenging. She found occasional work as a dressmaker and, later, as a translator.

Luise was particularly concerned that her daughter received a good education. In 1939 Barbara was sent to St Martin's School of Art in London, to learn fashion design. However, when Luise discovered that she had decided to learn life drawing instead, she immediately pulled her out of the course. She was worried about what training would be best for her daughter's future and, knowing that secretarial work was always in demand, she set Barbara an ultimatum. She had set aside a small sum of money and offered to finance a shorthand and typing course at Pitman's College; the alternative option would be working in a factory. Although reluctant at first, Barbara enrolled at the college in 1940 and soon began to appreciate its benefits. Her description of her training at Pitman's is quite comical: twenty students hovering over the keyboards learning to type to the strong regular rhythm of marches being played on the gramophone and the call of the teacher, 'carriage return'! This mechanical way of learning words, through sound rather than meaning, had an unexpected advantage. Until that point Barbara had not formally learnt English, and she later admitted 'after 10 months at Pitman's I suddenly realised I could understand English without any knowledge of grammar. I just picked it up, the rest is history'. Now she could go to the cinema, read newspapers and mix with Londoners. Previously she had spent all her time with German and Jewish refugees.

Although this training would stand her in good stead in the coming years, it was inevitable that Barbara would find secretarial work intellectually unstimulating. Her first employment was at

Fashion sketch, pencil and watercolour on paper,
signed 'E. Feistmann 14. Juni 1939'

New Skin, a company that produced adhesive plasters. After typing invoices for two weeks she decided to leave, and this was followed by a succession of short-term jobs. As Barbara later commented: 'I changed jobs as often as my underwear'. She took on numerous secretarial jobs: becoming an assistant for an accountant, a typist for a tyre merchant and assisting elderly ladies in wheelchairs on outings, to name but a few, but she soon realised 'this is not a career for me'. Finally something attractive came along. A friend, the singer Agnes Bennell, was leaving her job at London Films and offered it to Barbara. The film studio belonged to the internationally-renowned Hungarian-born British film producer and director Alexander Korda. Not only was the environment exciting, but the pay was higher than anywhere else. Her task was to be an assistant to Zoltán Korda, Alexander's brother, although he was in the United States for the duration of her employment due to visa problems. This meant she was being well paid for hardly any work, and she described her time there as 'magic'. Barbara could arrive late for work and spend her day watching films being made, such as Laurence Olivier's *Henry V* (1944). She was fascinated by how water-drenched naval scenes, streets with terraced houses and cobbled alleyways were all filmed indoors, and marvelled at the perfection of the illusions they created. It must have been extraordinary watching famous stars such as Vivien Leigh and Noel Coward.

Ironically, on the day Zoltán Korda finally arrived in England, Barbara arranged for his luggage to be transported from Liverpool to London (her only task for him), and then had to return the office keys. The Labour Exchange had called her up for the war effort and she was assigned to work as a factory labourer at Kelvinator, a London company which manufactured ice-boxes and domestic refrigerators before the war. During wartime the company had been transformed into a manufacturing plant for aircraft components, which would withstand freezing temperatures at high altitude. The foreman took one look at her and commented 'this is not your cup of tea', however the chief engineer recognised her potential and gave her an office job. She soon understood how to implement a newly-introduced time and motion study system that was incomprehensible to other members of staff, and before long had a pay rise. Barbara even found she had some spare time during work and discreetly managed to earn a little extra money using her creative talents and a sense of enterprise. Among her productions were lamps made from broomsticks, metal, string and parchment. The metalworkers in the company helped her weld frames together for the parchment shades. Sandals were impossible to obtain during wartime, so she started making them with a little instruction and materials from Kelvinator's enamelling and metal-bending workshops, including leather straps used in the machines. All Barbara required were leather soles and crepe rubber, and fellow staff and friends were pleased to be her clients. One day she was caught by the managing director with her feet up on the desk taking measurements. He was outraged and wanted her fired, however her services were much admired by the chief engineer who threatened: 'If you fire her, I am leaving'.

In 1941 Barbara had met the artist René Graetz (1908–1974) through the Free German League of Culture and in 1943 she began a relationship with him. Born in Berlin, Graetz had been sent to an internment camp in England for being German despite not being Jewish, before being deported to Canada and then returning in 1941. He was much older than Barbara and eventually broke off their liaison to marry the Irish-born author Elizabeth Shaw in 1944. They moved to East Germany as Graetz was offered citizenship and joined the Communist party. They remained friends with Barbara until his death and she admitted he was influential to her development. However it was in 1944, during her time working for Kelvinator, that Barbara's personal life would take a new and life-changing direction.

Emma ('Bobbi') Feistmann, c.1943

An Unusual Love Affair

'One May evening in my local, The Wheatsheaf, in Rathbone Place, I saw this drop-dead gorgeous young man'. So Barbara described the beginning of a whirlwind romance in 1944 which led to a life-long marriage. The story of how Barbara and Derrick Cartlidge met could be the script for a very entertaining film.

In the 1930s and 1940s the Wheatsheaf pub in London's Fitzrovia was a well-known meeting place for bohemians and intelligentsia. Authors, artists and entertainers gathered there for lively conversation and conviviality. In 1936 the pub had been the setting for a tumultuous love affair between the poet Dylan Thomas, who was a regular, and Caitlin Macnamara, a dancer of Irish descent, whom he married a year later. Barbara described how it was packed every night during the war; everyone knew each other. It was a place where she was happy, even when London was being heavily bombarded, and she found the atmosphere and characters inspiring.

Although Barbara and Derrick first met in the Wheatsheaf, their story has an unusual prologue. It began with a portrait photograph of Barbara taken by the Hungarian refugee Zoltan Wegner.

He was the official photographer for the Courtauld Institute of Art and a sought-after portraitist. Barbara was a willing and ideal sitter for many photographs. For some unknown reason, a passport-sized version one of these photographs ended up in a dustbin not far from Charlotte Street, where Barbara was sharing a flat with an art student whom she met at St Martin's School of Art before the war. Derrick Cartlidge was living nearby and going through an unhappy phase in his life. His long-term girlfriend had tuberculosis, and her recovery in hospital was expected to last a year. Vic, a friend of Derrick's, knew he was in need of some distraction and showed him the photograph he had picked out of the bin. Derrick took an immediate shine to Barbara and told his friend she was 'just perfect'. Vic struck a deal: he'd reveal who she was for a cup of tea worth twopence, and for an extra spam sandwich worth fourpence he'd let him know where to find her! Sixpence was all Derrick had, but time would prove it was the best investment he ever made, as he admitted in his autobiography *Wild Oats and the Wooden Pillow*.

Derrick was then twenty-one years old, a drifter with a warm heart, great charm, charisma and good looks. He had experienced a miserable childhood. Abandoned as a baby, all attempts to find his parents had failed. He had been brought up by an elderly spinster who ran a boarding house for orphaned children, but she was in constant debt and frequently absent in prison. Neglected as a child, he never received a formal education, and was twelve years old before he learnt to read and write. Derrick learnt 'how to cope with the uncopeable', in Barbara's words. It was not until he had met an older man known as 'Uncle', whose name has never been revealed, that Derrick was sent to school and experienced some luxuries in life, such as trips to the South of France. Uncle came from a large family, but adored Derrick as an 'adopted' son.

Barbara remembered how, when she first set eyes on her future husband, he was elbowing his way through the crowded pub to reach the bar. Being penniless, he asked the barman for a glass of water which caused a moment of silence, but caught Barbara's attention and sparked the conversation Derrick had hoped for. In his autobiography, Derrick described his first impression of her as having a slight resemblance to Ingrid Bergman and 'her long legs might have made [Marlene] Dietrich envious'. He admits he was besotted with her. After several attempts at approaching Barbara he over-heard a conversation that she was looking for someone to stay in her flat, as her flatmate had left London to escape the heavy bombing. Derrick quickly seized the opportunity and accepted her invitation to move in. Barbara could not believe when he arrived that all his worldly possessions fitted in one paper carrier bag. In his autobiography, he stated: 'All I need is a change of underwear and a shirt plus my shaving tackle … Being able to travel light and at a moment's notice gives me a sense of freedom'. Their first evening in the flat was momentous for Derrick and his description of it betrays the unhappiness of his early life and how much this encounter meant to him: 'Never before had I seen an intimate meal for two being prepared before. Bobbi couldn't have known it, but un-wittingly, she had given a twenty-one-year-old orphan his very first glimpse of what family life was all about, and I took to it like a duck to water'.

That night they heard the deafening sound of German V1 flying bombs, nicknamed 'buzz bombs' or 'doodlebugs' by Londoners, and the returning British anti-aircraft shells. The following morning, after Barbara had gone to work at Kelvinator, Derrick had a lucky escape. Leaving the flat and walking down the street, a doodlebug suddenly crashed very close to where he was, and on impact flattened three houses to the ground. At the flat, windows were smashed, the black-out curtains were torn and dust was everywhere.

Not all was plain sailing, as Derrick had doubts about whether Barbara would 'start up a relationship with an uneducated, uncultured and penniless Soho bum'. After an embarrassing scene with Barbara's then boyfriend, a medical student, she broke up with Derrick but it was not long before she returned to him. She found him sitting in Café Tony, his usual haunt, looking quite miserable and not believing his luck when she appeared.

By August of that year the bombing of London had significantly intensified with the first long distance missiles, the infamous V2 rockets, being fired night and day. That month Barbara was due her two-week annual leave from Kelvinator. Derrick suggested they go to Bude, in Cornwall, for a holiday. Barbara's status as 'Friendly Enemy Alien' meant that travelling beyond the 30-mile radius of London was only possible with transit visas from the Home Office. The visa to Devon was granted before the holiday started but the visa permitting her to stay in Cornwall had not yet come through. They set off by train to Exeter and then hitchhiked to Barnstaple in Devon, where Barbara hoped the visa could be picked up at the local police station. The police there had no idea what Barbara was talking about and suggested contacting the Penzance headquarters in Cornwall, who in turn referred them back to London. It was recommended that they visit the Chief Constable of Devon, who generously suggested the young couple come to his house. They were allowed to stay in Devon for their holiday although the Constable pulled Derrick aside and reminded him of his responsibilities: he should ensure that his German lady friend would remain loyal to the country that gave her refuge.

By their return Derrick knew Barbara was the love of his life. He persuaded her to marry him, despite the fact that Barbara, from what she recalled in later interviews, did not believe in formalizing marriage. However, she recognised she would be free to become a British citizen and shed her status as an alien. Barbara's mother, Luise, was not thrilled about her choice of husband and expressed concern that he lacked regular paid employment. Although Derrick had no immediate family, his benefactor, 'Uncle', took an instant liking to Barbara when they first met, and pulled out of his waist-coat a gold ring from his mother for their wedding ceremony.

The wedding took place on 9 September 1944 in the registry office at St Pancras Town Hall, only four months after they had met. It only occurred to Derrick in the morning that two witnesses were required. Luise could be one, but a second had to be found quickly. He hurried to his actor friend and previous flatmate, Peter Penn, to ask him, who, although astonished by the short notice, readily

Derrick and Bobbi Cartlidge on their wedding day, 9 September 1944

agreed. After the ceremony the newly-wed couple had lunch with Uncle and Barbara's mother, where the two met for the first time. It was only then that Luise learnt that Derrick was an orphan and one can only imagine what was going through her head. After lunch and just before leaving, she pulled out of her bag three enamelled saucepans which she had purchased from Woolworths as their wedding present. She had also given the young couple the gold wedding band from her late husband.

In the evening, to pay for a round of drinks at the Wheatsheaf, Barbara and Derrick rushed to the pawnbroker and pawned their gold wedding bands. After the festivities, Uncle's ring was sold to buy back Luise's. With these funds they had enough money to take a taxi to the Windmill Theatre where, they were led to believe, their friend Peter had invited them for tea. Once ushered up three flights of stairs, a door opened to reveal Peter standing on the top of a landing with the stairs leading up to him lined with the famous 'Windmill Girls' standing in the nude holding feathered fans and showering them with confetti! A bottle of wine and a cake bought from Patisserie Valerie were laid on a white tablecloth for them. The idea was Laura Henderson's (known as 'Mrs Henderson'), an eccentric and wealthy widow and renowned owner and founder of the Windmill Theatre, who had managed to acquire the treats despite wartime rationing. The wedding reception could not have been in a more fitting place for Barbara, as the theatre had become a symbol of defiance to Nazi threats. During the Blitz, Mrs Henderson decided the show must go on. Each night the staff showed great courage and, against the noise of aeroplanes and falling bombs, they continued to entertain and give the public a little cheer and distraction. Mrs Henderson remained defiant against government attempts to shut the theatre down during the war and their slogan became 'We never closed'.

For Barbara and Derrick the wedding paved the way for a long and occasionally bumpy marriage but a very loving and supportive one.

'He still loves me after 11 years':
Bobbi and Derrick Cartlidge,
August 1955

Making a Living

The much longed-for Peace was finally declared on 8 May 1945. After years of devastation, post-war Britain faced near bankruptcy and the late 1940s proved to be a time of rationing and austerity. Due to her marriage, Barbara's transition from refugee status to a settled existence in Britain was relatively trouble-free. She did not have to endure the problems other refugees were experiencing. Some were in danger of compulsory repatriation; others had to endure the long and worrisome process of naturalization, which was not always granted.

Immediately after their marriage, Derrick recognised his aimless way of life had to come to an end, but the transition to full-time work was not an easy one for him. He had tried his hand at most jobs, including farmhand, merchant seaman and film extra, and even had a short stint as an army volunteer at Mill Hill Barracks before he deserted, due to his pacifist beliefs. But now he had taken on the responsibility of supporting a wife. Barbara was finally free from the Labour Exchange. It could no longer dictate what work she was obliged to take on and she gave up her employment at Kelvinator. The challenges facing both were enormous, but they helped each other. Money was always short and their attempts to find a place to rent were plagued by bad experiences.

Barbara found a temporary job painting dolls' faces at home at the kitchen table, while Derrick got involved with a shady business knocking up black market divans in Islington. When the orders dried up, and his partner was caught by the Board of Trade, Derrick was given the opportunity to stand in for the actor Herbert Lom in the film *Seventh Veil* at London Films. The offer turned out to be false but he did take up another offer of introduction to a theatrical agent and to gain some acting experience, as he knew good looks would not be enough. He was given various theatrical acting parts which entailed a considerable amount of travelling around the country, to cities such as Norwich, Birmingham and Manchester. Barbara always accompanied him and at one point they were entrusted with organising and taking a show on tour. Barbara was given the management role and had absolutely no idea what was required, but as Derrick described in his autobiography: 'In the bleak wartime evenings, plays as awful as our show played to packed houses because there was simply nothing else to do to amuse yourself'. In the post-war years, going out to the theatre, the local dance and cinema were ways of maintaining morale. Derrick was given a part in a production of Oscar Wilde's *The Importance of Being Earnest* at the Theatre Royal in a suburb of Wolverhampton. It was such a dreadful experience that they decided they had had enough of this itinerant way of life.

By 1945 Derrick had resigned from his travelling and acting jobs, disappointed that he had never been given a promised part to act opposite Jean Simmons in the film *Blue Lagoon*. The need to find regular employment was now urgent, as Barbara was pregnant with their first child, Tony, who was born in January 1946. In desperation, and as a challenge, Derrick took a job as a waiter in the up-market restaurant L'Etoile near Charlotte Street, but the position did not last long. Derrick's contacts were very much linked to his life as a foster child and he found himself working for borderline villains from the West End. His instinct for survival and desire to support his family led him into one particularly ill-considered and dangerous scheme. Under the Exchange Control Act of 1947, gold had a higher value in Britain than in France. A group of London gangsters tried to exploit this situation by smuggling gold across the Channel. They hired young couples with small children, like Barbara and Derrick, to drive over to France as if they were on the perfect family holiday and even gave them some spending money. Once they had reached their destination in Paris, the car's petrol tank was partly filled with gold, partly with petrol. On their return to Britain, they would be paid a lump sum. Tony later stated: 'I was used as a decoy'. These trips became ever more hazardous and the profiteers more greedy. On his last trip Derrick was ordered to create an accident by driving the car into a tree, as, by law, car wrecks of British vehicles were required to be returned by train. The tank could therefore be completely filled with gold. Somehow Derrick got away with it, but it was his last journey as Barbara was now pregnant with their second child, Michelle (born October 1950). When Tony asked his father what would have happened if he had been caught, Derrick replied: 'I had a plan, I would go to prison [but] not reveal the gangsters names under the condition they would care for Barbara and the family'. They finally decided to distance themselves from this criminal world, especially after a frightening incident when some gang members came to their house and held Barbara and Tony at gunpoint.

Barbara's mother Luise left Britain for the United States in 1946 and stayed with her son Eugene and his family in Chicago. In 1947 she continued to Mexico where her son Rudi was living, and finally settled in Washington, D.C. By 1948 she had found employment, including working for the cosmetic firm Avon. Regular correspondence with her daughter survives from April 1947 until the late 1950s and the letters give a detailed insight into daily life at the Cartlidges. The letters from Barbara to her mother are nearly always addressed to 'Dearest Headmouse', and are mostly written in English with the occasional German phrase or paragraph.

During this period Luise was continually sending the family food parcels, and, later, clothing. Their favourite treat was packaged noodle soup, but they were also sent basics such as tinned food, tomato puree, cheese, rice, sugar, soap flakes and even chocolates and tea, as rationing was severe in England. Barbara wrote: 'Your parcels are an enormous help, but I understand you also have obligations to Rudi and Leni'. Barbara continually bemoaned the financial problems they were having, and in some letters she hoped that her brother Eugene might help, but this was impossible for him at the time although he and his wife occasionally sent food. Eugene was not a frequent writer, much to Barbara's disappointment, but they kept in regular contact after Rudi's death in 1950 and Derrick was also very fond of him. Despite the difficult circumstances, on 16 May 1947 she wrote to Luise 'We are very happy and believe me, I say more than once a day to myself, what a very lucky person I really am'.

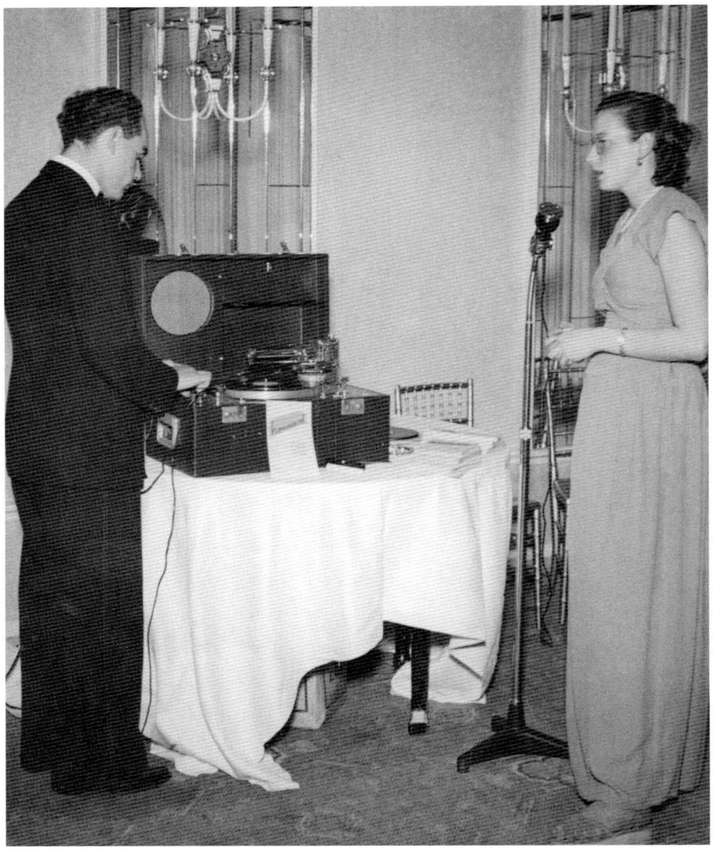

Derrick and Bobbi Cartlidge recording an event for their company Homecord, 1949

Barbara clearly felt the need to assure her mother that Derrick was trying hard to find employment. She described his various attempts, such as acting in an advertising film for Aspro and as a miner for a Ministry of Information film. In August 1947 they were excited that Derrick might get a big part in a film but it did not materialise. By 13 January 1948 Barbara wrote: 'We have given our future a great deal of thought. Derrick has decided to give up the stage entirely …' He was determined to learn a profession and start from scratch. Barbara wrote hopefully 'Our life is taking a new turning'. However Luise was not easily convinced and continued to voice her concern. On 7 November 1948, she wrote a very frank letter to her daughter, in German, remonstrating that for two years Barbara had been the breadwinner, nothing had changed, she continued to struggle and everything fell upon her shoulders. In 1949 Luise visited the family in London but by then, fortunately, Derrick's career had taken a turn for the better.

Derrick grew into his role as a father and family life suited him. He adored his son Tony, and wanted to shower him with everything that he himself had never received in life. It was one day in March 1949, when Derrick heard Tony making his first sounds, that he had the novel idea of setting up a business recording children's voices. He had finally found his vocation and over the next few years the business – named Homecord – grew slowly but steadily. Derrick was never technically-minded, but, with the help of a friend, soon learnt how to work the machines. The orders started to come in. They made home visits for the recordings, while Barbara looked after the office work and organised advertising. In a letter dated 24 March 1949, Barbara reports how the business had started to expand: 'We already have a lot of orders from people with young children, concert pianists and amateur musicians or people who make a speech or something like that.' Uncle gave them a financial jump-start which covered the expense of a car and the equipment. Luise was even asked to check on prices in the United States as they were cheaper and quicker with delivery. By October the business had expanded and the Dorchester Hotel had 'put them on the map' by including an advert for the business in their hotel brochure.

On 14 November Derrick was asked to go to the Savoy Hotel to record political speeches by the former Prime Minister of South Africa, Jan Christiaan Smuts, by Sir Anthony Eden, later Prime Minister of the United Kingdom, and by the Rt Hon. Viscount Samuel of the Liberal Party. Adverts were printed in *The Times*, *The Daily Telegraph* and *The Jewish Chronicle* and by December 1949 the demand for recording at Jewish weddings, bar mitzvahs and bat mitzvahs were a major source of income (although Barbara mentioned in one letter how much they preferred working at the Savoy as they were given free food and drink). In early 1950 Luise was sending her nylon stockings to be worn at special recordings and offered to send a velvet dress, as Barbara needed to be smart for her new role commentating during the ceremonies. A little later Barbara mentioned she needed another dress as recommendations between friends for Homecord's services meant she was meeting the same people at different events wearing the same outfit. On 13 November 1951 she proudly stated 'I am collecting nothing but compliments for our commentaries – they prove to be an actual selling point now and we are getting recommendations with people asking particularly for my voice on it'. Homecord ventured into recording background music for theatre productions and by 1953 added sports recordings to their repertoire, with commissions coming as far away as South Africa. On 20 March 1955 Barbara noted 'Recording is so busy we don't know where we are, all sorts of interesting jobs have come up lately'. These included interviews with famous film stars from London Films (founded by Alexander Korda) such as Vivien Leigh and Diana Dors, all arranged by the radio film broadcaster Lilian Duff. They resulted in endorsements to prominent film directors of the time such as David Lean and Carol Reed. In the same letter Barbara states '… altogether we are having a wonderful time'.

By the middle of 1953 Barbara and Derrick had also started a new endeavour, looking for a change in direction. On 8 April Derrick had bought a 1930s old convertible taxi for five pounds. Their new business, initially named Taxi-Lift, would operate successfully for the next 40 years. Early on, they

Bobbi Cartlidge taking a phone call
for Taxi-Lifts or Taxi-Trucks, c.1953

discovered that many customers were wanting to transport small items of furniture and goods, rather than people, so the business developed into what was to become Taxi-Trucks. Barbara was able to look after the children at home while taking on the responsibility for advertising and bookings. Local businesses recommended them and the local tobacconist had their business card. Further drivers were hired: 'Basher Bill' as one employee was known, and Benny Sirota, later the co-founder of Troika-Pottery. In later years a number of artist-jewellers represented in Electrum Gallery also helped out, such as Claus Bury, Alan Craxford, Wally Gilbert and Fritz Maierhofer. Taxi-Trucks was a personal success story for Derrick, but only possible through the support and commitment of his wife and the stability she provided in their home life. They made a formidable team.

A Political Conscience

A book written about Barbara without a mention of her political activism would be unthinkable. Her work with German refugees and the Communist Party of Britain during the war and post-war years was the beginning of a lifetime of political involvement driven by a defiant optimism and, to a degree, idealism. For a long time she was active in the British Peace Committee with the aim of alleviating the misery suffered by politically suppressed people. Her attitude was doubtless fuelled by her personal experiences as an exile from Germany.

In a speech given to the Congress of the Patriotic People's Front in the early 1970s, Barbara outlined her personal goals and that of the Committee, which represented many political factions:

The activities of the British Peace Committee cover a wide range of ground as the fight for peace has to operate on many different levels. We are at the moment much concerned with the question of European Security and are organising many meetings, demonstrations and publishing material particularly on the aspect of NATO. Foremost in our concern is the question of Vietnam. As the Peace talks in Paris continue our press and television coverage is diminishing and we have to make great efforts to keep the British public informed on the developments and emphasise how very serious the problem still is. We have issued a declaration demanding the complete disassociation of our Government from American policy in Vietnam, the withdrawal of all US and allied troops and the implementation of the 1954 Geneva agreements.

As did many of her generation, Barbara felt very strongly about the injustice of the Vietnam War, which began in 1955 and did not end until the Fall of Saigon on 30 April 1975. The charity Medical Aid Committee for Vietnam was founded in 1965 by the London doctor Joan McMichael (1906–89), who had experienced first-hand the horrible suffering of people in Hanoi through lack of medicines and surgical equipment. Barbara was a member by 1966 and was hugely committed to fundraising for the cause. In 1990 Barbara reflected on her activities with great pride: 'With Joan's drive, determination and enthusiasm, and the often self-sacrificial willingness of everybody involved, we tackled some truly ambitious projects with amazing results'. The charity is still active although re-named Medical and Scientific Aid for Vietnam, Laos and Cambodia (MSAVLC) and has actress Dame Judi Dench as its president.

Barbara and Derrick Cartlidge
at a political rally, c.1968

MSAVLC's website contains an account of a blood donation campaign in the 1960s and early 1970s and records that by the end of 1971 a total of 6,567 pints of blood had been flown to Vietnam. Barbara devoted much time and energy to this campaign, collecting blood and ensuring it was delivered to those most in need. Her relentless efforts have been acknowledged in a number of newsletters over the years. In February 2016, MSAVLC published a tribute to Barbara and all the volunteers who helped support the charity in its early days. An article she wrote in 1985 for the 20th anniversary newsletter of MSAVLC is so informative and revealing that a long excerpt was republished in the tribute and is repeated here:

Vietnam's heroic fight for independence, against enormous odds, was a fact with which I was familiar in the 1960s but when Stanley Foreman telephoned me one day in 1966, asking if I had a bit of spare time to help a newly-formed Committee for Medical Aid I had little notion of the tremendous tasks and deep involvement that lay ahead. Then and since, people would ask me why I did it – and the answer is still the same: to do SOMETHING to counter the unspeakable horror and hardship forced on Vietnam. Moreover, this was one Committee dedicated to spare no efforts, where few words were followed by swift and concrete actions. The keynote for MACV was always a sensible, practical approach, terrific team-work among the many specialised volunteers over the whole country and abroad, and close contact with Vietnam itself.

Among the many different jobs I did in the course of many years, one was the responsibility of getting the blood donated at our many Donation Sessions to a blood bank in Sutton, Surrey within a few hours. To be honest, I felt pretty sick the first time I handled the body-warm fluid in its soft plastic container. Moreover, on the first few occasions I had to cool it down in my domestic fridge and forgot to tell my husband – who recoiled with horror when he opened the fridge door to get a pint of milk. We got quite professional soon afterwards, with special boxes which had frozen inserts to keep the blood at the right temperature. These inserts had to be prepared 24 hours ahead in a deep-freeze, a task I entrusted to our local ice cream manufacturer. Packed with inserts and full of blood, each box weighed 24 kilos, and I grew muscular like Popeye humping them in and out of the car. The routine for many years, sometimes every week, was to get the blood to Sutton on Sunday night after a session, then fetch it again the following Thursday, leaving home at 6am, and deliver to LOT, the Polish airline, at London airport. If the flight was delayed, they would telephone me and I would have to go back to Heathrow, collect the boxes and return them to Sutton, because even in those special containers, it could not remain for longer than eight hours.

In the early 1970s Gordon Schaffer and I were delegated by the Peace Committee to attend a Peace Congress, in Budapest, Hungary. I was never a great public speaker, in fact, I have always avoided the task, but as soon as we got there they clamoured that I should tell them about our aid to Vietnam. I discovered it was quite easy, at any rate to address a large audience who didn't speak English, so every two or three sentences I could pause and think while the interpreter rambled on in Hungarian. In the resplendent main chamber of the Hungarian Parliament, decked out in gilt and plush, I elaborated on the various and many activities of our Committee. Their reaction was in some ways unexpected – they were used to their aid for Vietnam being organised by the Government. They were amazed that we did all this work unpaid, making our own decisions, and some thought it sounded 'romantic'. I was quick to tell them how unromantic it is to lug ten to twelve boxes of 24 kilos each for weeks on end in the small hours of the morning.

During the height of the war in the 1960s and 1970s a vital part of the charity's work was to raise funds to provide aid for the Vietnamese people, both in the North and the South. Barbara was deeply involved in organising art shows at different London venues, but mostly in Hampstead. She once stated 'My part in it was as manifold as ever, from the sublime to the ridiculous'. Many jewellers Barbara would come to know through her own work and through Electrum Gallery backed her efforts. For a reasonable price spectators could purchase artwork and be made aware of the situation in Vietnam. Other volunteers

Barbara Cartlidge setting up an art exhibition
for the charity Medical Aid Committee for Vietnam,
c.1970

organised concerts, theatrical events, recitals and speeches, and many influential members from society and the acting world supported the work of the charity. As she continued in her article:

I do not give the impression that it was all hard slog and nothing else. When I joined the Events Committee, I helped with the organisation of concerts and later the Art Exhibitions to raise funds. Of course it was a lot of hard work, but it was always interesting and good to see such a large variety of paintings on the walls, talk to prospective clients and generally help people to understand the problems that faced Vietnam. It was exciting and rewarding to have so many willing and sympathetic artists, many of whom gave their work entirely or shared a generous portion of the proceeds of their sales with us. Beryl Bainbridge enjoyed her first success as a painter with us, before she became a famous writer. Patrick Proctor, David Hockney, Ron Kitaj, Philip Hughes, Keith Grant, Hilda Bernstein, Harold Elvin, Ken Sprague and Peter de Francia were among the hundred or more participants. Not only did they respond to our appeals time and again, but often helped to hang up the pictures as well. In our hey-day we raised sums exceeding £10,000, though as Vietnam receded from the headlines, it became progressively harder to achieve large turnovers.

After acknowledging the efforts of many other volunteers, Barbara also summarized her own inspirational journey to the country:

Certainly one of my personal highlights in all those years was my visit to Vietnam itself in 1975. It came as part of my helping with the co-ordinating programme of the European Committees, at a time when the war was in its final stages. After a meeting with the Medical Aid Committee in the German Democratic Republic in Berlin, it was decided I should fly out with a large consignment of medical supplies to Hanoi to investigate at first hand the possibilities of shipping still larger quantities of aid, either by bigger aircraft or by boat to recently liberated ports. I flew from East Berlin via Moscow, Tashkent, Dacca and Karachi to Hanoi. We were just three passengers, four flight crews, and a huge amount of packing cases in a fairly small Illyushin 18, belonging to the German Democratic Republic airline, Interflug. Aboard we kept European time till we got there twenty-six hours later. We slept on top of the packing cases (much more comfortable than ordinary passenger flights). The reception at Hanoi was as warm as the spring air. By sheer coincidence, the war finished on the day of my arrival – and hardly anyone could believe it. There was a kind of stunned reaction, with sporadic outbursts of jubilation which was most touching. I was the only foreigner there with an 8mm cine camera, and allowed to film everywhere, including some of the spontaneous celebrations. I travelled over several areas of the North, to Haphong and Ha Long Bay, saw much of the devastation and destruction. But I saw also much of the incredible vitality, industriousness and warmth of the Vietnamese people. Their hopefulness, their resilience and their ability to cope with such horrendous adversity was an impression which made an indelible mark on me. The beauty of the country, the friendly warmth and generous hospitality of its people made my trip unforgettable.

Barbara's film footage of this journey is now held by the Imperial War Museum, London.

Derrick was a dedicated pacificist, and backed Barbara's political activism in every way. She also recalled the support and interest shown by her children, Tony, Michelle and Katrin (born 1961), and how they joined in with odd jobs, and helped with circulars and invitations for events of the MACV. It is astonishing how Barbara would manage to juggle family life with supporting Derrick's enterprises, realising her own passions for making and later promoting contemporary jewellery, and also find the time for her political commitments. Barbara's political conscience was so strong that nothing would hold her back helping people in need, especially those affected by immoral governments or politics. Her conviction was to work for a 'world of friendship, co-operation and abundance'.

Barbara in her studio in Hampstead,
c.1960

A Jeweller Emerges

By the mid 1950s, the success of Taxi-Trucks meant that Derrick could employ more drivers and office staff. After all the years Barbara had supported him in the business, he felt it was time for her to follow her own interests. He was adamant that Barbara should do something she enjoyed and encouraged her to go back to her creative roots. As a young girl in Berlin she showed a talent for fashion design, producing semi-professional artwork which included fabric samples and was signed 'Emma Feistmann 35'. These have miraculously survived, as have life drawings, mainly in charcoal and pencil, which she made during her brief time at St Martin's School of Art in 1939.

In 1957 Barbara decided to approach the Central School of Arts and Crafts in London to study part-time. She enrolled without even arranging an appointment to see the different departments. Her original intention was to register for painting or sculpture and she brought along her portfolio from before the war, but on arrival she spontaneously asked at the front desk if they also had a course for jewellery. Barbara later remembered how the head of the Silversmithing and Jewellery Department, Arthur Robert Emerson, was surprised by her sudden arrival and rather sceptical of her plans. He reminded her that the school would not take beginners. However much Barbara was confident in her metalworking skills, he was unconvinced about her abilities to master the course, having lacked any prior training. In her inimitable way, Barbara negotiated a probation period of six months, for three days a week, and if she proved to be unsuitable she would be obliged to leave.

In Caputh, Barbara had learnt how to work with metals and hammer a bracelet or bowl into shape from Neusilber, a nickel silver. She was now excited about broadening her experience. Within the first week the students had to prove their basic skills: to make chain links, saw out cufflinks and decorate their frames, and copy an Anglo-Saxon brooch using resin instead of enamel for colour. The teachers were technically skilled craftsmen from nearby Hatton Garden workshops, but Barbara remarked on their lack of imagination. They would often pass her bench and question what she making, shake their heads and walk on. However, Barbara passed her trial period and was to prove very successful. Her designs captured the mood and fashion of the time and were popular with several London outlets even during her student days. She stayed in the School until 1960 although her hallmark was registered at the assay office in Goldsmiths' Hall, London, in 1958, which Barbara enthusiastically reported to her mother Luise on 14 November of that year.

On 13 February 1959 Barbara proudly told Luise about her newly created stationery headed 'Barbara Cartlidge / Hand Made Silver Jewellery' with the Hampstead address. There was also an explanation for her change of name: 'How do you like my letter heading? I am a bit miserable having exchanged the Emma for Barbara, I don't really know what started that except that someone introduced me as Barbara at Liberty's and it sounded better at the time, now I really think it was a bit silly but as most people here think that Bobby derives from Barbara, and both Emma and Barbara are on all my papers, it is perhaps just as well. Anyway, I delivered my second lot to Heal's yesterday and although Liberty's are interested very much, they haven't yet bought anything but said they want to start with my things in the second half of the year'.

Barbara's studio in Hampstead,
c.1960

Whilst still a student, Barbara had befriended the furniture designer Christopher Heal of Heal & Son Ltd, whose flagship store was on Tottenham Court Road. Under Christopher and his brother Anthony, the company would become renowned for promoting modern styles in Britain, such as Scandinavian design and 1960s Pop, and for employing young designers. One day in 1958, a friend of Barbara's, who worked in the bedding department, mentioned that the company had recently introduced an area called 'The Craftsman's Market' for handmade goods which expressed a contemporary aesthetic. As jewellery was not yet shown there, she should present herself to the woman in charge, a Mrs Pollock. Barbara's first approach in December 1958 failed, but in January 1959 her jewellery was eagerly accepted. The first ten pieces were sold almost immediately and Mrs Pollock had commissioned a ring for herself. On 10 September that year Barbara wrote to her mother: 'Yesterday I went to Heal's because they wrote me a letter asking for new stock (what a change from six months ago when I had to smuggle my things through the back door) and they bought a pretty big amount as well as offering me a solo exhibition in Spring of new designs and with special feature publicity. Isn't that wonderful?' In April 1960 Barbara made 65 pieces of jewellery for her first solo exhibition at Heal's, a great triumph for a budding jeweller. They sold 40 per cent of the exhibition pieces but the rest were stolen. As Barbara later recalled, in those days displays were often on open shelves. It was a great achievement for Barbara, and a stepping stone. The excitement of meeting the public and having her work so well received by the press so early in her career was thrilling.

Barbara's first workshop was the kitchen table in the family house in Hampstead. She soon moved to a bench in a narrow passageway and finally to the conservatory at the back which she transformed into a goldsmith's workshop, with an array of tools and a view into the garden. Fritz Falk, former director of the Schmuckmuseum Pforzheim, who became good friends with Barbara and Derrick, has fond recollections of watching her work in this small studio and the beautiful vine which formed a natural cover to the roof. Many artist-jewellers have described how they assisted her in this workshop, and later in the basement of Electrum Gallery.

Ring and two bracelets by Barbara Cartlidge, 1960, silver and gemstones

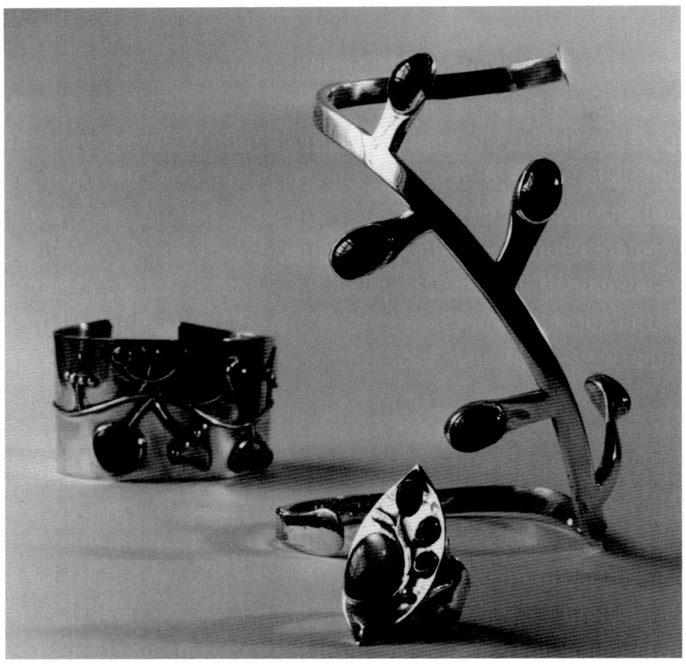

Bangle by Barbara Cartlidge, c.1968,
silver and pink tourmaline

Ring by Barbara Cartlidge, c.1968,
silver and amethyst

Her breakthrough at Heal's in 1960 snowballed into further successes and sales. Various outlets in London marketed her jewellery, mainly craft galleries, such as Primavera on Sloane Street, Anschel on King's Road and Ewan Phillips on Maddox Street. Some pieces were also exhibited in the newly opened Design Centre on Haymarket. Barbara's early jewellery fitted very well with the spirit and fashions of the time. Between 1966 and 1968 her bold designs seemed to have caught the eyes of fashion photographers and many of her rings and bangles were worn by models in popular fashion magazines, such as *Harper's Bazaar*, *Vogue* and *Queen*. In 1968 her jewellery was even featured in *The Daily Telegraph magazine*, worn by the model and actress, Veruschka, who loved Barbara's designs.

In 1966, in a letter to Luise, Barbara described her forthcoming visit to Idar-Oberstein, a German city internationally known for gemstone trading, to acquire higher quality gemstones than her mother had been sending her from the United States. Barbara also mentioned a company for whom she had been asked to design a whole collection of jewellery, but there is no further mention of this in the family archives. On 9 August 1966 Barbara proudly announced: 'I had a lot of interesting commissions, and have just finished making an episcopal ring with amethyst for the future Bishop of the Isle of Man who invited me to his investiture on 29 September'. He also commissioned his wife's wedding ring. After 1968 the family archive is less revealing as Luise returned to England that year and the letters between them cease.

Barbara had a passion for gemstones. It was the feel of them, their tactile quality, which she loved. She found stones with imperfections and inclusions more exciting as they bore the fingerprint of nature. In an article called 'Striking it Rich' for *Harper's Bazaar* in June 1968, Barbara admitted, 'invariably it is the stone that decides the design and I will use [just] about any stone, provided it looks exciting. I am not terribly concerned about the cost of it – if it has some sort of life, some magic, some mystique about it.' Quartz slices with fascinating formations, rutilated quartz with its crystalline structure and natural random patterns and cabochon stones, preferably in their natural

Barbara Cartlidge
with Fritz Falk, c.1984

Necklace by Barbara Cartlidge,
1968, silver, gold and agate

Earrings by Barbara Cartlidge, c.1968,
gold and agate

Silver ring with agate by Barbara Cartlidge in the Ewan Phillips Gallery, *Queen*, 1966

Ring by Barbara Cartlidge, 1968, gold and agate.
Alice and Louis Koch Collection, Swiss National Museum, Zurich

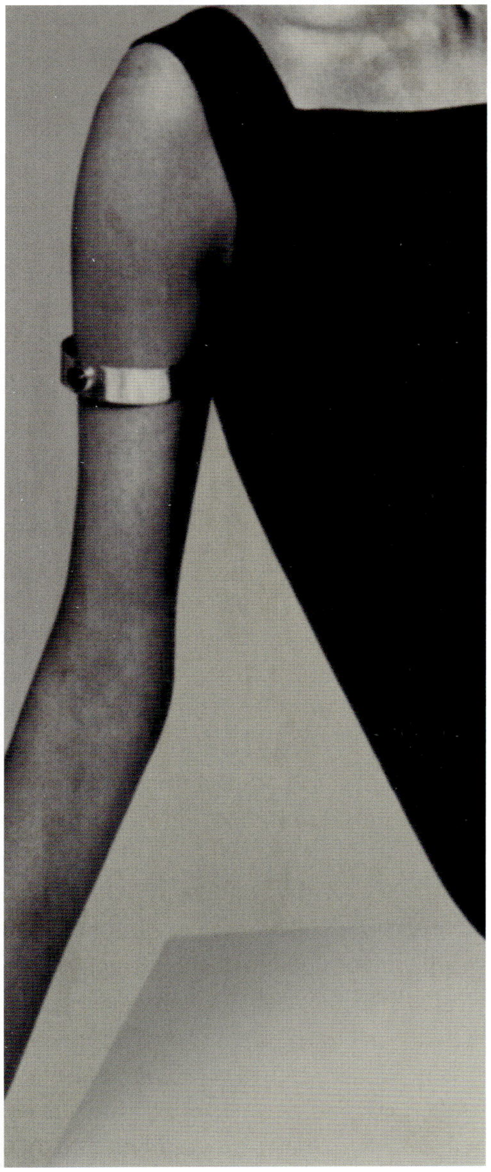

Jewellery by Barbara Cartlidge,
Harpers Bazaar, October 1966

OF CABOCHONS AND RINGS

Heralding the new spring scintillation— a panoply of jewels rich in memories of mediaeval courts. Great gilded chain of office, far left, a pendant or belt in a series of sparkling Maltese crosses with fabled and fiery stones. 50 gns, at the Ken Lane Boutique. On a man's pure sky blue silk shirt, tucked, pearl buttoned, 12 gns, at Turnbull & Asser. Important black papier mâché cufflinks, ringed in gilt, set with sea deep sapphire stones. Large lustrous gold-dipped papier mâché armlet, near left, bright with swirls of ruby rose and rhinestone. Both by Siboa, 5 gns, at Dickins & Jones. Grand cardinal red cabochon ring embellished with curls of gold. By Adrien Mann, 21s, at Liberty. Finely wrought gilt belt interspersed with splendid cabochon stones like pigeon's blood rubies and night dark sapphires. By Adrien Mann, 10 gns, Marshall & Snelgrove. On a slip of silky blush pink twill, flared and hung on diamanté ribbon straps, 9 gns, at main Wallis branches. Crème de Rose nail varnish, by Lenthéric. Glittering galaxy of rings, right. Star cluster of garnet and pearl, 17s. 6d. Oval opalescent cabochon moonstone, 35s. Both by Adrien Mann, at Marshall & Snelgrove. Sombre Indian jewels in a circling sea of silver. By Four As Agency, £3, at Sunas, Radnor Walk. Beautiful cool blue stone in gilded lacquer black papier mâché. By Siboa, 3½ gns, at Dickins & Jones. Luminous lilac quartz cabochon set high in a studded crown of silver. 12 gns, at Biba. For other shops and colours, see Stockists

Jewellery by Barbara Cartlidge worn by model Verushka, *The Daily Telegraph Magazine*, 27 September 1968

Bangle by Barbara Cartlidge,
1971, silver and amethyst

Bracelet by Barbara Cartlidge,
c.1968, silver and amethyst.
Victoria and Albert Museum, London

and irregular shapes, were her favourites. Her most favoured combination of materials, however, was amethyst set in silver. Her office at home had purple walls, and her favourite colours to wear were (and still are) silver and purple.

Her jewellery repertoire included neckpieces, pendants and earrings but she chiefly made finger rings, because she liked wearing rings best. This was an unusual preference as her designs were very complex and working with three-dimensional forms at such a miniature scale would not be to every jeweller's taste. The variety of her designs was exceptional and she tried, unsuccessfully, to patent one of them, her take on the traditional seal ring. The set stone design incorporated a container which concealed a rubber stamp, which, when removed, could be used to stamp the wearer's address on an envelope. Barbara once teased the officials at Checkpoint Charlie in Berlin with such a ring, when having to fill out numerous forms to visit friends behind the wall in East Berlin. The chief officer on duty was so impressed by it that he ordered her first commission of this design! Some ornamental motifs recur in her designs, becoming almost trademark signatures, such as ornamental friezes with small triangular shapes in combination with globules, as found on a pendant and ring in the Victoria and Albert Museum, London, and on an earlier bangle and a later ring. The same motif forms the border pattern on the invitation card, which she designed and made, for her first solo exhibition at Heal's.

Barbara's jewellery designs of the 1960s reflected her admiration for Scandinavian design, very much in vogue at the time, in particular the work of the designers at Georg Jensen in Copenhagen. She shared with them clarity of form, clean outlines and simplicity of design with a minimum of

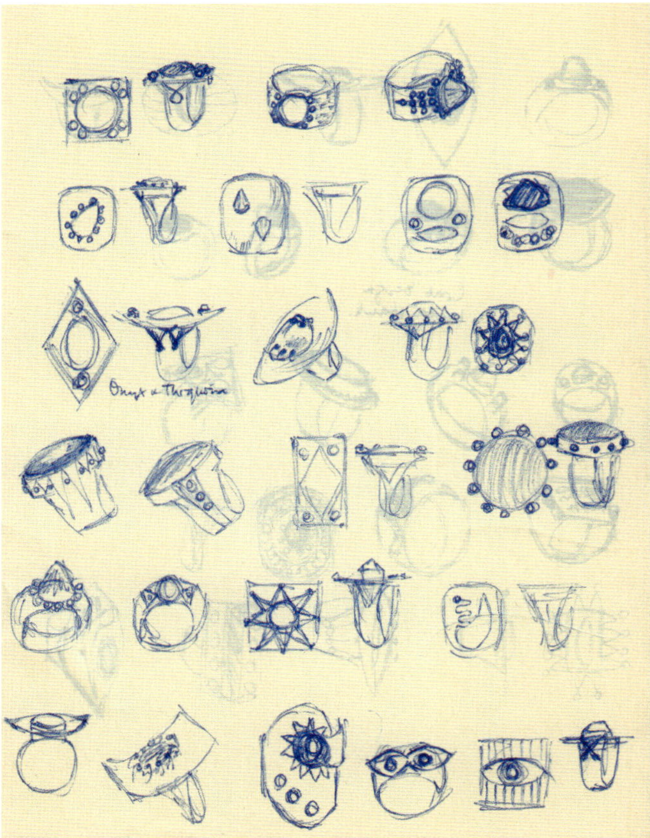

Drawings of rings
by Barbara Cartlidge,
date unknown, pen on paper

ornamentation. When Barbara had made her surprising decision to specialise in jewellery at the Central School of Arts and Crafts in 1957, it had been sparked by a chance encounter with Scandinavian design during a holiday in the south of France with the family a few months before. The Swedish jeweller Torun Bülow-Hübe (1927–2004) was unknown to Barbara until she was mesmerised by a display of her jewellery hidden in a glasshouse at the back of a villa in the picturesque Provençal village of Biot. Here Torun lived with her family and had a workshop. The sheer simplicity and bold forms of Torun's jewellery designs were awe-inspiring for Barbara. The clean cut lines, oval and round shapes and use of asymmetric gemstones or pebbles found on the beach had a lasting effect on her and the encounter would prove a major turning point in her life. In 1967 Torun joined the Danish company Georg Jensen as designer and gained fame as one of the most innovative designers of the second half of the 20th century.

British jewellers of the late 1950s and 1960s such as Gerda Flöckinger, Helga Zahn, Sah Oved, John Donald, Andrew Grima and David Thomas also experimented with natural stone formations, irregular cabochons and pebbles, and settings were randomly formed. Barbara caught the mood of the moment and admits to having been influenced by fashionable trends in jewellery. Graham Hughes of The Goldsmiths' Company wrote an article in the 1963 edition of *The Saturday Book* about 'The New Jewellers' stating: 'The best jewels are now the most imaginative, not necessarily the most expensive'. In 1961, in association with the Victoria and Albert Museum, he had organised a ground-breaking exhibition at Goldsmiths' Hall, the *International Exhibition of Modern Jewellery 1890–1961*. Jewellery was finally being recognised as an art form. It was an exciting period, traditions were being broken and a new freedom of expression was evolving. Barbara's passion for jewellery came at the right time.

Invitation to solo exhibition at Heal's, 1960,
designed by Barbara Cartlidge

Pendant with chain by Barbara Cartlidge, c.1967,
silver and agate.
Victoria and Albert Museum, London

Rings by Barbara Cartlidge, 1968, silver and agate, 9ct gold and aquamarine

Ring by Barbara Cartlidge, 1968, silver and amethyst. Victoria and Albert Museum, London

Ring by Barbara Cartlidge, c.1973, silver and aquamarine

Electrum Gallery

Barbara experienced personal success with her jewellery designs throughout the 1960s, with work displayed in various galleries in Britain and abroad. One of these was the Ewan Phillips Gallery in Maddox Street, London. She knew the founder and his family, wealthy Dutch Jews who had also been forced to leave their home country due to political circumstances. In 1965, Ewan Phillips opened an art gallery for modernist painting and sculpture, and, unusually for the time, he decided to include jewellery in his range. He asked Barbara if she would like to display some of her work in a special exhibition, *The Renaissance of Modern Jewellery in Britain*. Forty jewellers participated in the exhibition, some better known than others. The accompanying leaflet called them 'artist-craftsmen', and its recognition of 'a renaissance in modern jewellery' was exceptional for the period. The comments from the press, such as 'Revolution in jewellery design' (*What's On in London*), and '… [a] break away from the traditional …' (*Vanity Fair*), were revealing. Their response, together with the influence of Graham Hughes' 1961 exhibition at Goldsmiths' Hall, showed that modern jewellery was finally getting the recognition it deserved, its status moving away from the applied arts to the fine arts.

It was in the Ewan Phillips Gallery that Barbara first met Ralph Turner, who had recently moved to London from South Wales to become an actor. Having discovered an enthusiasm for the art world through exhibitions, his focus turned towards contemporary jewellery. Soon afterwards the Ewan Phillips Gallery discontinued selling jewellery and eventually closed down in 1968. Fortuitously, the British Peace Committee was looking for an outlet to raise funds for their causes, as was already common practice in other European countries. Barbara seized this opportunity and was influential in organising and running a new venue, which was well situated in St Christopher's Place, just off Oxford Street. The gallery was named Pace, from the Latin and Italian words meaning peace. The gallery sold mainly glass, pottery and jewellery. In November 1969 it held a specialised exhibition

21 South Molton Street, c. 1970

on jewellery with a small accompanying catalogue. Of the 37 artist-jewellers represented, a number of them had previously exhibited at the Ewan Phillips Gallery, but there were also some new well-known names from Europe and the United States. By this point Ralph Turner had joined the team but the business was running into difficulties. Barbara was still very active raising funds for the charity Medical Aid Committee for Vietnam and even though the Pace gallery was successful, she realised it was not easy working for a committee who had little understanding of what was being sold. Before long she was confronted with the situation of not being able to pay the artists, and it emerged that the secretary of the committee had defrauded funds. Despite financially subsidizing the venture, Barbara decided to resign and take a loss. The committee subsequently forced Ralph Turner to leave and by 1969 it ceased to exist.

From failure grew success, and the idea for Electrum, an independent gallery dedicated exclusively to contemporary jewellery, was born. Derrick was quick to grasp that a new gallery could be a success, and suggested that Barbara could 'start your own thing', and, as Ralph Turner was then available, he could assist in running it. Derrick was again the driving force behind the idea and after much deliberation they both began to search for suitable premises for a new gallery. When they were offered a shop previously rented by a distinguished tailor in 21 South Molton Street they instantly accepted. The location was perfect, connecting Oxford Street with the luxury shops on Bond Street. Little did they realise this was more than the beginning of a new business venture. It was to become a huge part of their lives, especially Barbara's, as her passion for jewellery would continue to flourish.

The six months before the gallery opened in June 1971 were very busy, and exciting. Even though Derrick generously supported the costs of the gallery, expenses needed to be kept to a minimum, as resources were not limitless. Ralph Turner became co-director and manager, with a view to earning a partnership through commissions, as he was initially unable to contribute to the business financially. Barbara was very keen to preserve the original features of the historic building, but the interior

Electrum Gallery, 21 South Molton Street, 1974

Electrum Gallery, interior view, 1979

needed to have a modern feel. Wall cladding and a false ceiling simply painted with white emulsion created a neutral setting to allow the jewellery to stand out. Helga Zahn designed modular showcases which were then built by a customer of Derrick's, and these lasted well into the 1990s. The system consisted of flexible units which could be adapted to what was required, and for each exhibition the appearance could be transformed without great effort.

The search to find a suitable name for the gallery led to Electrum, a natural occurring alloy of silver and gold used by goldsmiths since ancient times. Barbara felt it was a descriptive and up-to-date name, and liked the 'zippy' ring to it. The distinctive lettering – which became the trademark symbol of the gallery – was conceived by the young designer John Rice. Ralph brought in Raymond Carpenter, a graphic designer, who assisted with the stencils on the front window, the labels and other graphic details for the following years. Ray fondly remembers working with Helga Zahn on the text, design and production of the first catalogue. Graham Hughes, then Chairman of the Crafts Centre of Great Britain, wrote the foreword, praising the founders and outlining their aims: 'The admirable idea of Barbara Cartlidge and Ralph Turner is to concentrate on named artists, by promoting them for their creative contribution on jewellery. The gallery will emphasise that jewellery is art, not just bullion.' In Barbara's and Ralph's introduction to the gallery in the catalogue and, similarly, in the press release, they stated: 'The gallery will exhibit work chosen for its aesthetic quality and made from both the traditional materials silver and gold as well as some of the new materials that are being discovered by some of our designers.' Taken for granted now, the combination of precious and non-precious materials and the use of plastics and paper for jewellery were revolutionary for the time.

The grand opening night of Electrum Gallery was on 23 June 1971. The jeweller Wendy Ramshaw remembers the first piece to be sold on the night was one of her innovative ring sets with surgical mirrors, which was acquired as an engagement ring. To quote Ramshaw, 'Barbara was an exceptional person … the gallery was so key, it drew a lot of artist-jewellers because of its rarity, and was indeed very special.' As history would prove, Electrum Gallery was established at the beginning of a new trend in showcasing contemporary jewellery. Prior to the opening of Electrum, artist-jewellers whose work did not belong in a traditional jewellers shop found themselves exhibiting their pieces in craft galleries, which included ceramics, glass and textiles, among other craft disciplines. As Barbara had recognised there was a need to create a new platform for contemporary jewellery, and to find a new audience who would appreciate its novelty and artistic value. In the press release written by Electrum for the opening, their aim was clearly stated: 'We feel now that the time has come to establish a gallery for this art form and so give jewellery designers the same opportunity for exhibiting their work that is enjoyed by painters and sculptors.'

The early history of the contemporary jewellery movement is discussed in correspondence from 1984 between Barbara and gallery owners Marie and Peter Hassenflug. In Germany there was a different jewellery culture, which persists today. The wearing of jewellery was more widespread, and customers were more open-minded to modern trends, which might explain why dedicated galleries appeared there first. In 1968, the MAP Gallery, named after its owner Map Sauer, opened in Cologne to display and sell contemporary jewellery, with gemstones and minerals included in the displays. In 1969, Galerie Orfèvre in Düsseldorf was founded by Marie and Peter Hassenpflug exclusively for contemporary jewellery and celebrated its 45th anniversary in 2014. In 1972, a year after Electrum opened, Inge Asenbaum founded the Galerie am Graben in Vienna (closed in 1988) and in 1973 Helen Drutt gave her name to a gallery in Philadelphia which continues to support artist-jewellers. Although there was an overlap of artist-jewellers being represented, the choice often differed according to regional support and taste. These venues were the pioneers of the international contemporary jewellery movement and were soon followed by the next generation, such as Galerie Ra in Amsterdam (1976), Galerie Marzee in Nijmwegen (1978), Galerie Spektrum in Munich (1981) and Louise Smit in Amsterdam (1986–2012). Today galleries exclusively selling contemporary jewellery continue to flourish worldwide, with the remarkable exception of London.

Barbara Cartlidge with Wendy Ramshaw
at the Victoria and Albert Museum, London,
1982

Barbara Cartlidge with E.R. Nele, 1978

From left to right: Monika and Fritz Falk, Barbara Cartlidge, Therese Hilbert, Otto Künzli and Hubertus von Skal, 1978

'Hallway' pendant and
'Door' pendant and ring
by Barbara Cartlidge, c.1973,
silver and gold

'Door' Pendant by
Barbara Cartlidge, c.1973,
silver and gold

'Chest of Drawers' ring by
Barbara Cartlidge, 1974,
silver and gold

'His Master's Voice' ring by
Barbara Cartlidge, c.1973,
silver and gold

To understand this phenomenon one needs to look back on how jewellery making changed in the post-war period. By the 1960s, jewellers in Europe and the United States could learn how to make jewellery at art schools, rather than through the more traditional route of apprenticeships. This was a novel approach to teaching the subject. In Britain, Gerda Flöckinger, a leading avant-garde jeweller, set up a new and experimental course in modern jewellery at Hornsey College of Art in London. Jewellery was no longer simply seen as adornment or restricted to a period style. It developed independently from dress fashions, becoming an expression of the individual artist-jeweller and a reflection of their contemporary world. During the 1960s, jewellers broke away from tradition in search of new forms and techniques to create a modern aesthetic. It was all about the individuality of the maker and the wearer.

Those who knew Electrum Gallery from its early days have commented how quickly it gained national and international recognition. There was a general feeling that this gallery was something very different to anything that had been seen before. During an interview with the author, Raymond Carpenter summed up what Barbara and Ralph had achieved in so short a time: 'by end of 1971 they were on the map, it was definitely a place to be'. The first exhibitions created a storm with the press. In the aftermath of the opening in June 1971, articles appeared in *Country Life*, *The Sunday Telegraph*, *Design* and *Retail Jeweller* magazines (the latter with the title 'New Jewellery showplace run on art gallery lines') and *Harpers & Queen*. Later in the year the gallery featured in *The Lady*, *The Guardian*, *The Observer*, *Evening Standard* and *What's On in London* magazine.

British design was also finding international recognition in the 1970s. In 1971, Wendy Ramshaw, Catherine Mannheim and Barbara were invited to represent British jewellery at the opening of an exhibition on all aspects of British design in the Musée des arts décoratifs in the Louvre, Paris, where Princess Margaret gave the opening speech. In that same year, the work of jewellers such as David Thomas, Peter Hauffe and Wendy Ramshaw were displayed at a landmark exhibition in Nuremberg

'Train' bangle by Barbara Cartlidge, 1972, silver and gold

marking the 500th anniversary of Albrecht Dürer, entitled *Gold+Silber Schmuck+Gerät*. In 1973, in association with The Goldsmiths' Company, Electrum Gallery organised an exhibition on British jewellery in the Deutsches Goldschmiedehaus in Hanau, Germany, with a small catalogue written by Ralph Turner.

It was during this period that Barbara made some of her most recognisable jewellery which she called 'toys for adults'. She made a series of rings and pendants, in silver with gold details, showing scenes from inside her home in Hampstead. When opening a hinged door one might enter a miniature house with a view of a hallway and staircase, or a sitting room with sofa, lamp and flowers on a fireplace, a kitchen with a sink and pots, or a bathroom with a shower. Such details as plants, pictures on the walls, patterned curtains, lamps and clocks were lovingly recreated. One of her favourite miniature objects, which she described in detail in an interview, was an ornately curved 18th-century cupboard. Two rings stand out: one in the form of a chest-of-drawers with drawers that open and surmounted by a fruit bowl on a runner; the other a wind-up gramophone, which opens to reveal a record, with the emblem of HMV (His Master's Voice) on the lid. The most spectacular creations are her small series of bangles, each consisting of a wide band supporting miniatures. One featured a model railway with an engine and three coaches moving around a circular track, surrounded by houses and pine trees; another, a carousel with six golden horses. The hidden technical trick is that these central motifs can be pushed down when worn on the arm and, when taken off the band, they can function as miniature toys. The jewellery proved to be immensely popular. The collection was sold out and more had to be made. Claus Bury, a 'surrogate son' as Barbara called him, remembers helping out and sending a small group of goldsmiths from Germany to assist in the production. At one point, two thirds of the income of the gallery came from sales of Barbara's jewellery.

However exciting these early years were, the fascination for jewellery as an art form was not enough to keep the gallery afloat. Derrick was very generous in his financial support. As Barbara wrote in

'Wardrobe' pendant by Barbara Cartlidge, 1972, silver and gold

'Kitchen' pendant by Barbara Cartlidge, 1972, silver

one of her many recollections about the gallery, 'While Electrum raised a lot of dust with challenging exhibitions, it failed to make the connections that might have turned spectators into clients'. It took time for an audience to fully appreciate 'new jewellery' and have the wish to own and wear it.

By 1974, the two very strong personalities who were instrumental to the setting up of Electrum, and devoted to the cause, were at odds. For a number of reasons – and plenty of rumours surrounded this incident – Barbara asked Ralph to leave. They went their own ways and individually continued to support the movement in major publications and numerous exhibitions. Ralph went on to work for the Crafts Advisory Council (now known as the Crafts Council). With subsidies at his disposal, he had the freedom to show avant-garde exhibitions in Europe and in London which were more like art exhibitions, often with accompanying catalogues, and not dependent on sales. Interestingly, he also chose to move away from the concept of showing jewellery alone, and instead mixed it with other media. Some artist-jewellers preferred this cross-fertilisation. The decorative arts were gaining in status, with glass, pottery, textiles and other media being accepted as art forms in their own right. The split between Ralph and Barbara meant that a number of the British artist-jewellers found their loyalties lay with one or the other, while some were able to maintain a balance. The situation was common knowledge among the gallery exhibitors, whom Barbara described as a 'brotherhood', but had less impact on the international artist-jewellers, who were thrilled to be shown at Electrum Gallery. 'Swinging' London had increasingly become an important centre for the arts, and Electrum was the place for jewellers to show their work.

After Ralph left, Barbara had to rethink the future of Electrum. She was very much aware that running such a specialised gallery was not going to be hugely profitable, but at least it should make its own way. With Derrick's support and Barbara's dedication they kept the business going, but it would take another two years before the gallery broke even. From there it would steadily prosper. To use Barbara's own words from 1996, on the occasion of the gallery's 25th anniversary, 'it grew in

'Bathroom' pendant by Barbara Cartlidge, 1972, silver and gold

'Carousel' bangle by Barbara Cartlidge, 1972, silver and gold

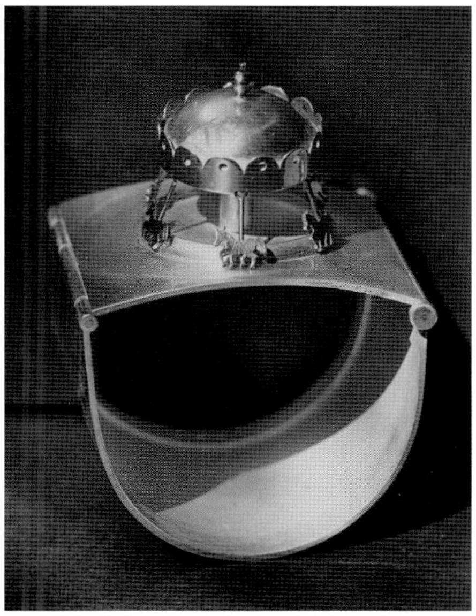

Electrum Gallery, exterior view, 1979

a steady upward direction, to be the kind of forum for artist-jewellers and clients from all over the world, which I had always hoped for'.

It took time for the public to accept the new style of jewellery and the use of new materials. These included acrylic, either on its own or combined with gold or silver; new metals discovered in the aftermath of space technology, such as titanium and niobium; 'high end' paper jewellery that the wearer could construct; materials not previously used by jewellers, such as felt, rubber, feathers and aluminium; and even found objects turned into wearable miniature, or not so miniature, works of art. Traditional metals, such as gold and silver, were being treated in a novel way. Settings for gemstones or pearls were redefined, often in asymmetric compositions, and the stones were cut in unusual shapes. The jewellery was unconventional, exceptional and, for some, perhaps even shocking. Barbara acknowledged that wearing works of art was demanding, unlike owning a painting or sculpture. For the wearer 'to have it actually on your person means you completely identify with it, via its creator it also becomes a statement of the wearer.' She saw her function as that of communicator between the artist and the public.

For Barbara, emerging talents were as important as established names. The 1970s was a groundbreaking decade when jewellers were experimenting with materials and forms in their search for innovation. By the 1980s, many artist-jewellers had gained public recognition and new ideas were discussed with enthusiasm. It was also the height of the conceptual art movement, in which the ideas behind works of art were considered more important than their finished appearance, and the question was asked: 'what is jewellery?' Many artist-jewellers tested the limits of wearability. Barbara was pleased to be a part of this significant development, and make her contribution through the gallery.

Over time, the gallery built up a clientele who appreciated contemporary jewellery, who sought out the unusual and would return to acquire more. Collectors and museum curators would come to South Molton Street from all over the world to see what was new and be inspired to add to their collections. Barbara very much enjoyed personal contact with the clients and, most of all, her conversations with the artist-jewellers. She had very open and frank opinions and was forthright in voicing them when the artists came to show their jewellery. Some makers found this intimidating but appreciated her honesty; many were in awe of her and found the comments constructive. Barbara was a jeweller herself and understood the intricacies of making, appreciating the work involved. One memory the jewellers nearly all shared was the cloud of smoke that perpetually surrounded Barbara. She was a chain smoker throughout her life, as can be seen in many photographs, and it almost became a trademark, along with her large glasses.

Through her charity work for the Medical Aid Committee for Vietnam Barbara knew many artists, authors, actors and musicians, and these contacts spread the word about Electrum. In an interview, Barbara mentions a few of the celebrities who visited the gallery, such as David Niven, Vincent Price, Robert Wagner, Natalie Wood and Elton John. From this period Barbara dedicated her time to the gallery and friends would help her with the daily running of it, such as Anna Britten, the wife of an eccentric director of *Vogue* magazine, and the actress Louie Ramsay, best known for her role in the Ruth Rendell Mysteries series on television.

In later years Barbara suffered from agoraphobia, an open secret but extremely debilitating for her. It took some time for the condition to be recognised, as nobody was willing to believe that someone as active, independent and well-travelled as Barbara could suddenly develop such a condition. She would not leave the house without a trusted person, and avoided crowds, suffering anxiety and other unpleasant symptoms. Wendy Ramshaw remembers accompanying Barbara to the gallery on a regular basis. Barbara's presence in the building was reducing, and it became important to find someone to whom she could hand over the day-to-day responsibilities. Barbara was particularly indebted to

Angela Cowall and to her longest standing member of staff, Janice Hosegood. She wrote about them in her exhibition text for the 25th anniversary: 'their efforts have been a tremendous help and great contribution to the continued success of Electrum Gallery'. Janice, who had studied Design & Crafts at Epsom School of Art and specialised in jewellery, began working for Barbara in November 1987. Having also been trained in business studies, she was perfect for the gallery, as she had a passion for creativity combined with an understanding for the commercial requirements of the business. Barbara and Janice would discuss in detail the exhibition programme and decide together which artist-jewellers should be invited. The exhibitions raised the profile of Electrum, but the gallery's main income came from a much larger group of jewellers whose work was on permanent display. Barbara and Janice were both excellent at spotting new talent, and felt it was important to give young designers and recent graduates a chance to exhibit in a commercial setting. Students, mainly from the Royal College of Art, were also employed to work in the gallery on a part-time basis. They learnt how to communicate with clients and understand the commercial side of their artwork. It was a tremendous opportunity and benefitted a number of young artist-jewellers who are well known today.

Barbara's decision to work with Niessing, a German jewellery manufacturer since 1873, has often been misunderstood. Because they were a company, rather than an individual, assumptions were made that they had some financial involvement but in reality their relationship with the gallery was exactly the same as the other artist-jewellers. Barbara admired their ethos of quality production and exceptional design. They employed talented designers, mainly German and Dutch, to create their collections. It was also during this period that Electrum had a makeover. Niessing provided workmen and designs for new cases, but the project was financed by Electrum.

South Molton Street was increasingly fashionable and an ideal location for a jewellery shop. Electrum was situated between Browns, the glamorous fashion store, and Butler & Wilson with its exuberant costume jewellery. Janice remembers Barbara's description of the diversity of clients who regularly visited the gallery: 'from baronets to barrow boys'. Often people would walk into the gallery and exclaim, 'I had no idea that something like this existed'. The discovery of jewellery as an art form was a revelation to many, who, after developing an appreciation for it, would then become regular clients. Janice recalls how rewarding it was to work with clients who were so interested and passionate about jewellery. She also remembers Barbara's idiosyncrasies, experienced by many. She was incredibly generous and loved to entertain, inviting the artists to stay at her house and enjoy her renowned dinner parties. On the other hand, Barbara could be quite frugal. Her handmade leather pouches, made from off-cuts or scraps of leather and hand stitched, were used regardless of whether a jewel was exceedingly expensive or inexpensive. Some clients were surprised by the pouches, and even hated them, while others collected them.

Barbara was always proud of her photographic skills and used many of her own images on the invitation cards to the gallery's exhibitions. Aesthetically, these cards were simple but effective. She nearly always included an informative explanatory text about the artist-jeweller(s) and had a great ability for capturing the essential points of their work. Writing came naturally to her, and her knowledge about 20th-century jewellery was extensive. Her book on the subject, *Twentieth-Century Jewelry,* published in New York in 1985, continues to be an important reference work. This was preceded by a contribution on 20th-century rings in *The Ring from Antiquity to the Twentieth Century* (1981). Barbara was invited to give lectures in Europe and the United States, and to be on judging panels for fairs, shows and competitions, for example in Hanau. Over the years she received many accolades. She became a freeman of The Goldsmiths' Company in 1978 and in 1987, the goldsmith and designer Friedrich Becker presented her with the Golden David Award from the Committee of the Forum für Schmuck und Design in Cologne. In his speech, he called her 'The Queen of the Scene' for her contribution to 'new jewellery'.

Barbara Cartlidge with cigarette in a cloud of smoke, c.1968

Anton Cepka, Beatriz Chadour-Sampson, Barbara Cartlidge, Manfred Bischoff, Dr Barbara Mundt and Eberhard Burgel: judging panel for the international competition Schmuck in Bewegung, Bewegung in Schmuck (Jewellery in Motion, Motion in Jewellery), Hanau, 1987

From left to right: Barbara Cartlidge, Kathleen Slater, Janice Hosegood and Angela Cowall, 1990

In 2007, after 36 successful years, Barbara finally took the decision to sell Electrum Gallery. It was the end of an era and a sad day for artist-jewellers. Today aged 93, and despite suffering dementia, Barbara has neither lost her feisty spirit, nor her eye for recognising good jewellery. When her main carer and friend Hanne showed Barbara an image of her jewellery displayed in a showcase in the William and Judith Bollinger Jewellery Gallery of the Victoria and Albert Museum, her face lit up with a lovely smile of acknowledgement. Whilst working in the family archive, the author would go and visit Barbara with her little Chihuahua dog Ruby, as Barbara found pleasure playing with her. On one of these visits the author encountered Barbara unwell in bed, thumbing through her book, *Twentieth-Century Jewelry*. She was looking at page 131 while following with her finger the outlines of a beautiful bangle by Giampaolo Babetto; in one of her interviews she described Babetto as her 'great favourite'. At the same time she wore on her wrist a few strands of amethyst beads (her favourite colour) used for crafting, and when the author politely tried to open the conversation about them, she shrugged it off, as if to say 'this is not good jewellery'.

The final sentence of Barbara's 1985 book sums up what jewellery is all about and especially what it meant to someone with a passion for the subject: 'It is of real importance for both jewellery-makers and wearers to understand the fundamental meanings and function of all forms of jewellery, which is as powerful and essential to the individual today as it ever was. Jewellery is very much a part of our modern culture and a vital component of our spiritual and emotional well-being.' The long list of exhibitions at the back of this book, containing the names of hundreds of well-known artist-jewellers from Britain and abroad, who contributed over thirty-six years, is proof of Barbara's perseverance and enthusiasm for contemporary jewellery.

From left to right: Yasuki Hiramatsu, Barbara Cartlidge and Janice Hosegood, 1995

Electrum Gallery,
interior view, c.1990

Epilogue: The Cartlidge Family

As parents, Derrick and Barbara's combination of creativity and entrepreneurship must have been stimulating, but it must also have been challenging for their children to prove themselves against such strong-minded individuals. The success they have all achieved in their fields, and the passion they have demonstrated for their chosen professions, can perhaps be seen as part of Barbara's legacy. The two daughters in particular, inherited Barbara's creativity and became accomplished in their own artistic endeavours.

Their youngest daughter Katrin (1961–2002) was an acclaimed film and theatre actress, first working backstage at the Royal Court Theatre in London, and then acting with the Royal Young People's Theatre Group. She played a regular role on the television soap *Brookside* in the 1980s and soon garnered attention with an impressive list of films and stage appearances. Her film roles in *Before the Rain* (1994) and *No Man's Land* (2001) brought her particular critical acclaim, and she is probably best remembered for her haunting role in director Mike Leigh's *Naked* (1993). Tragically, Katrin's life was cut short through a sudden illness. In her obituary in *The Guardian* on 13 September 2002, Mike Leigh wrote about her passion for the arts and her plans to direct: 'And, despite her inspired, genius ability to lose herself in the character and to behave as an actor should, she also had the objective eye of an artist. For that is what she was, in the broader sense of the word, and in the way that most actors are not. She drew her inspiration not only from life and people and experience, but also from painting and sculpture and much else, including world cinema. She often talked to me about her eventual move into directing. I am in no doubt that we have lost not only one of our greatest actors but also one of the most interesting new directors of the future'. In an interview, Barbara admits that of all the trials she had been put through during her life, her daughter's death was the toughest experience of all. The Katrin Cartlidge Foundation set up after her death continues to award young filmmakers with a bursary.

Katrin Cartlidge at the National Theatre, November 1987

Michelle, Tony, Derrick and Katrin Cartlidge, c. 1990

From left to right: Barbara Cartlidge carrying Katrin, a family friend, Helene Reinfrank, Derrick and Michelle Cartlidge, September 1961

Barbara and Derrick's eldest daughter Michelle trained as a ceramicist at Hornsey College of Art and the Royal College of Art, London, but found that her talent lay in drawing. Today Michelle is a successful author and illustrator of over 50 children's books. She shares the same fascination for mice as her mother and her aunt Leni. Many of her books feature mice and, fittingly, she lives in the fishing village of Mousehole in Cornwall. Clearly, some of her stories call on childhood memories. *Teddy Trucks*, the story of bears who run a company driving trucks and delivering goods, was turned into a thirteen-episode animated series by BBC Children's Television. Her love of animals is evident in her charming illustrations which can be also be found on greetings cards, tins and wrapping paper, and a 29-piece service by Wedgwood porcelain.

Tony however, the eldest of the children, is made from the same mould as his anarchist father, showing a similar disdain for authority from an early age. Today Tony owns a successful winery in the Napa Valley in California. The story of how he came to this profession follows true (Derrick) Cartlidge tradition. In 1969, after various jobs and helping out with the family business Taxi-Trucks, he decided to try his luck in the United States. Very much the entrepreneur, he had heard that vintage clothing, especially Victorian, were all the rage and fetched good prices in Greenwich Village, New York. He acquired a vintage black dress studded with sequins to take with him, but by the time it finally reached Greenwich Village, after the US customs officials had gone through the suitcase, most of the sequins had fallen off. His aspirations then took him northwest and on to Oregon, Washington, and Alaska driving logging trucks and cement mixers. A chance gift of a wine book led him 750 miles south in search of opportunities in Napa County. After a flurry of cold calling, fate led him to Helen Niemi, who provided him with a hat-trick of lucky introductions leading to a job as a guide at Rutherford Hill winery, then to Glenn Browne who became his partner in the Cartlidge & Browne Winery, and thirdly to his wife Sarah, Helen's daughter. All these events contributed to Tony setting down roots in the Napa Valley. Tony grew Cartlidge & Browne into a 120,000 case winery before selling the company in 2011. Since then, and supposedly semi-retired, Tony has bought the Dancing crow vineyard which grew the Sauvignon Blanc grapes for Cartlidge & Browne and in his typical style, is creating a new family business with his wife and two sons, Adam and Stefan.

Barbara Cartlidge and Electrum Gallery

Recollections of Barbara Cartlidge and Electrum Gallery

The 69 artist-jewellers featured in the following pages reflect the different generations who exhibited at Electrum Gallery over the 36 years of its existence. They were asked to comment on the significance of the gallery for their work and for contemporary jewellery in general, as well as their relationships with Barbara Cartlidge. The individual responses show a diversity of personal and honest reflections and varying levels of friendship and contact. The statements have been left in their original format as an expression of the wide array of opinions and experiences. These depict the reality of Barbara Cartlidge's strong character and the role that Electrum Gallery played for each and every artist. The works illustrated span pieces by artist-jewellers from the earliest days of Electrum through to more recent work by the gallery's contributors. Some of the artist-jewellers, who have since deceased, were chosen for the significance they had for Barbara Cartlidge and thus when possible, her personal words have been quoted.

These recollections have been preceded by statements from three leading authorities on contemporary jewellery: Dr Fritz Falk, Dr Elizabeth Goring and Rosemary Ransome Wallis.

Electrum Gallery featured over 190 exhibitions from 1971 to 2007. Alongside the exhibition programme there were continual displays of work from many other artist-jewellers. Over the years, nearly 1000 jewellers were shown in the gallery in South Molton Street – some for a short time as contributors to a group show and many others as much longer term members of the Electrum 'family'.

Barbara Cartlidge and Schmuckmuseum Pforzheim, Germany

Since the 1970s two addresses in London are inextricably linked in my memory of Barbara Cartlidge and her exceptionally amiable husband, Derrick.

One of them is in north London, near Hampstead Heath and only a few metres away from the two ponds with ducks and anglers and the nearby Rumbold Bakery, which sadly no longer exists. It is here where the house is situated in which Barbara (called 'Bobbi' by her family and friends) and Derrick worked; where they both enjoyed family celebrations and many discussions, argumentative as well as amicable, with their many friends from all over the world. In brief, a place where they led fulfilled lives. Under a glass roof, an annexe to the house in its small garden, there was a small goldsmith's workshop. There, covered by a grapevine that occasionally even bore fruit, Bobbi's own pieces of jewellery were created. These often included motifs which belonged to her personal life: pendants and rings, behind which tiny doors, when opened, reveal various interior views of her house on a miniature scale. Every piece was designed and made with such endearing imagination and artistic talent, reflecting her unwavering dedication to the task.

The second address is South Molton Street, situated in the heart of London, a short street just around the corner from New Bond Street and adjoining Oxford Street. Initially this street was quite insignificant, but over the years it developed into an important shopping area which, although small, has become all the more exciting. The extravagant shops, fancy galleries and cafés continue to this day to draw visitors from all over the world. It is here where those interested in the art of jewellery could experience the place that became such an essential part of Barbara Cartlidge's life, a life which was rich in exciting events and moments. She will remain known for her exuberant energy, her never-ending curiosity and, resulting from this, her continued strength to search for and find something new. Here in South Molton Street, Barbara, in partnership with Ralph Turner, founded Electrum Gallery which specialised in contemporary jewellery. Over the years Electrum Gallery became an institution, if not a place of pilgrimage, for artists, collectors or those who simply loved jewellery. During this early phase the gallery became a centre for studio jewellery, probably only comparable with Helen Drutt's gallery in Philadelphia or Inge Asenbaum's Galerie am Graben in Vienna. Rarely has any other gallery in the world matched the commitment which these three ladies have shown in supporting jewellery as an art form.

In these early years it was exceedingly difficult to capture the public's interest for this new jewellery – it was an uphill struggle. Without the determination and belief, not to mention the financial backing with which Derrick Cartlidge productively promoted his wife's visions, Electrum Gallery would never have survived. It was only through Derrick's support that the success which gradually developed over the years was even made possible. Barbara's knowledge, her sense for quality, and her receptiveness for something new – as well as her courage to champion jewellery designers which were hitherto unknown – all these were essential properties for the recognition of her amazing achievements. So many artists began their careers at Electrum Gallery! Barbara Cartlidge discovered and promoted them, organised solo exhibitions and group shows at the gallery, thus ensuring that they would become known and established names, including artist-jewellers from countries in the Eastern bloc. Barbara was most knowledgeable and had the ability to promote art jewellery, both verbally and in writing.

It is wonderful to think back on Barbara as a kind friend, who was so gifted as an artist and a gallery owner. For me these two addresses in London will always be linked with Barbara and her family.

Fritz Falk
Former Director of Schmuckmuseum, Pforzheim, Germany

Barbara Cartlidge and the National Museums of Scotland

The role of the highly-informed private gallerist in the ecology of public museum collecting is not often fully acknowledged or appreciated. The best have an enviable overview of their sector, their position at the interface between artist and purchaser allowing them to track emerging talent, nurture artists' development and offer a knowledgeable 'editorial' service. Barbara Cartlidge, a pioneer in her field, set the bar for gallerists very high indeed.

In early 1980 Barbara discovered that the Royal Scottish Museum (one of the institutions later to form the National Museums of Scotland) was thinking about adding some examples of contemporary artist-jewellery to its collections, and approached the Museum to offer her assistance. The Museum's contemporary collecting at that time was largely driven by the personal interest and knowledge of Revel Oddy, Keeper of the Department of Art and Archaeology, who curated the ceramics and glass collections. He had visited Electrum in its earliest years for his own interest. There was no curator specialising in jewellery at that time although Naomi Tarrant, Curator of European Costume and Textiles, was interested in the subject, principally in relation to her own curatorial area. Naomi sent Barbara the names of the 15 jewellery artists who were already represented in the collections from the late 1960s on, nearly all of them UK-based. Barbara suggested widening the collection's scope with work by important jewellers from Italy, Austria and Germany, an idea that could not be followed up at the time.

I arrived at the RSM in 1982, initially as the Curator of the Ancient World, but with a personal passion for jewellery. I offered to take on responsibility for modern jewellery, and was encouraged by my colleagues to do so – a bold decision on their part for which I am hugely grateful. By the summer of 1983 I had started researching potential contemporary jewellery acquisitions, at first alongside Naomi. I first visited Electrum in the spring of 1984. I made the visit alone and, as a newcomer to the field, I vividly recall feeling daunted both by the glamour of the gallery's façade and by the reputation of Barbara's formidable knowledge. I hesitated in South Molton Street for quite some time, plucking up the courage to enter. I needn't have worried: Barbara welcomed me with warmth and charm. My recollections of her at that first meeting are probably replicated by many other people: her mass of wild curls, the signature enormous glasses, the constant phone calls punctuating our conversation, the hoarse voice and, above all, the chain-smoking. I was overwhelmed by her energy and astuteness, and by the generosity with which she shared her knowledge. In July that year, I made my first RSM purchases from Electrum: Arline Fisch's delicate knitted silver and anodised copper Bell Collar and Tone Vigeland's stunning oxidised silver, steel and gold necklace, both 1983. These pieces still delight me, just as much as they did more than thirty years ago. In retrospect I see they set the standard for my aspirations for the quality and internationalism of the Museum's jewellery collections. I made my last acquisition for the National Museum's contemporary jewellery collections – a remarkable brooch by Gijs Bakker – in 2005. In starting that long journey, I could not have hoped for a better guide than Barbara.

As a footnote, I visited Barbara at her home many years later, I think in the late 1990s. Still the same hair, glasses and cigarette smoke, the same forthright manner, ferocious intellect and enthusiasm, the same generosity of spirit. I found myself departing with 'going-home' gifts: Barbara's silver 20 ring celebrating Electrum Gallery's 20th anniversary in 1991 and, rather more surprising, a vintage Denby Little Folks child's foot warmer. I'm still not sure why she presented me with the latter – but it sits on a shelf above my computer reminding me of Barbara every day.

Dr Elizabeth Goring
Former Curator of Modern Jewellery,
National Museums of Scotland, Edinburgh

Barbara Cartlidge and The Goldsmiths' Company

One of my first assignments when I joined The Goldsmiths' Company in the early 1970s was to be sent by Graham Hughes, Art Director of the Company, to deliver several items of jewellery from the Company's Collection to an exhibition at Electrum. Somewhat nervous, I entered the gallery to be warmly greeted by Barbara Cartlidge who showed me around. The impression was of bright modernity, not only in the gallery layout, but in the choice of the exhibits.

These were jewels of my time, highly individual, each chosen with the expert eye of Barbara knowing what would appeal commercially, but also educating her public in the latest designs. Her partner at the time, Ralph Turner, also made an impression on me later on at a talk about how jewellery could be worn – one illustration being an elephant wearing a necklace of pebbles designed by David Poston.

Rosemary Ransome Wallis
Curator and Art Director, The Goldsmiths' Company, London

Mike Abbott and Kim Ellwood

UK
Mike Abbott born 1963 / Kim Ellwood born 1956

Exhibitions:
1991 Ahead of Time
1991 20th Anniversary Show
2004 Anti-War Medals

I first met Barbara when I was a student at Middlesex University – I was writing my thesis and rang to ask if I could come and talk to her about contemporary jewellery. She was very welcoming and her forceful character, enthusiasm and knowledge of contemporary jewellery were both an inspiration and a spur to starting my own practice. After graduating in 1985, she exhibited my steel, enamel and gold-leaf pieces and I had a continuous presence in her gallery until she retired.

I was aware of and visited Electrum Gallery before I started my degree, and it was these visits and the energy and originality of the work shown which confirmed my decision to become a studio jeweller. I had not seen anything like this gallery before – it was a complete antithesis of the jewellery on the high street. I believe, through the gallery and her books and her liaison with Ralph Turner at the Crafts Council, Barbara inspired a new identity within the world of jewellery, which was no longer seen primarily as about status but more about artistic expression.

When I first showed at Electrum, I was working with enamel on steel. The steel allowed larger and finer enamelled forms than traditionally found when enamelling onto precious metal. The colour was an important aspect of my work and, over the years, after forming a 25-year collaboration with Mike Abbott who had also shown with Barbara since graduating from the Royal College in 1988, our work is still primarily concerned with colour. There is still an absence of precious metal in our work, which has not always been an easy road to travel, but the ethos of this new jewellery movement stays with us!

One of my most endearing memories of this time was being invited to Electrum's 20th anniversary, not least because this is where Mike and I cemented our relationship. We had a wonderful party at Barbara's house. There were many friends and great jewellers there – it felt like one big family of like-minded people. We were all given a silver ring made in the shape of 20 to mark the occasion, which we both still have to this day – treasured possessions!

Kim Ellwood

Abbott and Ellwood,
'Journey to the Mount' sculpture
2010
mixed metals, found objects

Mike Abbott,
'Hang Luce' brooch
1990
brass, enamel

Kim Ellwood,
brooches
1988–90
steel, enamel

HANG-

Vicki Ambery-Smith

UK
born 1955

Exhibitions:
1981 Electrum – the tenth year
1982 New Figurative Jewellery
1991 20th Anniversary Show
1993 The Magic of the Ring

I first went to Electrum as a student at Hornsey Art College in 1975 or '76 – it was a 'must see' destination for all designers of contemporary jewellery. A year after graduating, I received a 'setting up' grant from the Crafts Council followed by an exhibition at the Oxford Gallery. I took these exhibits to show Barbara with the hope, naturally, of showing in Electrum. I was a timid twenty-something and my first impression of Barbara was spellbinding. She sat behind the desk in a cloud of smoke from her cigarette while holding all present in rapture while she told a story (alas I can't remember what it was about), swearing like a trooper! I'd never heard the like in my sheltered home town of Oxford. I thought she was very glamorous and exotic. Barbara immediately took the pieces and asked to see the next creations.

My first exhibition there was in 1982 with Sophie Chell and Martin Page – it was terrific. I've been hugely lucky in that I got established quite quickly, and Electrum certainly played a part in that. For several years the gallery sold some piece or other every month, as well as a few commissions. I had little connection with Electrum in its last decade, being busy with other exhibitions and commissions, but it remained important that it was there. It is very sad that the gallery came to an end and a big loss for our (small) world of contemporary jewellery. Barbara nurtured a friendly community amongst us jewellers whom I'm sure I first met at the many private views and at the parties at her home in Hampstead.

'Sydney Harbour Bridge' ring
2013
silver, 18ct gold

'Globe Theatre' brooch
1982–3
silver, red and yellow gold

Malcolm Appleby

UK
born 1946

Exhibitions:
1973 Aspects of Modern Jewellery
1985 *Twentieth-Century Jewelry* book launch
1991 20th Anniversary Show
1993 The Magic of the Ring

Because I lived in the northeast of Scotland, I can't remember if I even met Barbara more than once or twice, but over the telephone we got to know each other very well. I used to phone her in the evenings, putting on a slightly nasal Peter Cook voice, saying 'I'm sending over a ring made from a blue bicycle ring but you must only sell it to boys'. She'd request things from me such as artist statements, which I find so damned tedious, so I would write things like 'everything I touch turns to gold, baby', which she absolutely loved. What I liked about Barbara selling my work was that she was able to do so quite expensively, which set a much higher standard for my work, so from that point of view, Electrum Gallery was very good for me.

'Ring Ring' ring
1991
bicycle bell
Alice and Louis Koch Collection,
Swiss National Museum, Zurich

Brooch
2015
iron, gold, rainbow moonstone

Rings
c.1980
Damascus iron, 24ct and 18ct gold

Giampaolo Babetto

Italy
born 1947

Exhibitions:
1985 *Twentieth-Century Jewelry* book launch
1991 20th Anniversary Show
1996 The Innovators – 25th Anniversary Exhibition

I met Barbara at Electrum Gallery in 1975. I was young and intimidated, the gallery was very important and in a large city. It was my first experience, but when I arrived she immediately made me feel at ease. I had started making jewellery in 1967 but it was a few years later that I presented my work and so for me it was all very new – it was great when Barbara had agreed to show it.

Fundamentally, there were very few galleries that dealt with contemporary jewellery. Electrum was perhaps the most important then and even more so as it had also published a very important book on the subject. When I had my exhibition at the gallery I stayed at her house in Hampstead Heath and she was always very kind – every so often she would invite me to dinner. I think, because I was skinny at the time, Barbara was concerned about my health. It was a great experience when growing up in my work, above all from a human aspect.

Brooch
1974
18ct gold, ebony

Necklace
2012
18ct gold, pigments

Gijs Bakker

The Netherlands
born 1942

Exhibitions:
1971 Opening Exhibition
1972 Objects to Wear
1973 Aspects of Modern Jewellery
1985 *Twentieth-Century Jewelry* book launch
1991 20th Anniversary Show
2006 Midsummer Madness – 35th Anniversary Show

After a successful presentation of our aluminium collars at the Stedelijk Museum in Amsterdam, Emmy [van Leersum] and I decided to try our luck in England. At the Ewan Phillips Gallery we met Ralph Turner, who went completely wild when he saw the pictures of our work, which resulted in an exhibition in that same gallery in 1967. In 1972 we returned to London, this time at the invitation of Electrum Gallery's Barbara Cartlidge and Ralph Turner. It was one of the first exhibitions at Electrum Gallery and I vividly remember the mannequins in the front of the gallery wearing our white elastic jumpsuit designs and our aluminium bracelets displayed in the gallery room behind.

Barbara (generous as ever) welcomed me, Emmy and baby Aldo to stay at her Hampstead family house. Derrick, who was always in his trouser shorts and working from his home office, offered to babysit Aldo together with Katrin, while Barbara, Emmy and I were busy installing the exhibition at the gallery. Quite soon, it appeared that the partnership between Ralph and Barbara would misfire. Emmy and I have always distanced ourselves from the differences in their relationship and have maintained a friendship with them both. Regarding our working relationship, we never discussed work or jewellery design any more. Also, when Margaret Thatcher came into power, this wasn't very helpful. From that moment on there was hardly any exchange between continental and British artists. I have always considered Barbara a very dear friend and was always surprised by her outstanding cookery and hospitality.

Bangle
1971
aluminium

'3 point 7' necklace
2014
aluminium, gold, jade, plexi-glass, stainless steel, tantalum, titanium

Friedrich Becker

Germany
1922–97

Exhibitions:
1985 *Twentieth-Century Jewelry* book launch
1993 Friedrich Becker, Hermann Jünger, Bruno Martinazzi
1991 20th Anniversary Show
1996 The Innovators – Electrum 25th Anniversary

Graham Hughes, responsible for the ground-breaking exhibition *Modern Jewellery* at Goldsmiths' Hall, London, in 1961, recognised the talent of Friedrich Becker and invited him to take part. This was followed by a solo exhibition in Goldsmiths' Hall in 1966 where Becker first showed his kinetic jewellery to the public. With great appreciation Becker acknowledged these London exhibitions as stepping stones in his career. London was a city he loved and visited frequently with his students from the Fachhochschule (University of Applied Science) in Düsseldorf where he taught, and they regularly visited Henry Moore in his studio. After the opening of Electrum Gallery in 1971 a visit to South Molton Street and Barbara Cartlidge was always on the agenda. He admired her life and achievements in the world of jewellery.

Becker was the inventor of kinetics in jewellery – making jewellery with moveable parts. Having been an aeronautical engineer during the war and later training as a goldsmith, this was the culmination of his technical abilities and creative talent. In the 1950s he developed invisible settings that allowed the wearer to interchange gemstones, followed by jewellery offering multiple design permutations. This included the much copied 'two-point' setting of gemstones. Due to his background in engineering, precision and purity of form were his trademarks. His designs are timeless.

Beatriz Chadour-Sampson

Kinetic ring
1997
gold and diamond
RSV Collection

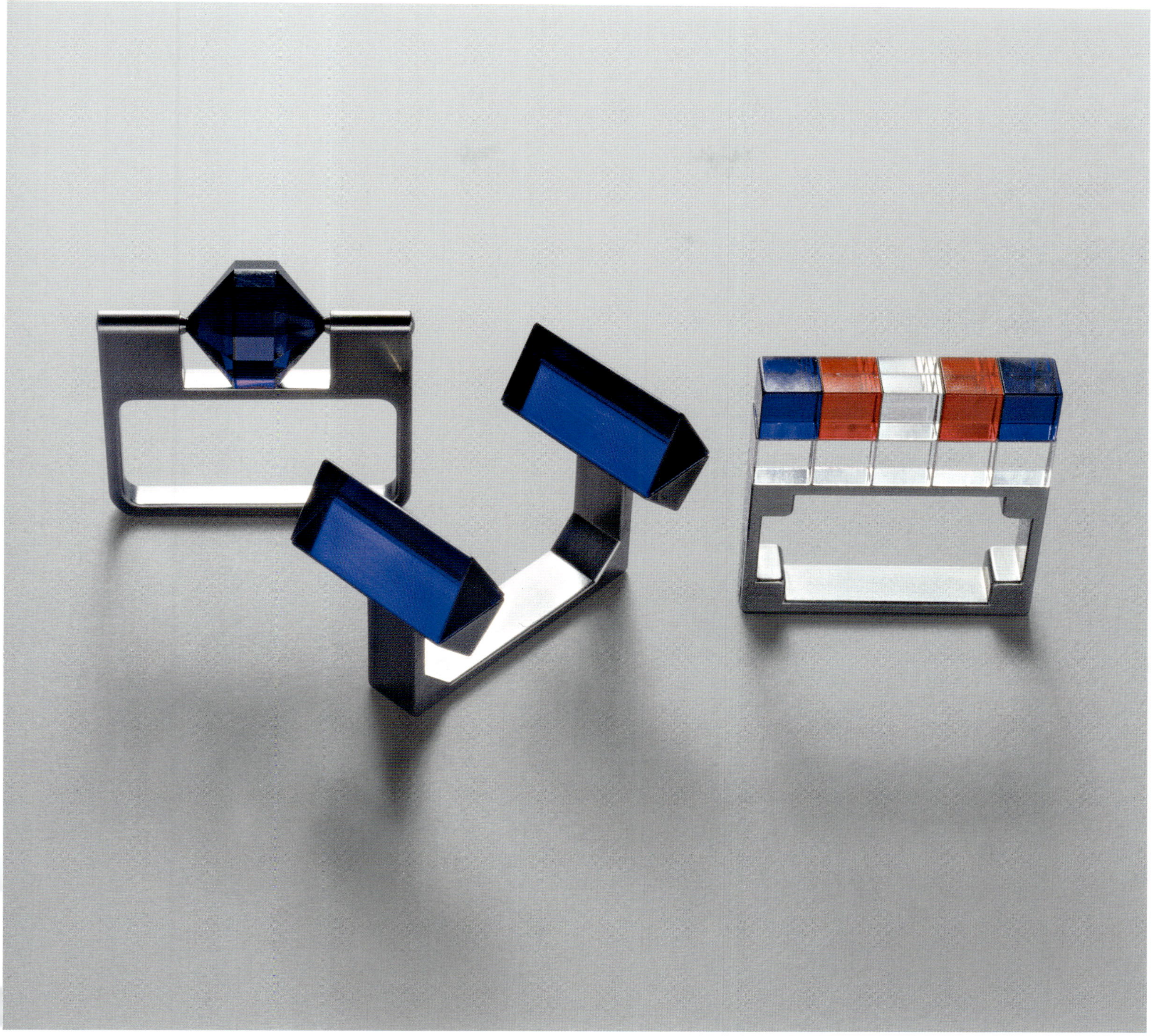

Rings
1991
steel with synthetic stones

Toril Bjorg

Norway
born 1944

Exhibitions:
1991 20th Anniversary Show
1988 Norwegian Jewellery and Textiles
1993 Toril Bjorg

Our great [Norwegian] jewellery artist Tone Vigeland called me in 1981 and told me about her show in Electrum Gallery and how advanced the gallery was, and of Barbara and her strong views and opinions. I understood immediately that I had to go to London to see with my own eyes the new radical jewellery and the new way to show it. Every year after that I went back to London to visit Electrum.

It took some time before I introduced myself but I did not dare to ask if Barbara was interested in seeing some of my works. Until then I had only read about the new jewellery in Barbara's book, and others by Peter Dormer and Ralph Turner, and I assumed that my work was uninteresting compared with all that. But in 1986–7 I brought with me some of my knitted works, went to the gallery and showed them to Barbara. She liked them and wanted to see more! For me it was fantastic and it was the start of a fruitful cooperation for more than 20 years.

For my career, Barbara and Electrum meant that my work was shown to the world. Coming from a small country with a small audience, that was so great that it is hard to describe. My meeting with Barbara has been vital to me and my career. Barbara's very strong views and opinions, and her direct way of putting them, was inspiring and has given me new insight in to my own work. The importance of Electrum Gallery cannot be underestimated for the development of contemporary jewellery.

My work now is slightly different from when I first showed at Electrum, but my artistic expression has the same strength as it had then, and which I think Barbara appreciated. The essence of my meetings and friendship with Barbara was not only her dedication to jewellery as art but also her generosity, her invitations to dinners at her home where I met with famous colleagues and her husband and late daughter Katrin. She gave a wonderful dinner with friends in an Indian restaurant after the opening of my one-man show in 1993.

Necklaces and bracelets
1988
silver, 18ct gold

Toril Bjorg

Necklace
2005
oxidised silver

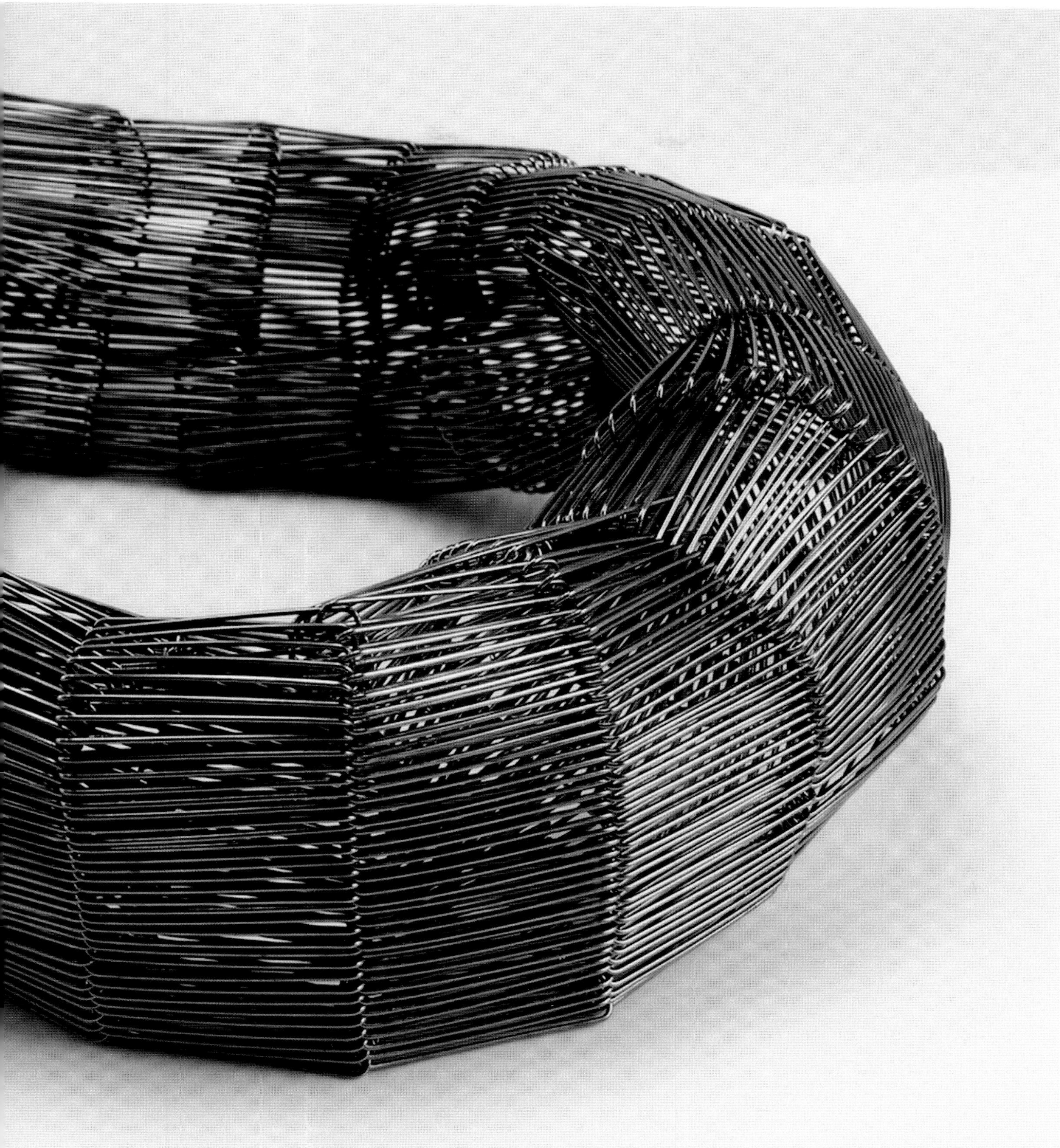

Caroline Broadhead

UK
born 1950

Exhibitions:
1973 Aspects of Modern Jewellery
1985 *Twentieth-Century Jewelry* book launch

I met Barbara through Electrum Gallery, although my first contact there was through Ralph Turner. When it opened, I remember thinking how exciting it was that there could be an exhibition of contemporary jewellery. I hadn't realised that Electrum was the first ever gallery for just jewellery until recently. I exhibited there when I was starting out in my career and finding my professional feet. It was extremely useful to have feedback on my work and sales and, in its first few years, it did have considerable international impact because of the challenging and innovative work that was shown there.

The first pieces I showed there were necklaces made up of buttons and, later, I exhibited carved ivory pieces. Over 40 years or so, my work has developed from making jewellery to dance performance, installations and sculptural objects. I remember Barbara smoking a lot and once inviting a group of gallery jewellers to come to her house in Hampstead to discuss the future of the gallery.

Sculpture
2015
re-conditioned stool, vintage stool, glass beads, linen thread

'Knot' necklace
1973
silver, ivory

Claus Bury

Germany
born 1946

Exhibitions:
1971 Opening Exhibition
1972 Concepts of Modern Jewellery
1972 Twenty Modern Jewellers
1972 Objects and Acrylic Jewellery
1973 Aspects of Modern Jewellery
1981 Electrum – the tenth year
1985 *Twentieth-Century Jewelry* book launch
1991 20th Anniversary Show

In 1969 I came to London to work with Andrew Grima and there I met Fritz Maierhofer, who was in charge of the Omega jewellery collection. He introduced me to Catherine Mannheim and through her I met Ralph Turner, who was at that time director of Electrum Gallery. At the end of 1969 I met Barbara Cartlidge and her family and we have been close friends since then. In 1972 I moved in with Barbara and Derrick in Hampstead. They lived in the main house and I had my room on the first floor overlooking the garden, where the daughters Michelle and Katrin often played with their cat. Their older brother Tony moved to California in 1969, where he built a very successful winery, and his global trade operates to this day.

Barbara and Derrick adopted me very quickly as their second son and they were also like new parents for me. I cared lovingly for my room and paid no rent, working instead for Barbara in her studio which was located in the conservatory directly behind the kitchen. We created many rings – small constructions with 'interiors', doors for example, with pull-out drawers – and bangles with moving circles. On the ground floor we had breakfast in the kitchen, always smelling of burnt toast, which Barbara spread with much salted butter and orange marmalade. Derrick preferred Marmite with the bitter orange, a combination that was unknown to me, and he always prepared Assam tea with fresh milk.

In 1972 I taught two semesters at the Royal College of Art in the Jewellery and Silversmithing Department, and at Hornsey School of Art. After returning from college I would sit with delight in Barbara's workshop while Derrick sat close by in his office – he controlled his fleet of 'radio controlled taxi-trucks' throughout London from there. Occasionally I went with Barbara, Derrick and the two girls to Southend-on-Sea. Barbara always sat at the wheel of her Rover with provisions of sandwiches and of course Derrick's tea in a thermos flask. How this British family liked being in the car and looking at the sea or walking in strong winds on the hills of Southend for New Year – it was always something special.

Barbara drove almost daily to Electrum and I often visited her there to see the exhibitions in the ground floor and basement showrooms, which had very beautiful, rectangular glass cases in which they arranged individual or several pieces of jewellery. At this centre of British jewellery, I met Wendy Ramshaw, David Watkins, Helga Zahn, Catherine Mannheim, Gunilla Treen, Pierre Degen, Karel Bartosik, Roger Morris and Edward de Large – also artists from the continent such as Emmy Van Leersum, Gijs Bakker, Friedrich Becker, Reinhold Reiling, Herrmann Jünger, Gerd Rothmann, Jens-Rüdiger Lorenzen, Fritz Maierhofer, Lisa and Helfried Kodré, Anton Cepka, Babetto and Pinto from Italy and Robert Smit from Holland. After the shows, which were always very well attended, we went to Derrick's favourite Chinese restaurant in Soho, not far from Shaftesbury Avenue. It still makes my mouth water when I think about it.

Brooch
1970
acrylic, silver, gold
Die Neue Sammlung –
The Design Museum, Munich

Claus Bury

'Bitterfelder Bogen' bridge,
in Bitterfeld-Wolfen,
Saxony-Anhalt, Germany
1995–6
steel

Alan Craxford

UK
born 1946

Exhibitions:
1991 20th Anniversary Show
1994 Alan Craxford
2006 Midsummer Madness – 35th Anniversary Show

In the early 1970s … I had heard of an interesting new place which showed very different jewellery from what was generally available. Ewan Phillips had closed by then so I went along to this new place called Electrum in South Molton Street and I must say felt somewhat unnerved. The street was narrow and had seen better days but was very attractive nonetheless – indeed an intriguing street, where even my great hero William Blake had lived. The chap, whose desk was in the back gallery, seemed friendly and we got to talk and, yes, he'd be interested to see my work, so a few weeks later I took a group of work along to show. The chap I talked to was, of course, Ralph Turner and he immediately offered to show my rather odd collection of pieces in a loose group exhibition called *Contemporary Jewellery '72*. He actually sold a couple of pieces and this was my first proper connection with Electrum. A successful working relationship was maintained until the gallery's unfortunate closure in 2012. Just under 40 years!

Now Ralph was always a rather urbane figure and it was his decision to show my work. On that occasion there was mention of his partner in the gallery Barbara (or Bobbi). However, she was a rather shadowy figure in the background until one day I arrived with some pieces and there was Barbara, sitting in the front gallery behind the big black desk. Where Ralph was charming and courteous, Barbara was a big character – big specs were in fashion at the time and Barbara had big specs, and do I recall leather trousers?! No, she had no idea why Ralph had decided to go but now she was 'going to get this baby up and running'. I remember the determination in her voice and the look in her eyes that said she was going to do what she said she was going to do! I was left in no doubt about that. In fact for quite some years I found her rather terrifying.

The gallery had become an important part of my life as it gave credibility to my work, although I couldn't make a full time living from it. Yet the gallery's reputation in the art world helped me enormously to get teaching work. In a way, I feel she respected the lack of compromise in the work which the teaching enabled. As I began to get to know Barbara I eventually realised that she rather liked me, although she could still be rather intimidating. It was clear she knew everyone who was anyone worth knowing in our world and her strength of personality was very much part of bringing that about.

By this time, other galleries and exhibition opportunities had opened up but it was interesting that the Electrum model was often followed. The work on show is what's important and the gallery space is kept modern, neutral, well-lit and simple. What seems obvious now was at the time highly unusual and we jewellers loved it for that very reason.

'Hidden Gold' pendant
2014
silver, gilding,
rhodium plate, diamonds

'And the morning stars –
sung together' hair comb
1973–4
silver gilt, blue enamel

Susan Cross

UK
born 1964

Exhibitions:
1991 20th Anniversary Show
1992 Susan Cross, Wally Gilbert, Barbara Tipple
1993 The Magic of the Ring

I remember my first meeting with Barbara very well – at Electrum with a case of all my recent degree work in 1986. These were the days before shows like New Designers so one had to take the initiative and make an appointment with galleries. I had just finished college and was of course a little nervous of meeting the director of such a prestigious gallery. Electrum had an international reputation for contemporary jewellery and I knew this was the right place for my work to be represented. Electrum (and Barbara) were intimidating for a young and inexperienced new graduate like me.

The gallery was quite dark and full of cigarette smoke (Barbara chain smoking throughout our meeting) and as I was unpacking boxes and laying all the work out on the display tray, I really had no idea of what her reaction would be. After having very carefully and closely looked at all the work and being silent for what seemed like an age, Barbara began to explain that she didn't usually take recent graduate work, owing to the fact that it might not be backed up and developed outside of college study. She normally only accepted work from someone who at been out of college for at least five years. However, on this occasion she explained, she was going to take a chance and break with her own house rule. I was then asked if I would leave everything with her at the gallery that day – she was clearly excited and enthusiastic about the work. This was great! But then I had to explain that I needed to get the work photographed and could I bring it all back in a week. She was not best pleased and I was given orders to return as soon as possible. Barbara subsequently purchased one of the pieces from this body of work (an 18ct gold crocheted ring) for her own collection and this has since been exhibited internationally over the years.

As I got to know Barbara over time I found her a very generous and giving person and one who certainly encouraged and nurtured my own development as a jeweller. I have every respect for her and for all that she has done for the subject.

Two rings
1986
18ct gold, iron
gold ring Alice and Louis Koch Collection, Swiss National Museum, Zurich

Gloves
1991
silver

'Crimson Trace I & II' brooches
2015
oxidised silver, enamel

Charlotte De Syllas

UK
born 1946

Exhibitions:
1971 Opening Exhibiton
1985 *Twentieth-Century Jewelry* book launch
2006 Midsummer Madness – 35th Anniversary Show

I moved in around the corner with Jasper [Vaughan] and met her because Jasper knew her from childhood. I refused to reproduce a piece on show early on, so Bobbi asked me to take all my work away. This was not a problem and we still met each other from time to time. I worked entirely on commissioned pieces until I turned 60. I then needed to show work to gain new clients. Bobbi was very welcoming and I stayed with Electrum until it closed. It was immensely important and a stop off for all foreigners who collected modern jewellery when visiting London. Electrum had the capacity to sell inexpensive and very expensive modern jewellery.

Charlotte De Syllas

Derrick and Bobbi used to visit Asa and Pip (my parents) in our old Elizabethan house in the country near Tenterden, Kent. We three brothers Jasper, Paul and Mark would often witness them all arguing over politics while playing a card game called Canasta. Derrick and Bobbi were vehemently Communist and Pip and Asa were anarchist artist and poet. They were sat at the end and both sides of our long dining table copiously drinking Algerian Burgundy wine – then imported to England as cheap good quality drink – throughout the Canasta game. They all got very drunk and shouted louder and louder and the game of Canasta, as I remember, always ended in confusion without any winners. This left me with very clear visual impressions of their exaggerated political arguments and extreme intellectual opinions.

Jasper Vaughan

'Flight' necklace
2014
white Russian nephrite jade,
18ct white gold
The Worshipful Company
of Goldsmiths, London

Ring and box
1968
Damascus steel, silver,
gold, stone

Elisabeth Jesus Gu. Defner

Austria
born 1931

Exhibitions:
1973 Aspects of Modern Jewellery
1980 Elisabeth Kodré-Defner
1981 Electrum – the tenth year
1985 *Twentieth-Century Jewelry* book launch
1991 20th Anniversary Show
1992 Of Crystals and Magnets
1993 The Magic of the Ring
1998 The Colour Red
2001 Contemporary Jewellery from Austria

Of course, Barbara was one of the most important persons on the scene and for the whole development of modern jewellery but I can't remember the year Helfried Kodré and I met her for the first time. We met many colleagues in the gallery, such as Wendy Ramshaw, David Watkins and Paul Preston, who became a good friend. So many years Barbara and I were working together and we had great fun. She was very open and interested to know about my different ideas in my work, which have changed through the years. How much she meant to me I can't tell in few words – I hear her voice, her laughter, I see her smoking, Derrick barefoot coming in, Katrin and Michelle – what a wonderful family. I am so grateful for the time I was allowed to spend with them.

'Ginkgo' ring
1985
gold, ruby, opal

Pendant
2012
silver, black walnut and leaves,
green moonstone, rutile quartz,
pieces of a CD

Joel Degen

France / UK
born 1941

Exhibitions
1971 Opening Exhibition
2006 Midsummer Madness – 35th Anniversary Show

Barbara first invited me to show my work at her gallery in 1971, which I was so chuffed about as I still felt a little bit of an outsider on the contemporary British jewellery scene. Until then, I had been showing my work in several mixed crafts-come-art shops/galleries. As a jewellery-only gallery, Electrum managed successfully to present two aspects of the best of contemporary jewellery, namely well-made, well-designed, very wearable modern work alongside innovative, sometimes controversial, work. Also, crucially, by featuring international as well as British contemporary work, Electrum was unique and incredibly important. It soon became part of the select 'club' of international galleries which, by showing innovative work from vastly different horizons, acted as a forum of exchange of ideas for many of us, and the public of course. For my part, seeing for the first time the work of Claus Bury, Fritz Maierhofer and Norbert Muerrle sent my mind racing!

Without any doubt, seeing such work was an important factor in determining my future approach to my own work, in terms of materials (non-precious), techniques (non-orthodox) and design philosophy (sculptural/engineered yet comfortable to wear objects). Barbara's often repeated remark that 'no one uses stones anymore!' definitely prompted me to produce, in the mid 1990s, a new range of titanium rings that incorporated precious stones.

There is on my wall a small painting by Robert Farquhar which I bought at an exhibition sale of contemporary art at Hampstead Old Town Hall in 1973. Barbara, as a representative of the British charity Medical Aid of Vietnam, had organised it, asking makers and artists to donate a piece of work each. Of course, many of us responded gladly. And there were the parties, the very welcoming, generous parties at her house. Everybody was there – David, Wendy, Gerda, Jackie … and the much missed Helga Zahn.

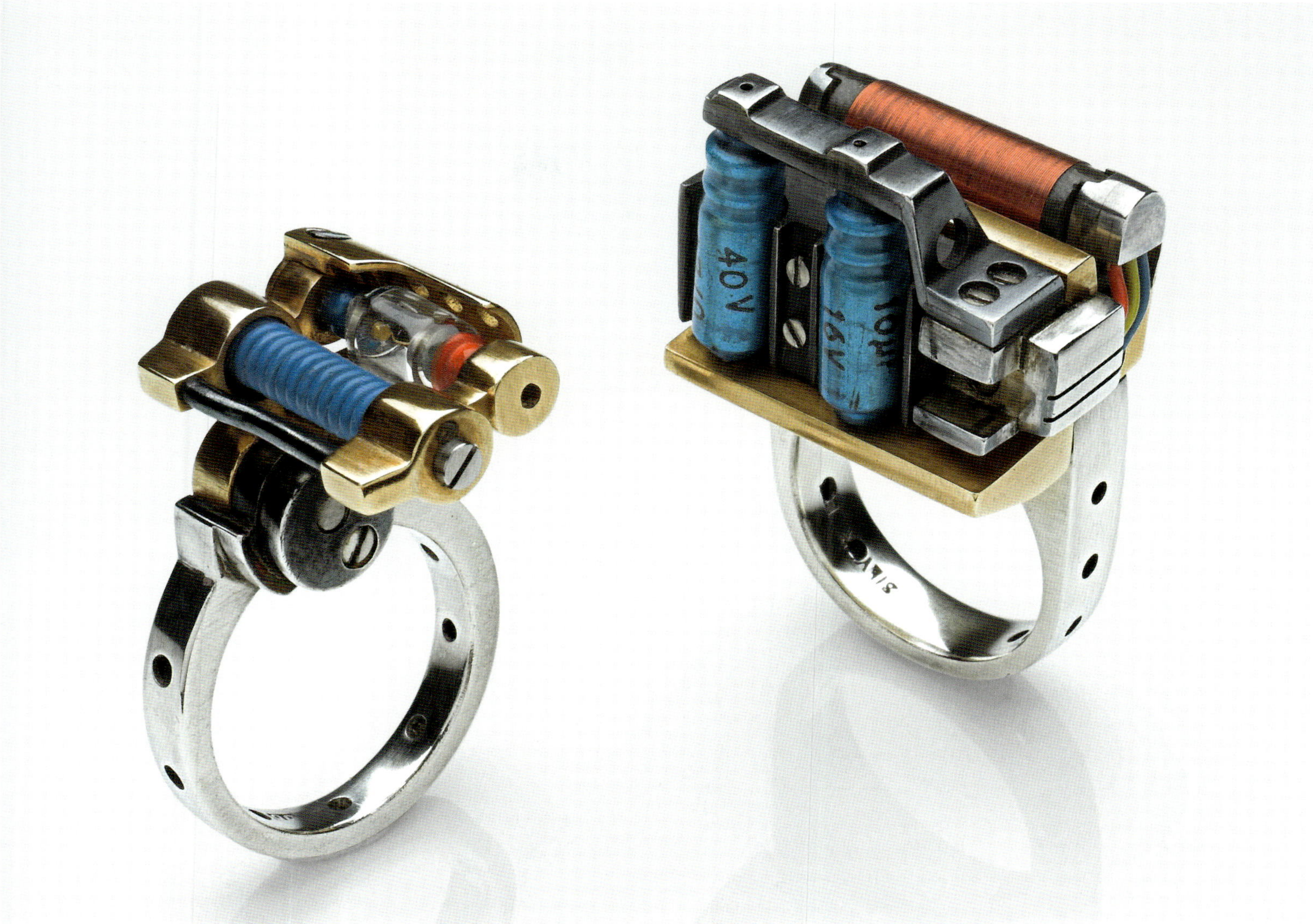

Rings
c.1970
gold, silver, electronic components

Rings
c.1990
titanium, gold, gemstones

Arline Fisch

USA
born 1931

Exhibitions:
1976 Six Contemporary American Jewellers
1980 Arline Fisch
1981 Electrum – the tenth year
1983 Arline Fisch
1985 *Twentieth-Century Jewelry* book launch
1987 Woven Gold
1991 20th Anniversary Show
1996 The Innovators – 25th Anniversary Exhibition
2006 Midsummer Madness – 35th Anniversary Show

I met Barbara in the early 1970s when I went to look at the gallery for contemporary jewellery that she and Ralph Turner opened in a small space in Central London. I made regular visits fairly often as I travelled through London to various other places in Europe, and eventually asked if she would carry my jewellery in the gallery. Barbara was very supportive of my work and I had my first solo exhibition at the gallery featuring work done in London during a year-long residence.

Her efforts resulted in great press coverage and some photographs in *Vogue* magazine. Barbara's enthusiastic support of my work over so many years even as it changed rather dramatically, was highly encouraging to me personally but also a strong factor in the course of my career. I learned over the years of many patrons of my work who regularly visited Electrum (including many Americans) and who acquired significant pieces as a result of seeing them at the gallery.

Electrum had an important role in the development of contemporary jewellery from the beginning as *the* place to be shown and sold. Many significant British and European jewellers were represented by the gallery, and it was always an important place to visit for collectors, authors, museum curators as well as artists and gallery owners. Graduating students of the RCA not only visited the gallery regularly but also showed their work to Barbara in the hope of being shown there. She was always encouraging even while, perhaps, not accepting the work as yet ready for the gallery. She had a very good eye for new and important work, and was most encouraging and enthusiastic about new ideas and new approaches in concept and materials. I never felt constrained to produce a certain kind of work for the gallery and was always pleased and gratified at the acceptance and support of my most recent work. I think that Electrum was important to the development of contemporary jewellery around the world as a showcase for artists. Electrum set a high standard in both concept and presentation but it also encouraged artists to evolve, to try new things. And it also introduced artists to each other which helped to create an international network which continues to flourish.

Barbara was always the most generous of hosts. I was invited to dinner whenever I was in London, sometimes in a favourite Indian restaurant but more often at home with her and Derrick. One Christmas, when I was living alone in London, she invited me to join a 'family and friends' house party somewhere in Kent where Barbara was the chief cook and organiser. It was a warm and wonderful occasion where I saw Barbara in another context, but equally as charming and witty as I had always known her. Her family was important to her and I was privileged to become a part of it, as had so many other jewellers from around the world.

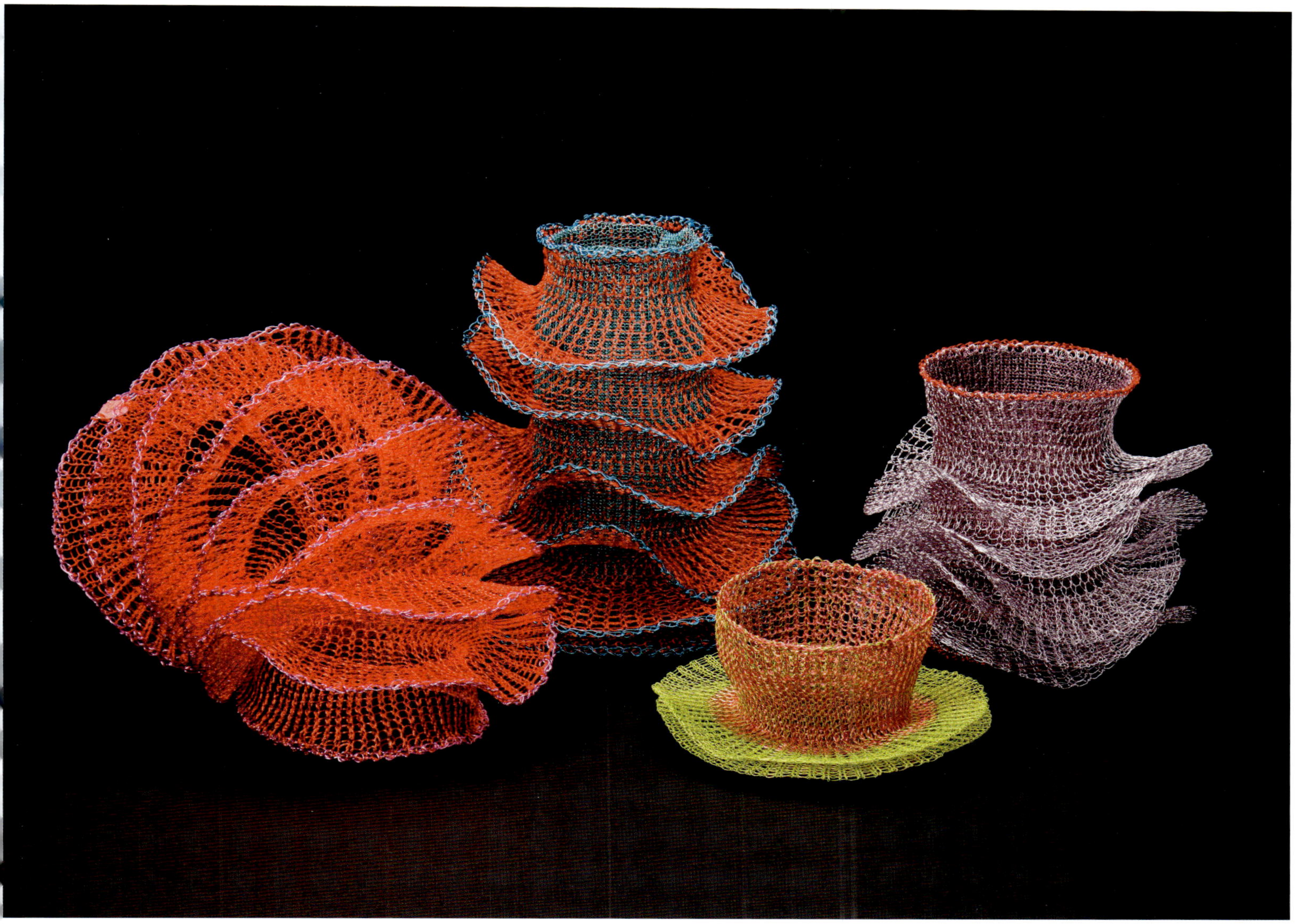

Bracelets
2009
coated copper wire

Ring
1978
18ct gold, Chatham
emerald crystal

Gerda Flöckinger, CBE

Austria / UK
born 1927

Exhibitions:
1971 Opening Exhibition
1972 Concepts of Modern Jewellery
1972 Twenty Modern Jewellers
1973 Aspects of Modern Jewellery
1977 Diamond Story
1981 Electrum – the tenth year
1985 *Twentieth-Century Jewelry* book launch
1991 20th Anniversary Show
1993 The Magic of the Ring
1996 Straight for the Heart
1996 The Innovators – Electrum 25th Anniversary
1996 Classic and Wild Earrings
2006 Midsummer Madness – 35th Anniversary Show
2007 Gerda Flöckinger, CBE

With the benefit of hindsight I have realised that whatever of my work I chose to show at Electrum Gallery, it was welcomed and exhibited, and that I was with the gallery for the whole period of the thirty-six years of Barbara's great venture.

Gerda Flöckinger

Gerda Flöckinger's jewellery is a definitive statement of her individuality, but beyond that, it reflects a deep involvement, both emotional and intellectual, and a superb understanding of the true meaning and function of jewellery. In a constant process of research and refinement, Gerda Flöckinger has evolved a style which is uniquely her own. This is not the work of a 'designer', a quick, intuitive brainwave to serve pure ornamentation and the whim of fashion trends, an aspect that is probably more common in the field of jewellery than it might be in other media of art. In fact, it was the advent of Gerda Flöckinger's jewellery that brought the dispute on the question of whether jewellery could be 'art' once more in to the foreground.

Barbara Cartlidge, July 1986. Foreword to exhibition catalogue Gerda Flöckinger, 15 October – 30 November 1986, Victoria and Albert Museum, London

Ring
1969
18ct gold, beige quartz (cut GF), tourmalines

Necklace
1995–9
silver, 18ct gold, cultured pearls, coloured diamonds, moonstones

Pair of rings
1993
18ct gold, diamonds, cultured pearl, moonstone, brown diamonds

Wally Gilbert

UK
born 1946

Exhibitions:
1978 Wally Gilbert and Sue Carney
1981 Electrum – the tenth year
1991 20th Anniversary Show
1992 Wally Gilbert, Susan Cross, Barbara Tipple

I took work to show Barbara at the gallery in, I think, 1975. I had dropped out of Chelsea School of Art's sculpture course some years previously and had been making a living by part time work including making and selling bespoke candles and jewellery to Biba. I had no contact with jewellers but had become intrigued by making jewellery using silver wire. Barbara and her gallery introduced the jewellery world to me though I didn't properly appreciate at the time that this was something special, probably because it came too easily to me. I was fearfully naive, probably still am, in the ways of the art/craft world. I was at the time primarily curious about jewellery making and showing at Electrum gave me a point to aim for and base myself upon. Barbara was hugely helpful and supportive to me but I didn't really have the wit to seek, heed or understand her advice properly.

At the private view to the last group exhibition in which I took part at Electrum, I met Seymour Rabinovitch who gave me my first silversmithing commission. This was important to me because I was becoming curious about silversmithing. Electrum Gallery was and is the first important professional milestone in my life. Showing at Electrum gave professional credibility and standing. I would say that Electrum was critical in the development of contemporary jewellery by showing innovative work from across the globe and supporting and encouraging such a range of work. I did not, at the time, properly realise the unique nature of the gallery but looking back, Barbara had a very even handed, non-partisan approach. This is not the first time that I have found myself wishing I had said this to somebody at the time.

My work has always been changing, for better or sometimes for worse. I was drawn to jewellery as small scale objects I could make with very limited resources and then became intrigued by the materials. My work developed through showing at Electrum but I then became interested in other ways of working and so moved away from what I thought of as 'studio jewellery'.

Pendants
1978, 1984, 1985
silver, gold

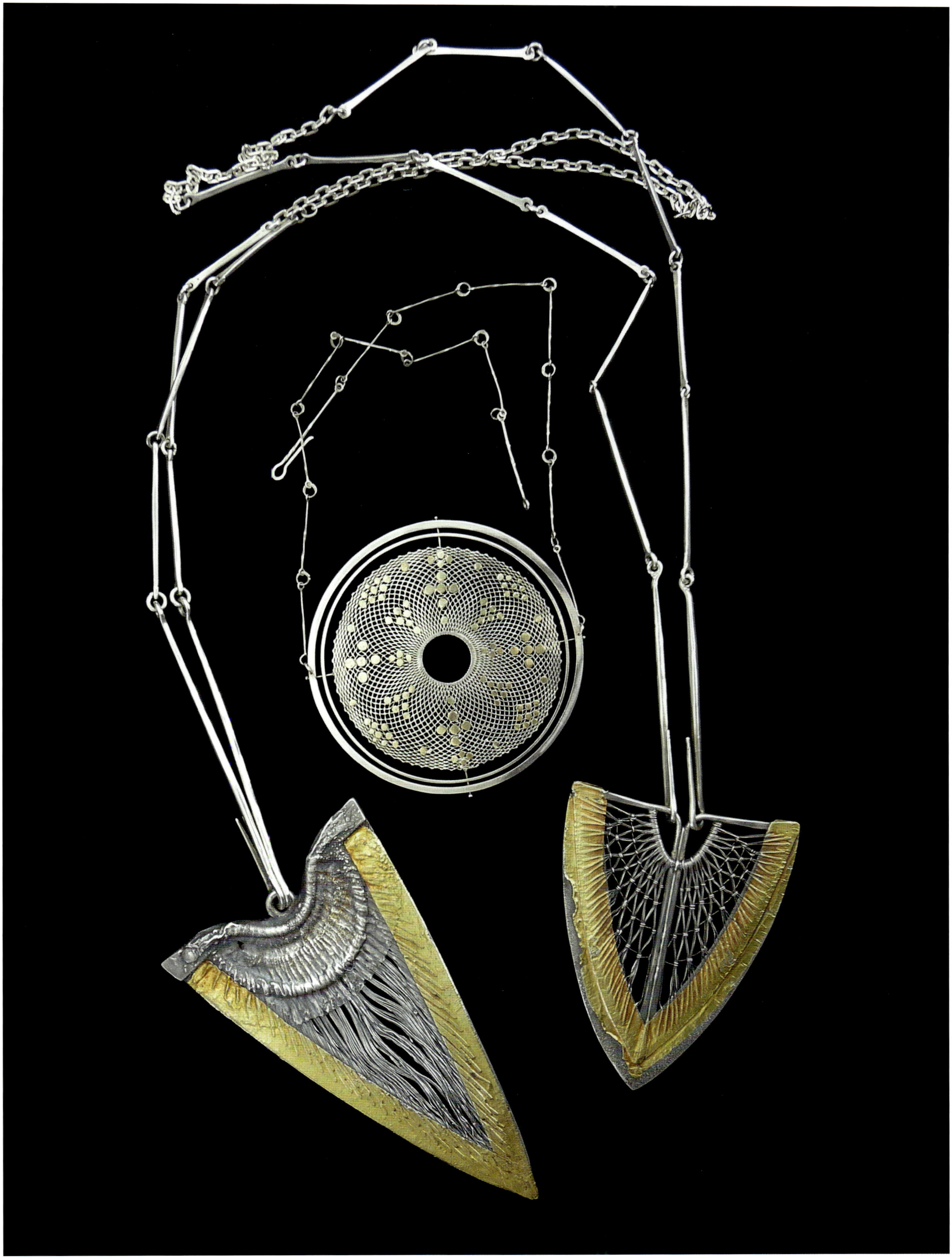

Barbara was kind and generous though also rather intimidating. I remember the warmth with which she would refer to her husband whom I met once. I had the impression that, for him, we jewellers, his wife's protégés, were from another world to his. A mature student of mine, no shrinking violet herself, never found the courage to pass Barbara at her desk in order to penetrate the inner regions of the gallery. Barbara put on an exhibition, my first solo of jewellery with my partner, my wife, showing collages on the wall. This I think showed both flexibility and generosity to both of us.
I caught 'flu once after seeing Barbara and I always attributed this to leaving Electrum in a heavy perspiration to stand in the cold waiting for a bus on Oxford Street. Thinking about it now I realise that Barbara was very special as a gallery director in a way that I couldn't, because of inexperience, properly appreciate at the time. I am sure she must have given many besides myself extraordinary opportunities with a complete absence of the sectarian cliquishness that I think of as common in the art world. I might have been somewhat intimidated by Barbara but never put down.

Chalice
2015
925 and 960 silver,
23ct gold, topaz

Rita Greer

UK
born 1942

Exhibitions:
1971 Opening Exhibition
1973 Aspects of Modern Jewellery
1973 Figurative Jewellery
1974 Christmas at Electrum featuring Rita Greer
1983 Mouse Gallery

Electrum Gallery was more than a breath of fresh air, rather a rushing mighty wind for modern jewellery and craftsman jewellers. Normally, the jewellery trade crams its windows with jewellery, concerned with bullion and cut precious stones. At Electrum it was quite the opposite. There was space and light with the emphasis on the artists/craftsmen and their work, not investment value and swank. At Electrum it was about art. Stones were more likely to be natural crystals and the value of the work was in design and hand craftsmanship. Pieces were one-off or limited edition, not an endless supply run off a machine, everything the same and anonymous. Precious metals were not obligatory. Resin, leather, enamels, fossils, wood, dried seeds, feathers, raw crystals and non-precious metals could all be featured. Barbara encouraged it all.

Considering Barbara's role in contemporary jewellery, I regard her as one of the most important influences of the 20th-century renaissance that took place. Electrum was at the centre of this. We were kept out of the trade because most of us were women and they hated our work. Most of us worked at home in a corner. Barbara and Electrum gave us a stage, protected our status, looked after us, encouraged us and allowed us to make our name and reputation. I feel very privileged to have stood under the Electrum umbrella right at the beginning of my varied career and even more privileged to have known Barbara. In the world of 20th-century contemporary jewellery Barbara Cartlidge was a visionary force. As a friend she was amazing.

'Robert Hooke as a boy on Isle of Wight'
painting
2005
oil on board

Pendant
c.1971
silver

Castello Hansen

Denmark
born 1965

Exhibition:
2001 Solos

I only met Barbara a few times at Electrum. It was during my final year at the Royal College of Art in 1995 that I approached Electrum with my work, and it was Janice Hosegood that I found there. I never spoke with Barbara more than a few phrases of politeness and in reality for me, Janice was 'Electrum' and if it is not too late I would like to thank her for being an ambassador for my work, taking me in and representing me at the gallery. It was a very important event for me at that time and I'm very happy that I was a part of the history of Electrum Gallery.

Brooch
2002
fine gold, acrylic,
oxidised silver, steel pins

Brooch
2015
900 gold, reconstructed coral,
ebony, 590 white gold, steel pins

William Harper

USA
born 1944

Exhibitions:
1979 William Harper
1985 *Twentieth-Century Jewelry* book launch

I was introduced to Electrum on my first trip to London in 1974. I was too intimidated to introduce myself to Barbara considering the high standard of work that she was showing and my non-reputation in Europe at that time. I first met Barbara in 1978 at Goldsmiths' Hall, London, for a show titled *Rings and Rattlesnakes: Four Americans.* The title partly derived from one of my pieces in the show, 'Pagan Baby #4: The Serpent', which had an appendage of a real rattlesnake tail. It was later owned by Helen Drutt, and is now in the collection of the Houston Museum of Fine Arts. If I recall correctly, it was at that time that Barbara proposed a one-man exhibition of my work at Electrum in 1979. The only other time I ever met her – I did not attend the Electrum show – was at a dinner at her home in November 1989 which she hosted for the four artists who were then guesting for David Watkins at the Royal College of Art.

I cannot say whether the Electrum show had a great deal of impact on my career, except for the fact that Wendy Ramshaw bought a pair of earrings from it. Of course, I felt honoured to have had the exhibition in such a prestigious place. As an American, Electrum, in my mind, was the crème de la crème of private spaces in which art jewellery was exhibited and explained. Also, she featured a full page picture in her book *Twentieth-Century Jewellery* of my brooch 'Grey Mystery', 1978, now in the collection of the Yale University Gallery of Art, New Haven, Connecticut. With the exception of a few English artists – Wendy, David, and Kevin Coates – Europeans, for the most part, have been rather hostile to my work because, early on, it did have content beyond formalism. Barbara understood that, and was a wonderful advocate for what I was doing.

'Enclosed Taboo' pendant/brooch
1979
gold, silver, enamel

William Harper

My strangest, and in retrospect funniest, experience with Electrum occurred trying to get my work back from the one-person exhibition in 1979. I cannot remember just exactly how the work got to London from the US, but it was not exactly 'kosher', and thus made getting it back a nightmare. At the time the show was over, I was a guest professor at Parsons School of Art in NYC. I had a student at that time who was going to London to visit her mother for the Christmas holidays, and who understood my predicament. She volunteered to go to the gallery to retrieve the work. It was fortuitous that it was fairly small, because the student and her mother carefully packed it in two whole salmon and other foodstuffs to be smuggled back to the US on her return flight to NYC. I received all the work, minus the earrings sold to Wendy, safely back at Parsons when classes resumed in January and none of it even smelled 'fishy.' It was hard lesson for me in the problems of international shipping for commercial purposes.

'The Albino Siberian' brooch
2015
gold, silver, enamel, glass, pearls,
moonstones, mother-of-pearl

Cathy Harris

UK
1954–94

Exhibition:
1991 20th Anniversary Show

In an interview with the author, Wendy Ramshaw – a renowned contemporary of Cathy Harris – said 'she was a coming star'. Cathy Harris' untimely death came just as her career in jewellery making was flourishing. From 1982 she had her own studio, after previously having worked for Liberty of London and Butler & Wilson. She played a significant role in the New Jewellery movement in the 1980s experimenting with the boundaries of scale and wearability, placement on the body and jewellery as sculpture or painting.

A statement recorded in the Crafts Council Collection regarding her large red neckpiece (opposite) gives, in her own words, a reflection of her thoughts when creating her pieces, 'The neckpiece satisfies my desire to create something large with the context of jewellery'. And of a large brooch, also in this collection, Harris' comment was 'this fairly large brooch is rather like a small painting. This is further suggested by the stand on which it is displayed, as a decorative object in its own right. This brooch does not necessarily need to be worn'.

Her jewellery is bold and vibrant in colour and the materials she used were mainly non-precious. Her acrylic pieces, either translucent or opaque, showed a great array of techniques and finishes. The imagery and forms were often geometric, or stylized. She had an exceptional talent as a teacher too, as Janice Hosegood recalls, 'Cathy was one of those unique tutors at college who quietly helped to build your sense of self, and gave us confidence in our emerging abilities.'

Beatriz Chadour-Sampson

'Red Spiral' neckpiece
1986
acrylic
The Crafts Council Collection, London

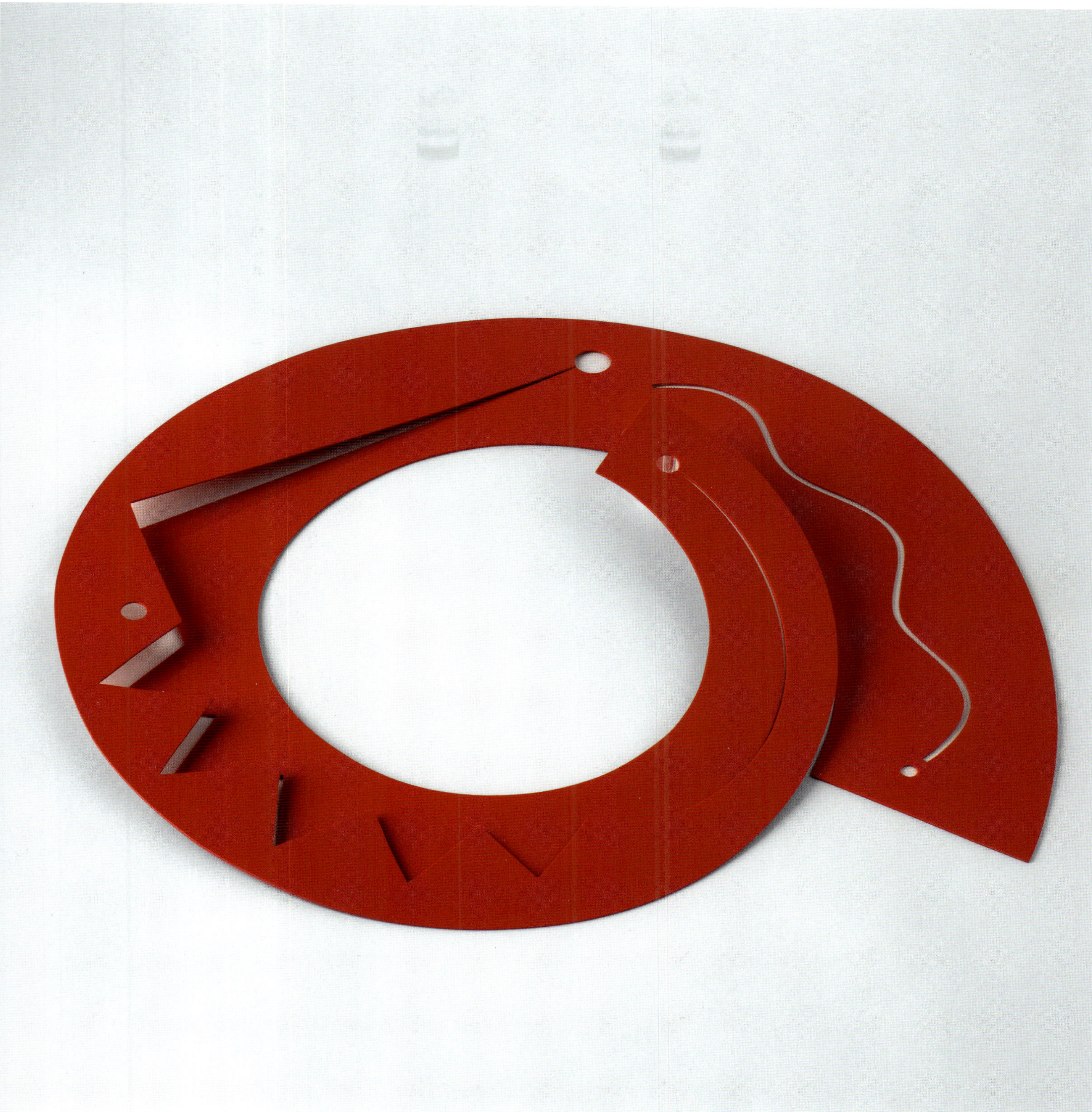

Cathy Harris

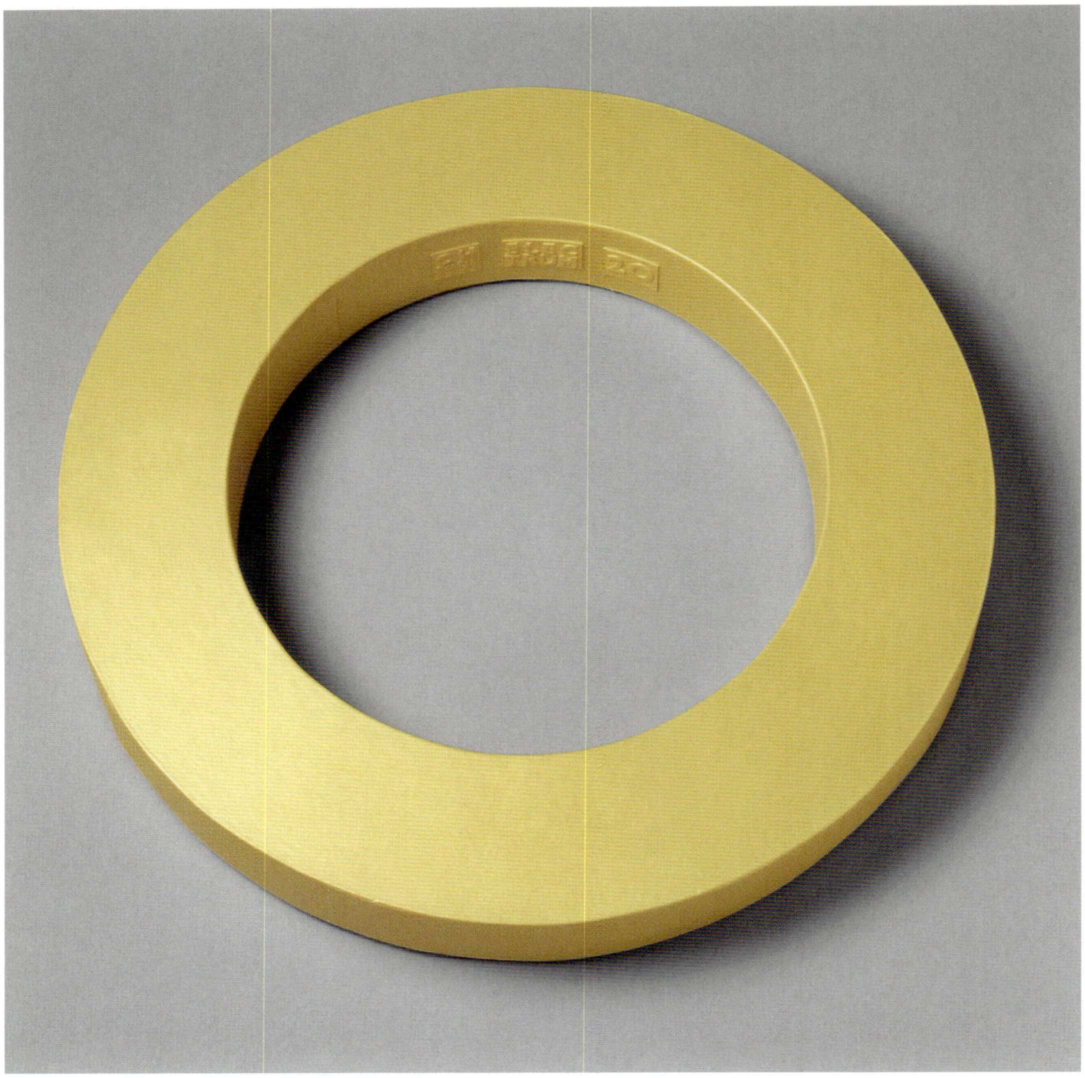

Ring box (closed / open)
1991
mixed paper

Godiva
TUNNOCK'S
CHOCOLATE
TWENTY
POUNDS
cresc

Jo Hayes Ward

UK
born 1975

I have very fond memories of Barbara, who gave me the opportunity to work as a 'Saturday Girl' at Electrum Gallery during my university studies. The experience gave me a fantastic insight into a huge range of eclectic designs and inspiring jewellery, and I was over the moon when my own work was chosen to be part of an Electrum Gallery showcase. My time with Barbara and at Electrum Gallery was certainly a launch-pad for my own business following my graduation and a huge support to so many other contemporary jewellers.

'Stratus' ring
2015
18ct gold, diamond slice,
brown diamonds

‘Lace Edge’ bangle
2006
18ct gold

David Hensel

UK
born 1945

Exhibitions:
1977 David Hensel and Rod Edwards
1978 Jewellery Grows on Trees
1981 Electrum – the tenth year
1982 Love Tokens
1991 20th Anniversary Show

Barbara was of great importance to me at an early stage of being taken seriously – very much the right connection at the right time for me. I came to making jewellery in a roundabout way. I didn't study it specifically, apart from a term at evening classes. Otherwise I was on my own. I've got scars going back to the age of six, from secretly borrowing my father's penknife and whittling at bits of wood. Throughout my childhood I collected and treasured fragments of nicely made things I found, such as a broken antique fountain pen, or the ebony and ivory keys of a smashed up piano found in a hedge, things which somehow were a window onto a world of, as I imagined them, stylish people of which in our rural Dorset we knew nothing. I came to love making and knowing how to make such things myself, and to use them as my way of discovering that world and connecting with those people, my way of making friends.

I've explored a number of different art forms, but jewellery more than anything else is, for me, about devising objects to serve as an interface between myself and others, and then for others to use similarly as an often rather romantic energy template, setting up patterns of self-defence and interaction in their lives. At that remove it becomes rather difficult for me, often too urban for my understanding, and that is the importance of such a gallery as Electrum, that it carries that responsibility of connections.

There had been encouragement. The Crafts Council at the time was supportive, as was Graham Hughes at Goldsmiths' Hall, and there were others. But Barbara was more significant. The first time I went there and showed her what I had, she said 'go home and work like stink and we'll do an exhibition in a year's time.' Fantastic! So we did that, we sold everything and that got it all started. She was good too in deciding on pricing, though as she once said 'you can't consider the time something takes to make in pricing', an important idea in that apparent value depends simply on getting it right. She said another thing of importance, after our success with that first exhibition when several new opportunities turned up: 'don't forget that you only have one pair of hands'.

Rings
1978
mixed wood

So it continued for years, the work developed in ways most of which she liked, some pieces less so, but she respected the need for it to grow naturally without interference. There were periods of less involvement with her, finding other ways and places to show and sell what I did. There's an alternative interpretation of Barbara's warning about only having one pair of hands: you can only listen to your own hands, do your own work, and I've long felt that the work of an artist consists largely of finding out what that work is. I think she knew she was genuinely a focus point for an important flowering of art jewellery, not just having a gallery and making her own work, but that she was able to bring to life an acceptance of the art form so to make a cultural contribution of great importance. I wish I'd got to know her better.

'White Man's Bliss' box
with objects
2015
rhino horn, African blackwood,
gold, glow-in-the-dark nose mask,
resin rubber, mammoth ivory,
Viagra pills, silver, silk, shark's teeth,
flower petals, tissue paper

Susanna Heron

UK
born 1949

Exhibitions:
1972 Susanna Heron
1973 Aspects of Modern Jewellery
1974 Susanna Heron
1985 *Twentieth-Century Jewelry* book launch

While a student in 1969 I made a costume from wire and tapes which spiralled around the body. The way in which the planes of the spiral defined the body, and the space created around it, established interests which have reoccurred in my work in various ways over the following years.

It was in 1977, however, when the scale of my work increased, that these ideas fully emerged in three large Jubilee neckpieces made for an exhibition at the V&A in London. I thought of these discs only in formal terms but their relationship to the form and function of great Elizabethan ruffs and ceremonial collars was often pointed out to me.

Later in the USA in 1978 I made the Cardboard Spirals which were surprisingly reminiscent of the costume of 1969. This time the spirals only related to the head and shoulders. They were never intended to be wearable objects but became the subject of a series of photographs made with David Ward. They did, however, also generate a lot of ideas to do with the formal relationship of hats and collar forms to the body. The Curves, made in New York soon after, developed one of these directions, defining as they do a spiral line from the collar bone, around to the back of the neck and down to the breast bone.

During the same period David Ward and I worked together on another series of photographs in which the torso is the subject defined, this time by various patterns of projected light.

Extract from Susanna Heron, *The Recurring Theme* (1982)

Necklace
1972
silver, resin

Susanna Heron

Necklace
1975
silver, resin

Yasuki Hiramatsu

Japan
1926–2012

Exhibitions:
1984 Contemporary Japanese Jewellery
1985 *Twentieth-Century Jewelry* book launch
1990 Yasuki Hiramatsu
1991 20th Anniversary Show
1995 New Japanese Jewellery

Perhaps Japan's best-known artist-jeweller, Yasuki Hiramatsu has exerted a crucial influence on the development of contemporary jewellery in Japan, both by his superb jewellery designs and his untiring efforts as professor at the Tokyo University of Fine Arts, as permanent director of the Japan Jewellery Designers' Institute and as chairman of the directors of the Japan Craft Design Association. Hiramatsu's favoured material was gold with its inherent beauty, but also silver or even aluminium covered with gold leaf. He re-interpreted traditional Japanese metalworking techniques and from this emerged a novel and unique form of artistic expression. With his magical use of metals either as ribbons, or from crushed, crumpled or even beaten sheet metal Hiramatsu creates surface textures which capture the light. Through the play of light and shade the surfaces come alive when worn.

Barbara Cartlidge, *Twentieth-Century Jewellery*, 1985

He once stated 'the metals which I mainly use are also like living things'. His avant-garde jewellery is minimalist in design, aesthetically pure and simple. These characteristics are captured in the subtitle of a book on his work from 2008, *The Essence of Form*, yet he also showed an endearing sense of playfulness.

Beatriz Chadour-Sampson

Ring
1998
18ct gold
Alice and Louis Koch Collection,
Swiss National Museum, Zurich

Bangles
1991
silver

Elisabeth Holder

Germany
born 1950

Exhibitions:
1981 Elisabeth Holder and Miriam Sharlin
1981 Electrum – the tenth year
1988 Elisabeth Holder
1991 20th Anniversary Show
1994 Elisabeth Holder, Helen Aitken-Kuhnen, Johannes Kuhnen

To me, Barbara Cartlidge and Electrum Gallery are and were almost synonymous. Back in the '70s, when I was studying at Düsseldorf, I was aware of Electrum Gallery in London and Galerie Orfèvre in Düsseldorf. As far as I knew, they were the only two galleries for contemporary jewellery at the time. Barbara Cartlidge gave me the opportunity to show my work at Electrum Gallery very early in my career and has supported me ever since. A solo show at Electrum marked the year when I moved to Düsseldorf to take up a post as Professor for Jewellery at the Hochschule (University of Applied Sciences), which I've held since 1988. The exposure Barbara Cartlidge gave my work extended beyond exhibitions and joint celebrations of anniversaries each decade. It certainly contributed to my work being seen also in international contexts. Electrum Gallery played a pioneering role for contemporary jewellery and was unfaltering in its support for a multitude of jewellers, not least owing to Barbara Cartlidge's big heart, acute sense for quality and her encyclopaedic knowledge of contemporary jewellery of the 20th century.

When first exhibiting at Electrum Gallery, and for a long time after, the concept of the autonomous object was important to me in my artistic practice. By this I mean that my jewellery, in addition to its obvious purpose to be worn as jewellery along with the ensuing functional requirements, should also be valid as independent objects that speak for themselves. To a certain extent, I can still identify with this concern today. However, this double requirement in the design of jewellery originally functioned for me as both a benchmark and a design premise. The objects should gain their meaning from two different contexts and can be both a staged object and a worn piece of jewellery. Looking back on that time, in this state of 'jewellery with a dual function', I can see that the view of jewellery as contextual art I hold today was already incorporated as an underlying pursuit. But today, from my present-day perspective, this concept of the independence of jewellery, in the sense of an object-like self-sufficiency that was initially important to me, stands in contrast to the concept of the contextual nature of jewellery. This includes worn jewellery in all its variations. In addition however, many other contexts for jewellery exist that can stem from all kinds of situations of our human environment, including the urban environment. For jewellery in such contexts I coined the term contextual art. This widened view of jewellery informs my own artistic research as well as my work with students.

Barbara Cartlidge strongly believed in what may best be termed an opulent style of display. This was in stark contrast to my own preference for minimalism, which she, for the most part, tended to tolerate when I set up an exhibition, but loathed from a selling point of view. Although we never agreed on this issue, today I can better appreciate her quite uncompromising stance.

Ring
1979
flint, gold

Elisabeth Holder

'Blickfang' sculpture
(eye catcher)
2008
mirror foil

Mary Lee Hu

USA
born 1943

Exhibitions:
1976 Six Contemporary American Jewellers
1981 Electrum – the tenth year

I first met Barbara Cartlidge in early 1976. My teacher, Brent Kington, had told me about Electrum Gallery and suggested I show them my work. I am not easily outgoing, but I mustered all the courage I could and went in. Luckily Barbara was in that day and, amazingly, she was very nice and took the time to look at the photos of work by a very young, unknown jeweller. She said that she was about to have a show of American jewellery and would I like to take part. I decided that it was something I could and should do. I had met all of the other Americans being asked to exhibit, so they entrusted their pieces to me and I packed them in two big suitcases and went over to the UK. I had looked into getting a Carnet, but it was so complicated and expensive that Barbara said just come over. I remember seeing Barbara waiting that morning at the airport when I arrived at customs and was diverted into the line with things to declare. They asked many questions. I was let out temporarily at noon to tell Barbara to report her about progress and then I was let out again at the end of the day … but not the jewellery. Barbara had to go to her bank to post the bond to get the work into the country. She said she would get the money back on any work returned after the show, but probably not for six months. I was impressed at the commitment this show was asking of her.

She hosted me at her home for the duration of my stay. She and her husband had bought a large house divided up into flats. They were letting any of the older residents stay there as long as they wanted, but as rooms became empty, she used them to let visiting jewellers stay while visiting London. I thought how generous and what a way of building a community! This exhibition was the first time I had shown my work in Europe, almost the first time out of the US. It is hard to know just what significance this show had on my career, but I do know that shortly afterwards, I began to be invited to show in other foreign venues and I wonder just how they heard of me.

Necklace
1969
silver

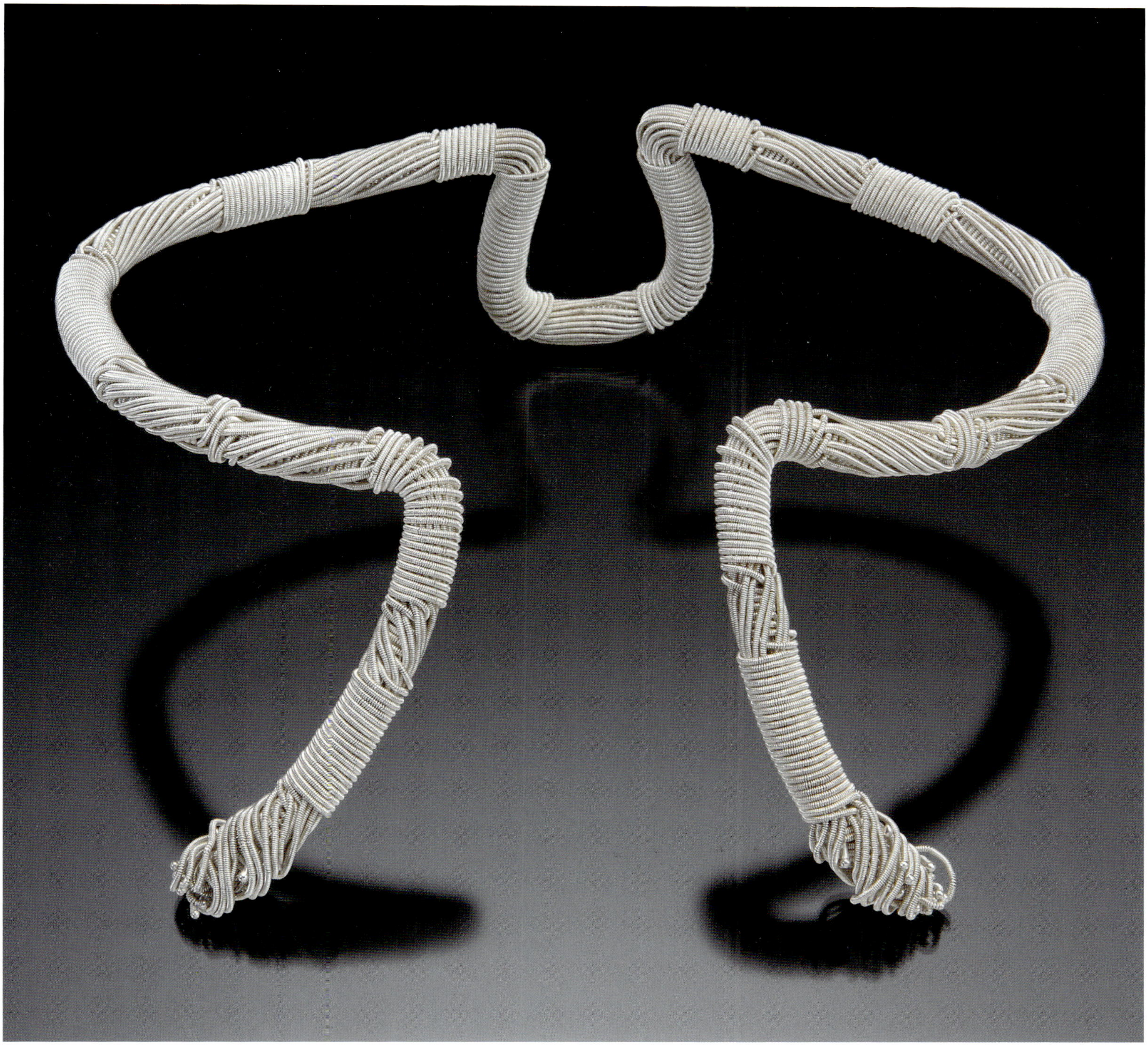

I was already doing wire work then ... I started that in 1966 as my Master of Fine Arts thesis. Some of the neckpieces were large, as we were doing in the 1970s, and I had a head/face piece there too. We were working large and exploring areas of the body that the regular fine jewellery did not. In 1985 I switched to using all gold and am still working in gold. One other thing that I sometimes tell people when reminiscing about that time ... I was out front helping put the lettering of the show on the front gallery window ... *6 Contemporary American Jewellers*, when some people walked by and I overheard one say to the others 'I didn't know America had six contemporary jewellers.' So I guess what we were doing was not well known in London in those days. I also remember Barbara, in referencing the work we sent which had several large necklaces, stating that European women do not wear large necklaces. If she saw someone walking past the gallery wearing a large necklace, she figured she must be an American.

Brooch
2015
18ct and 22ct gold

Bryan Illsley

UK
born 1937

Exhibitions:
1971 Opening Exhibition
1982 Love Tokens
1985 *Twentieth-Century Jewelry* book launch
1991 20th Anniversary Show
1996 Classic and Wild Earrings
2006 Midsummer Madness – 35th Anniversary Show

My partnership with Breon O'Casey ended in 1982 and therefore it must have been 1983 when I approached Electrum to see if Barbara would take my work. In agreeing to do so, her comment was that the work was really too primitive or 'ethnic' for Electrum, but that the exposure to the general run of more precise and sophisticated jewellery that she represented would in time affect my own efforts. Well, as you know, although that didn't come about and I continued in my rudimentary fashion, Barbara nonetheless treated me very well. Delivering pieces to the gallery, Barbara looking up from her desk and recognising me, a marvellous smile would alight on her face and she would say 'hello lovely' or some such kindly welcome. I went only to her house on the occasion of the 20th anniversary, after I recently met Catherine [Mannheim] who had known Barbara well for many years and been to the house often.

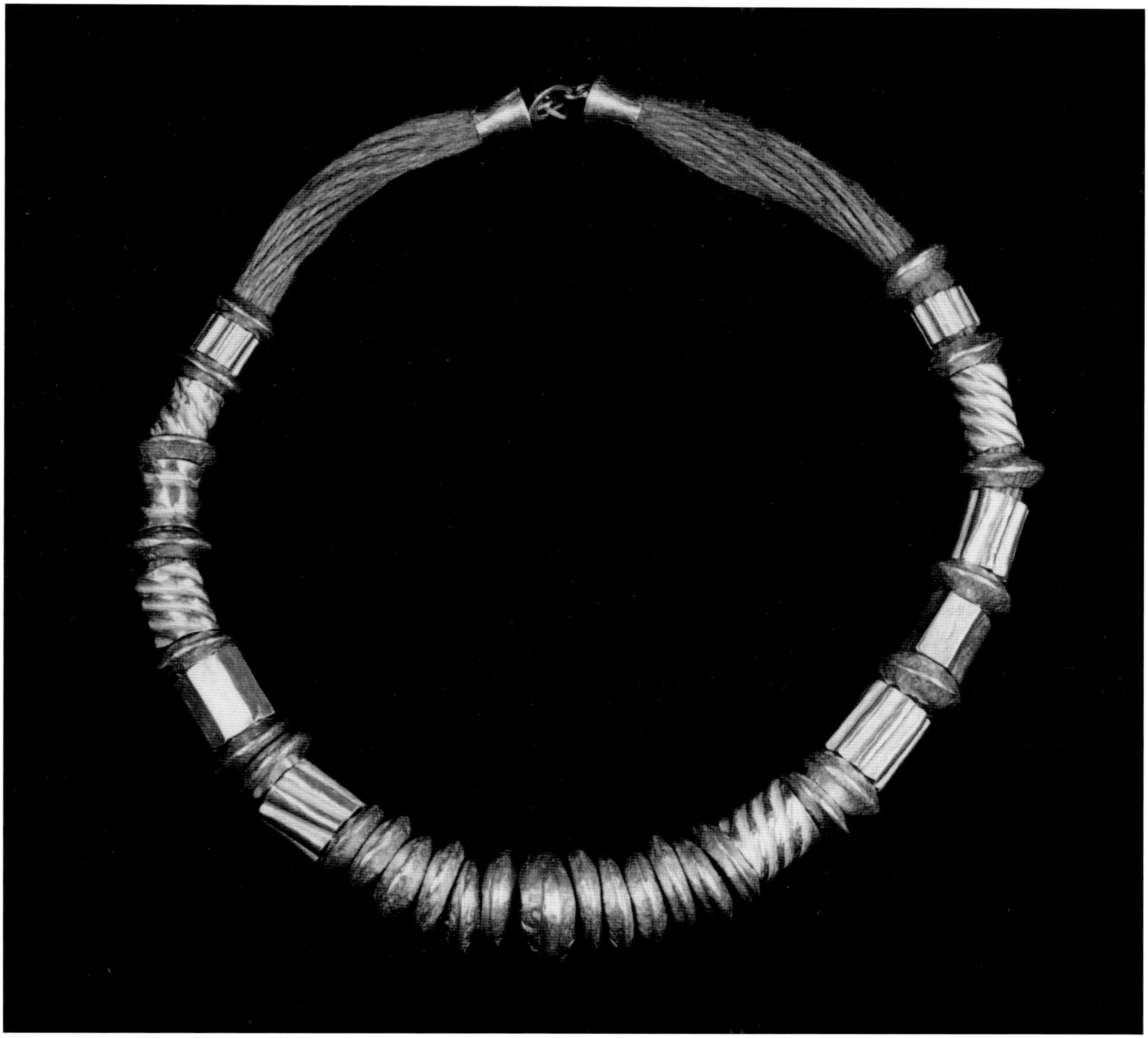

Necklace
1980
silver, string

Rings
2014
silver, 18ct gold, mixed stones

Kazuhiro Itoh

Japan
1948–2002

Exhibitions:
1977 Kazuhiro Itoh and Takao Mitsuyasu
1981 Electrum – the tenth year
1984 Contemporary Japanese Jewellery
1985 *Twentieth-Century Jewelry* book launch
1991 20th Anniversary Show
1992 Contemporary Japanese Jewellery
1995 New Japanese Jewellery

In *Twentieth Century Jewelry* (1985), Barbara Cartlidge describes how in Japan changing social patterns were reflected in changing attitudes towards jewellery. She describes how the young generation of Japanese jewellers, in the aftermath of the horrors of World War Two, 'began to create something different: jewellery that was contemporary, yet essentially based on their own cultural roots and images.'

Itoh was trained in painting at the Tama University in Tokyo and later in Munich at the Akademie der Bildenden Künste. In his early years he designed jewellery with pearls for Mikimoto, and later became Professor at the Hiko Mizuno College of Jewellery in Tokyo. Itoh played an important role in the new jewellery movement in Japan. Cartlidge defines his work as being 'Japanese minimalist' and states 'he reduces his forms to the absolutely essential, relying on a single contrasting colour or material to make his point'. Itoh favoured natural materials, such as cypress wood, wax, granite and marble often in combination with gold. His designs were unmistakably Japanese in concept, but applied in a contemporary way.

Beatriz Chadour-Sampson

Ring
1984
18ct gold, marble
Alice and Louis Koch Collection,
Swiss National Museum, Zurich

Brooch
1992
marble, 18ct gold

Hermann Jünger

Germany
1928–2005

Exhibitions:
1973 Aspects of Modern Jewellery
1975 Hermann Jünger and his students
1985 *Twentieth-Century Jewelry* book launch
1991 20th Anniversary Show
1993 Hermann Jünger, Friedrich Becker, Bruno Martinazzi
1996 The Innovators – 25th Anniversary Exhibition

In *Twentieth-Century Jewelry* (1985), Barbara Cartlidge conveys, in a few lines, the significant role Herman Jünger played in the New Jewellery movement in Germany, and ultimately how he inspired generations of artist-jewellers worldwide. 'A professor at the Akademie der Bildenden Künste in Munich since 1971, Herman Jünger has made a major contribution to the development of contemporary jewellery taken in the widest possible sense. Jünger was the first to break away from the traditional attitudes and concepts of jewellery; he brought an entirely new aesthetic into the field, and as an inspiring teacher, he has influenced whole generations of young artists/jewellers to think beyond conventional limitations and to strike out towards individualism and originality.'

Ralph Turner describes Jünger as 'an artist in metals'. In the 1950s and early 1960s he had already transformed traditional goldsmithing into a new artform, making abstract compositions and experimenting with non-precious materials and metals such as tombac. Randomness and compositional freedom gave his pieces an intentional 'unfinished' and mysterious aesthetic – his creative process was innovative. Jünger's use of enamel and insertion of gemstones had a painterly quality reflecting the spontaneity of his watercolour drawings. He was drawn by the medieval writings of goldsmiths, such as Theophilus Presbyter, a 12th-century monk, and the concept of the goldsmith as artist.

Beatriz Chadour-Sampson

‘Hand of Fatima’ pendant
c.1980
silver, gold

Hermann Jünger

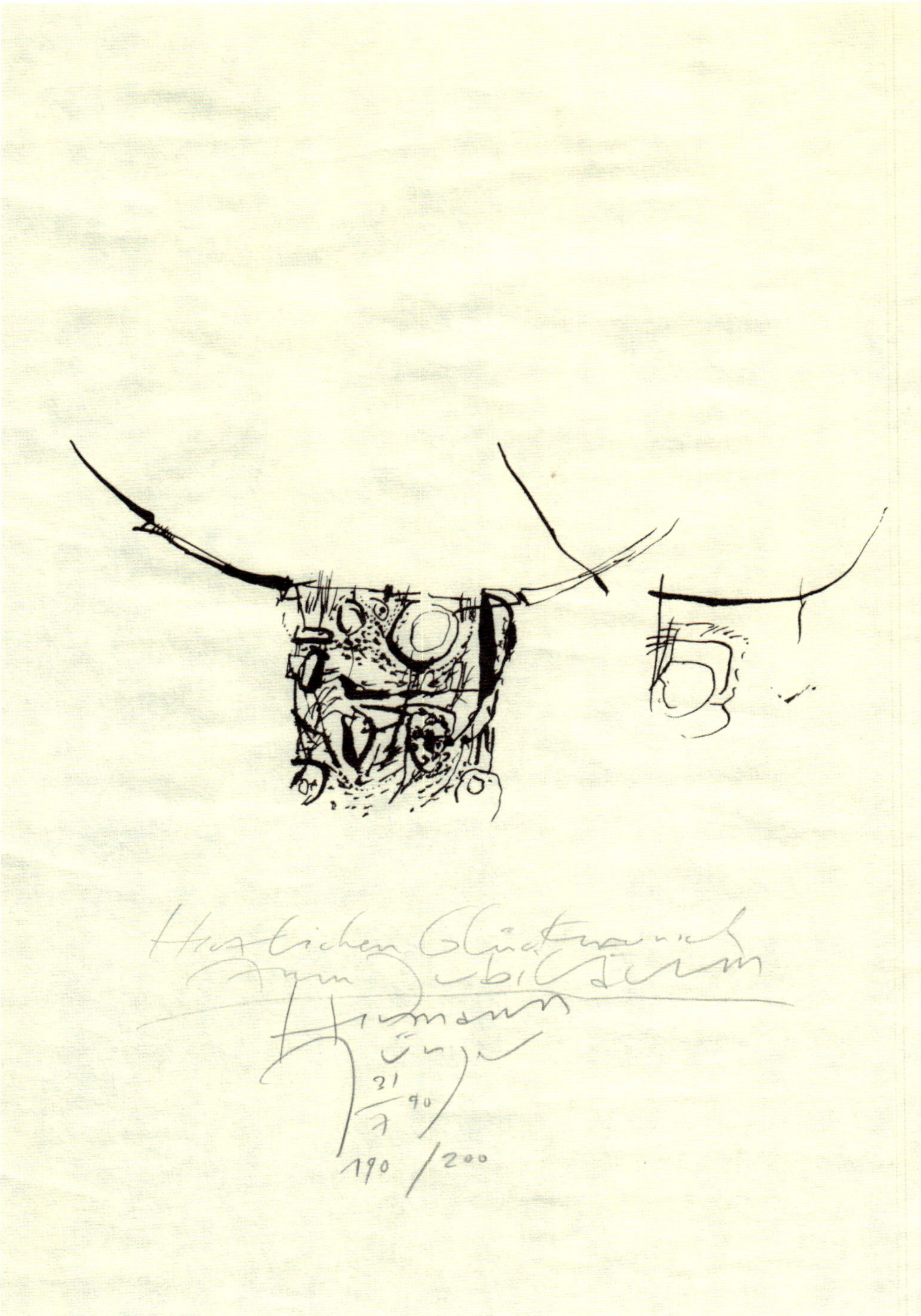

Drawing
1990
ink on paper

Necklace
1979
gold

Halsschmuck
1979

Sieglinde Karl-Spence

Germany / Australia
born 1943

Exhibitions:
1977 Diamond Story
1981 Electrum Gallery – the tenth year
1986 Australian Impressions
1991 20th Anniversary Show
2006 Midsummer Madness – 35th Anniversary Show

Barbara Cartlidge came to the Middlesex Polytechnic final year jewellery exhibition in 1977 where I was a final year student. She invited me to exhibit my work at Electrum Gallery which I continued until 2010. I was very aware of the gallery and its outstanding reputation even in those early days and often visited to see the work of Gerda Flöckinger, who particularly inspired me. My work was profoundly influenced by the gallery and the work shown there. Barbara was also wonderfully supportive and my career was definitely enhanced by showing my work there. I met many jewellers at the Electrum openings and made many, many friends.

Electrum Gallery was the bedrock of the contemporary jewellery movement both in England and abroad and certainly anyone who was serious about contemporary jewellery knew of its esteemed reputation. When I returned to Australia in 1982 my work changed significantly, but much to my delight Barbara was still very much interested in exhibiting this new work. I remember going to see Barbara to show her a new work which I had made and, as usual, she inspected it closely. She was very forthright always, and did not hesitate to tell me that the elaborate locking system I had made on the bangle was, in her estimation, a bit difficult to operate. I was rather upset, as she did not mention the fact that it was a rather stunning piece. It was sold within a month!

'Afterlife of the Rainbow' necklace
2007
lorikeet feathers, linen thread,
stainless steel

'Sun Journey' choker
1977
silver, gold

Helfried Kodré

Austria
born 1940

Exhibitions:
1973 Aspects of Modern Jewellery
1985 *Twentieth-Century Jewelry* book launch
1991 20th Anniversary Show
1993 The Magic of the Ring
1995 J. E. G. Defner and Helfried Kodré

If I remember rightly, it was in the early '70s, but not in the gallery, when I first met Barbara. As it is so long ago, I can't remember where it was, but I think it was Claus Bury who brought us together somewhere in Germany.

The situation was very different from nowadays – jewellery galleries did not yet exist. Electrum Gallery was very important because it offered the possibility to show my work and make contact with other artists and their work – most important in the times before the internet. The gallery was a meeting place of international jewellery artists, a place of interchange of ideas and networking. This is important for every artist's career – Electrum Gallery was important for the formation and development of mine.

I remember always liking my fortieth birthday that I spent with Lisa Defner and a friend with Barbara and Derrick. There was a small table of fireworks with many small rockets climbing like real fireworks, and then exploding – something I have never seen since. At this time, although I was not making jewellery, I had good contact with Barbara. When I returned to jewellery making in the '90s, I had an exhibition once again with Lisa Defner.

Brooch
2010
gold, silver

Brooch
1971
white gold, fine gold, ammonite, rubies

Daphne Krinos

UK
born 1955

Exhibitions:
1991 20th Anniversary Show
2006 Midsummer Madness – 35th Anniversary Show

I did not know Barbara very well but Electrum Gallery had a big reputation and was always my refuge whenever I happened to be in the West End during my student years. I loved going there and looking at all the beautiful and unusual jewellery and was intrigued by Barbara, who always sat on her desk, cigarette in hand, usually on the telephone, looking rather beautiful and stylish with lots of large rings on her fingers.

When I graduated, I decided to take my work there and show it to her. It was many, many years ago but I remember it so clearly. I was incredibly nervous. Barbara had a good look and picked up a few of my pieces (cigarette in hand as always), mainly work I had made at college, before she told me I needed to go back to my bench and start making some *real* work. She remarked that I showed 'promising signs' in my jewellery and I should maybe come again when I was ready. It was a great wake up call for me. I was still enjoying the tremendous response I had at my degree show and was beginning to believe it was all going to be an easy ride from now on. Her comments made me even more determined to set up my own studio and try to prove that I *was* indeed able to survive and make interesting work. I never went back to Electrum to show her what I was making a couple of years later. But I was incredibly pleased when she rang me up and asked to show my work at the gallery. I thought I had finally 'arrived'!

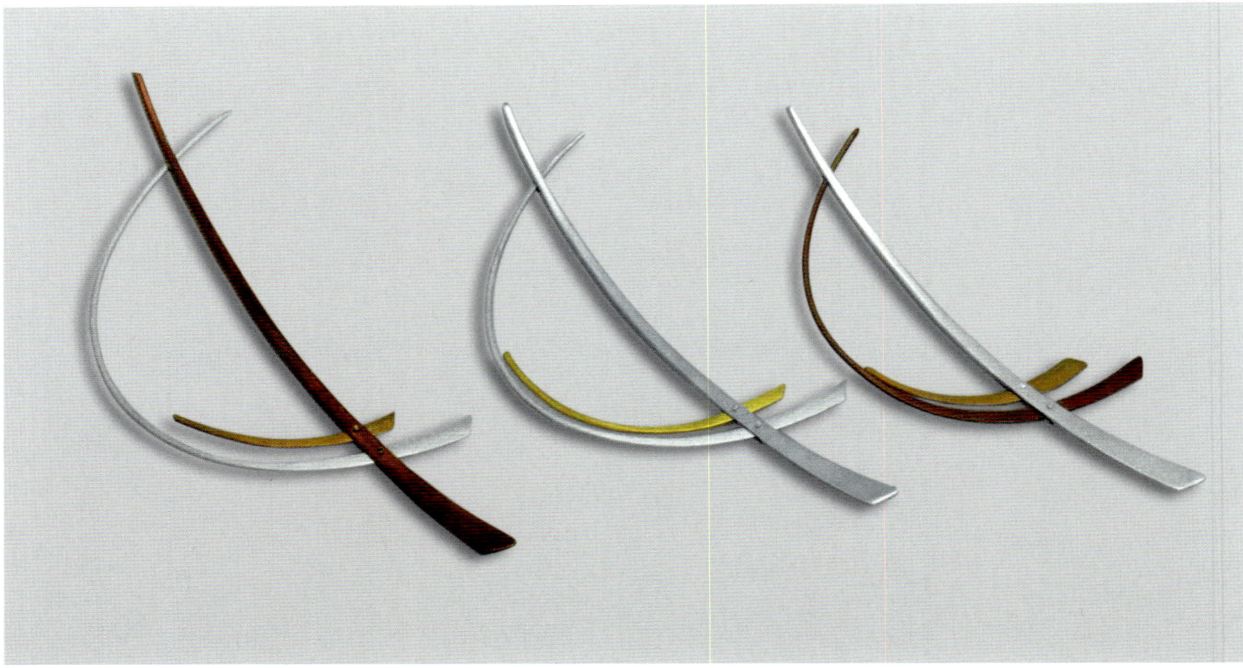

'Sun' necklace
2015
18ct gold, yellow beryl, silver

Brooches
1982
silver, titanium

Inger Blix Kvammen

Norway
born 1954

Exhibitions:
1998 Inger Blix Kvammen
2001 Inger Blix Kvammen and Lilian Busch
2006 Midsummer Madness – 35th Anniversary Show

In 1995, my family and I were on a week's vacation trip to London. It was pure coincidence that we passed a very interesting gallery in South Molton Street – a place where I really would like to exhibit – and what I could see from the street was jewellery of high quality. The door was locked and I dared barely knock. I had nothing to show off either, other than the bracelets I had on me. I was greeted by Janice Hosegood who looked at my bracelets and said that the owner would be there a few days later, and that I could have an appointment with her at 12 o'clock. On the Friday, my family waited for me at a restaurant across the street while I knocked on the door to Electrum for the second time, red in the face with nervousness. Barbara was a strong and determined woman, and radiated both warmth and humour and I liked her immediately. I showed her two bracelets. She said she had not seen anything like this before and was interested in my technique and the thinking behind them.

A few days later, there was a program on Norwegian television (NRK) about Tone Vigeland, where she explained that Electrum Gallery was the first international gallery where she had exhibited her work. She spoke about Barbara and how significant this had been for her. Then I realized who I had met. For me, this meeting with Barbara and Electrum has been the most important event in my life as a jewellery artist. It was the start of my relationship with Electrum Gallery and Barbara, who not only became one of the most important mentors for me as an artist, but also a close friend who I admired and was very fond of.

To be shown at Electrum opened doors internationally for me. Collectors and curators from around the world went by there. It was in this way that I came in contact with jewellery artist Professor Arline Fisch, who also showed her textile metalwork at Electrum. She invited me to take an Artist in Residency post at San Diego State University in 1999. Then she came on a 12-day study tour to my area in Norway with eight Masters students and we visited Norwegian, Sami and Russian artists. It led to the exhibition of American crafts at the Murmansk Regional Art Museum in Russia, the first ever American art exhibition in Murmansk.

Necklace
1995
silver, wild bear hair

In 2004 I was invited to exhibit at the first COLLECT contemporary art fair with Velvet da Vinci Gallery from San Francisco, run by Mike Holmes and Elizabeth Shypert. Electrum was not exhibiting at COLLECT, but I went there with Barbara and we talked to Mike and Elizabeth. They also had with them a small part of their exhibition *Anti-War Medals*, which was work by jewellery artists made as a protest against the war in Iraq. Barbara liked the concept and immediately invited the exhibition to Electrum. That was Barbara – impulsive, straightforward and quick to make decisions if there was anything she had faith in. Barbara was unique in her interest for people, stories, for justice, for human rights issues, and she gave her time and commitment to many unknown, talented artists, to victims of war in Vietnam, to the ordinary man in the street. Meanwhile, she had a sharp eye and flair for the unique, and she was keen on innovation. She was a founder and a courageous, independent woman ahead of her time. For me, she was also a role model.

On my first solo show at Electrum in 1998, my husband was present at the opening and met Derrick Cartlidge downstairs at the gallery. They stood chatting and continued during dinner afterwards. We were invited to visit Barbara and Derrick a few days after. They encouraged us to stay with them when we came to town, as they had plenty of room. It turned out that we had many common interests and similar views on lots of things. We live next to the Russian border with Norway in the far north, and my husband was working then as head of the Norwegian Barents Secretariat with regional cooperation across the east-west borders in the Barents Region. There were many interesting meals around the kitchen table, where we discussed politics and society and where we thus were fortunate to get a glimpse of the life that they had lived – one of a strong, uncompromising political stance and courageous, political and artistic commitment.

We understand that the home of Barbara and Derrick, over the years, had been open to artists from different parts of the world, as well as for neighbours and their children's friends. This was a warm home in London for many more than us. I have never experienced such gallows humour and self-irony that these two had, and the warmth, love, understanding and solidarity they showed one another – it was good to see. Youthful simplicity, the passionate commitment and curiosity for life, their interest in communities and individuals was not diminished over the years, nor the unique stories.

'Roots Tundra' bracelet
2015
silver, reindeer harness

Stanley Lechtzin

USA
born 1936

Exhibitions:
1985 *Twentieth-Century Jewelry* book launch
1996 The Innovators - 25th Anniversary Exhibition

I believe the first time I met Barbara was at Goldsmiths' Hall where I had my one-person exhibition in 1973. It was beneficial having a major European gallery dedicated to jewellery and it provided an important venue for 'art' jewellery makers and collectors.

'Pynch 2' brooch
2011
resin

Brooch
1969
silver gilt, agate, Biwa pearls

Hilde Leiss

Germany
born 1949

Exhibitions:
1991 20th Anniversary Show
1996 Classic and Wild Earrings
1998 Hilde Leiss and Jan Adams
2006 Midsummer Madness – 35th Anniversary Show

My role model, Barbara Cartlidge

In 1980 when I finished my studies as a jewellery designer at the Hochschule in Pforzheim, I had already learnt from my professors that Barbara Cartlidge had established Electrum Gallery in London, the most important gallery for contemporary jewellery. She was the first in Europe to show artist-jewellery with its sculptural qualities in contrast to more conventional jewellery. So I flew to London. With shaking knees and trembling hands I wanted to persuade Barbara Cartlidge to present my pieces of jewellery in her legendary gallery. I was deeply impressed by her charisma, her elegance and her humility, despite her fame as a jewellery designer and gallery owner, and how openly she received me – a young, unknown jewellery maker – and talked to me as one of her peers.

From the ensuing collaboration developed a lasting friendship. During my regular visits – initially once or twice a year – Barbara always cooked a wonderful dinner, and we had interesting talks about art, and of course about jewellery, but even more about paintings, the theatre and films. Of all the gifts I brought her the dearest were the German Schillerlocken (curled strips of smoked dogfish) – they were reminiscent of her youth in Berlin. In recent years we have rarely seen each other, but the memory of our meetings remains precious to me. From the very beginning in the 1980s, as a young artist-jeweller and aspiring gallery owner, Electrum was a great role model for me, especially the way it was managed by Barbara Cartlidge. This remains unchanged today.

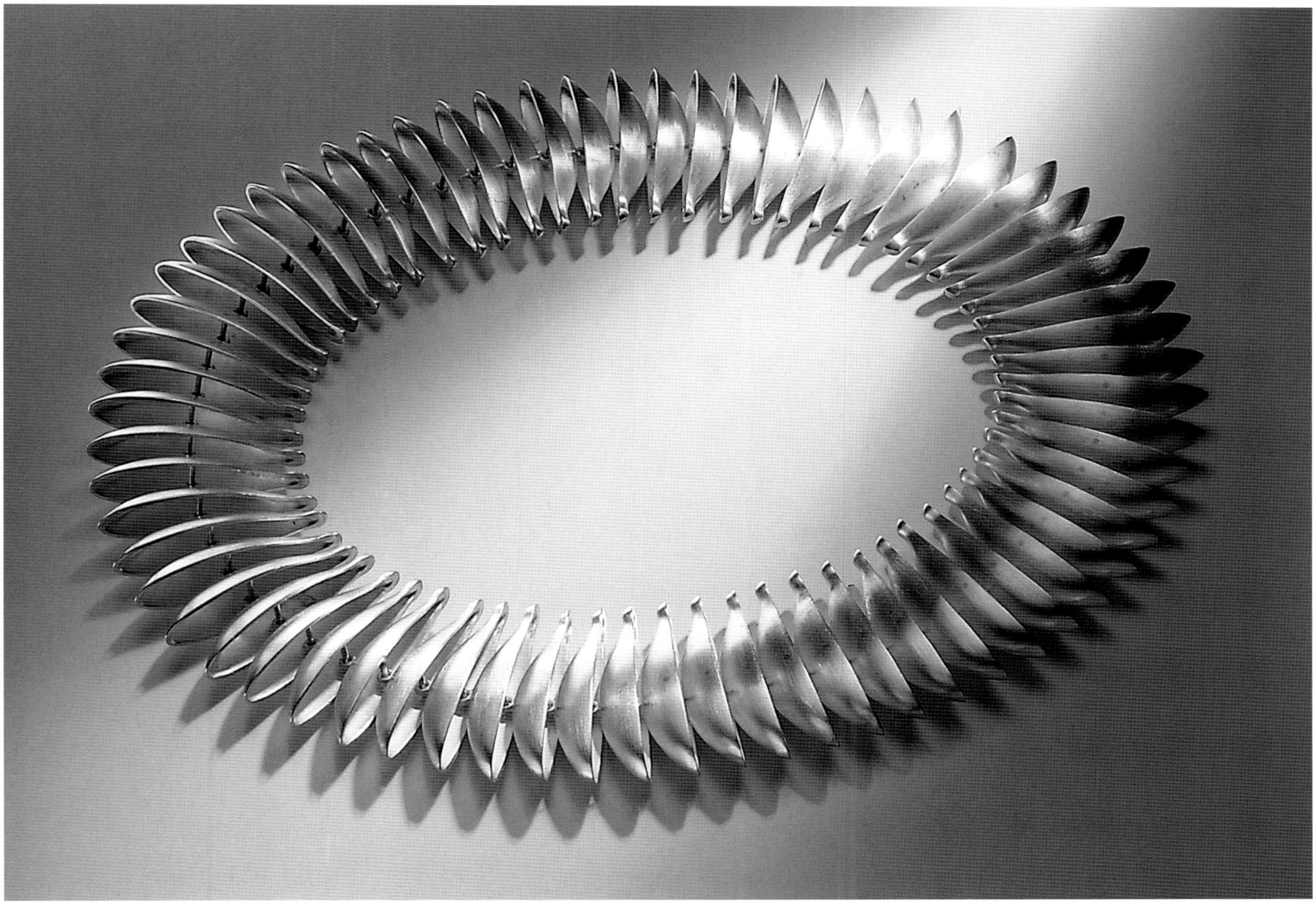

Necklace
1993
silver, 8ct gold

Brooches
2001
glass, 18ct gold

Fritz Maierhofer

Austria
born 1941

Exhibitions:
1971 Opening Exhibition
1972 Concepts of Modern Jewellery
1972 Objects and Acrylic Jewellery
1975 Gold and Acrylic Jewellery
1981 Electrum – the tenth year
1984 Base + Noble
1985 *Twentieth-Century Jewelry* book launch
1991 20th Anniversary Show

It is not easy for me to remember those exciting days. Everything we did at that time just fitted. Everyone experimented with new and different ideas – everyone in their own way! Hardly any photos exist. In those days, there were no digitals, no Facebook.

I came to London in 1967 to work with Andrew Grima and met Claus Bury when he came from Pforzheim as a student with Reinhold Reiling to visit Grima's workshop. This connection was a turning point for me by putting me in touch with Ralph Turner and finally with Barbara, when we met in her home. It all started and took shape – the puzzle came together.

London without Barbara would not have been the same for me. Later on when I travelled from Austria, there was always a stop at Hampstead: popping in, staying overnight, having a meal with some invited friends from England and abroad, breakfast in the morning with Derrick's heavy Assam tea and toast from the kitchen oven. Barbara liked white asparagus, which one could not get in England. Either I brought some with me, when it was in season, or I sent some to her house from Austria, well packed in damp cloth, so it arrived fresh in London.

Another memory is driving past Electrum in my car – there was no congestion zone back then – and seeing Barbara in her gallery behind her writing table being busy! All this formed my relationship with Barbara. Her incredible kindness was a natural gift. One could ask her for advice and talk it over with her. Humanity to her was very important. As the owner of Electrum Gallery it was not easy for her – we know all that. Above all she liked jewellery and was curious about new pieces.

Necklace
1970
silver and acrylic

Fritz Maierhofer

Brooches
2015
anodised aluminium

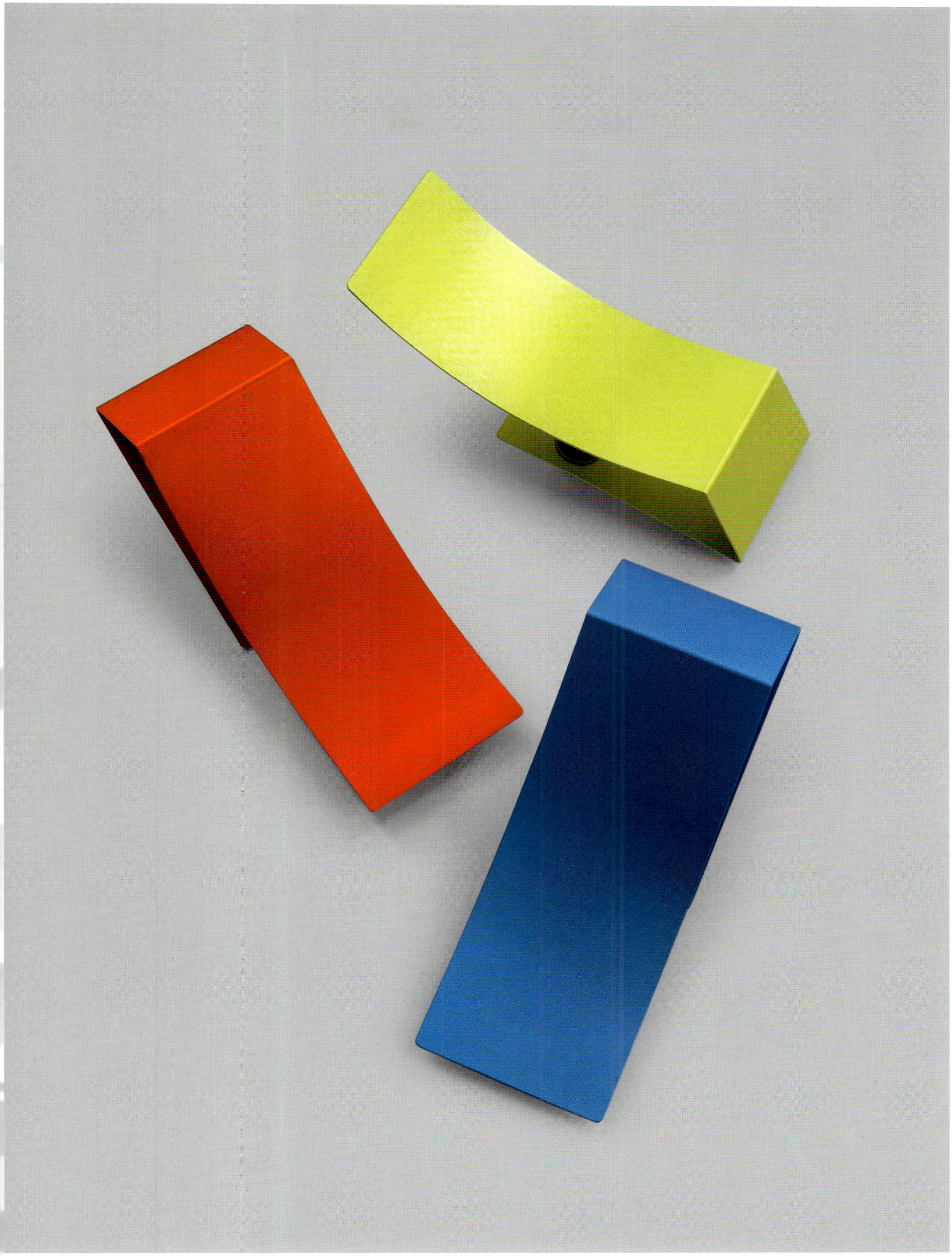

Julia Manheim

UK
born 1949

Exhibitions:
1978 Jewellery Grows on Trees
1981 Electrum – the tenth year

I first met Barbara at Electrum and although I knew that Barbara was the owner of the Gallery, I always thought that Ralph Turner was the mover and shaker when it came to showing what was new and radical at the time. He was the person I tended to talk to in my dealings with the gallery. Electrum Gallery had a huge significance for my work, as it expressed an interest in showing the enamelled silver jewellery that I had made while a student at the Central School of Art and Design. It showed and sold some of the silver and carved ebony pieces I went on to make after leaving college. In fact, I remember being extremely impressed by the beautiful black-and-white photographs which Barbara took of the silver and ebony work.

Electrum showed what was happening in contemporary jewellery, not just in Britain, but in Europe and the rest of the world as well. It brought contemporary jewellery to a wider public and, importantly, to the notice of other jewellers, when no one else seemed particularly interested in the wave of changes in materials, form and concept that were happening at the time. Electrum put on exciting shows which linked contemporary jewellery with other areas of the arts, such as dance, performance, sculpture and installation art. There was a real buzz about the place and the window onto South Molton Street always looked daring and exciting too.

My work has gone through various phases, both in jewellery and object making. It has travelled from jewellery to video via body wear, objects, sculpture, installation and public art. I have used many different materials from silver and enamel, to carved ebony and boxwood, thread, coloured resins, paint, plastic, PVC, re-used newspaper and wood. Exploring the boundaries where jewellery meets clothing and sculpture led on to making objects which were nothing to do with wearing, but still made reference to the body, culminating in large-scale sculpture which you could get inside.

I have had interesting and fruitful collaborations with architects, chorographers, poets, performance artists, clothing designers and musicians. I have also worked as lead artist on several public art projects and have been an integral part of the Quay2c Architects design team, since the practice was set up in 2000. Examples of my work are held in many public and private collections worldwide. Currently, I'm making very short films which often contain a performative element. Looking back, it seems as though this is something that has been latent in my work, surfacing every now and then.

Bangles
1974
silver, ebony

Film still from
'Inside Out' performance
2015

Catherine Mannheim

UK
born 1943

Exhibitions:
1971 Opening Exhibition
1973 Figurative Jewellery
1981 Electrum – the tenth year
1991 20th Anniversary Show
1996 Straight from the Heart
1996 Classic and Wild Earrings
2006 Midsummer Madness – 35th Anniversary Show

I first met Barbara at Pace Gallery in St Christopher's Place when I went to see her to show my jewellery. I know that she was the first person to open a gallery for contemporary jewellery and to show work from outside the UK.

To have your work at Electrum was to be accepted as a jeweller whose work was of a high enough standard in design and craftsmanship. Having your work at Electrum opened the doors to many other possibilities. By showing work there, I was invited to show in Europe and America and I was fortunate to exhibit my jewellery there until the gallery closed. My work was figurative then and I was one of the early jewellers to combine mixed metals, such as silver and gold, which was frowned on in those days. I also used spray enamel on my brooches, definitely not accepted, and I rarely used stones. I now work mainly in 18ct gold and use precious stones.

My main memory is of Barbara sitting in the back of the gallery with her over-large glasses and with a haze of cigarette smoke around her. She also held wonderful parties at her house in Hampstead. She scrutinised the work that you brought very carefully and you could be sure she would make an observation. There were wonderful openings and one could meet all the most eminent jewellers who would come from far and wide to be there. She was like a queen bee with all the workers around. Pre-openings, many collectors came to see the work to make their purchases. Barbara was supported by her lovely husband Derrick. In the earlier years, going to see Barbara would often take some time as there was bound to be a conversation. Our relationships with Barbara were very personal and one felt part of a large family of jewellers.

'Sections of the Earth' brooch
1973
silver, 18ct gold

Brooch
2004
18ct gold, platinum, ruby, sapphire

Bruno Martinazzi

Italy
born 1923

Exhibitions:
1973 Jewellery and the Human Form
1981 Electrum – the tenth year
1985 *Twentieth-Century Jewelry* book launch
1991 20th Anniversary Show
1993 Bruno Martinazzi, Friedrich Becker and Hermann Jünger

I first met Barbara at Electrum Gallery in 1971, when the gallery was inaugurated. I cannot remember if I had met Barbara prior to that, though possibly through Graham Hughes or Ralph Turner during my one-man exhibition *Jewellery by Bruno Martinazzi* at Goldsmiths' Hall in 1965. After River Gallery in Old Bond Street had ceased its activities, Electrum Gallery was my place of reference in London. In 1973 I presented my work in a group exhibition with Eberhard Burgel, Reinhold Reiling and Hubertus von Skal, and again in the years 1981 and 1991 at Electrum's 10th and 20th anniversaries and in 1993 with Friedrich Becker and Herman Jünger. It can be said with certainty that in those years Electrum Gallery was the most important gallery for artist-jewellery on an international scale.

I have always observed mankind with its passions and thoughts. For many years Barbara Cartlidge showed great passion for her work and she had a place close to my heart. I can say that my relationship with Barbara has given me warmth, in the same way as other art critics, galleries, and collectors. In those years the city of London, including Electrum Gallery, contributed to making my work known and appreciated worldwide. As I have mentioned before it was a long time ago and my memories seem far away in the past. Most certainly my thoughts about the significance of art, artist-jewellery and of beauty are fruits born from my encounters, my life and my work.

When approaching the final stages of life – *ultima linea rerum* – I embrace the memories of encounters which have enriched me and made me greater appreciate how to get closer to truth and beauty. At the moment when souls meet, each with a different voice, they join and become something greater, together more beautiful, more truthful.

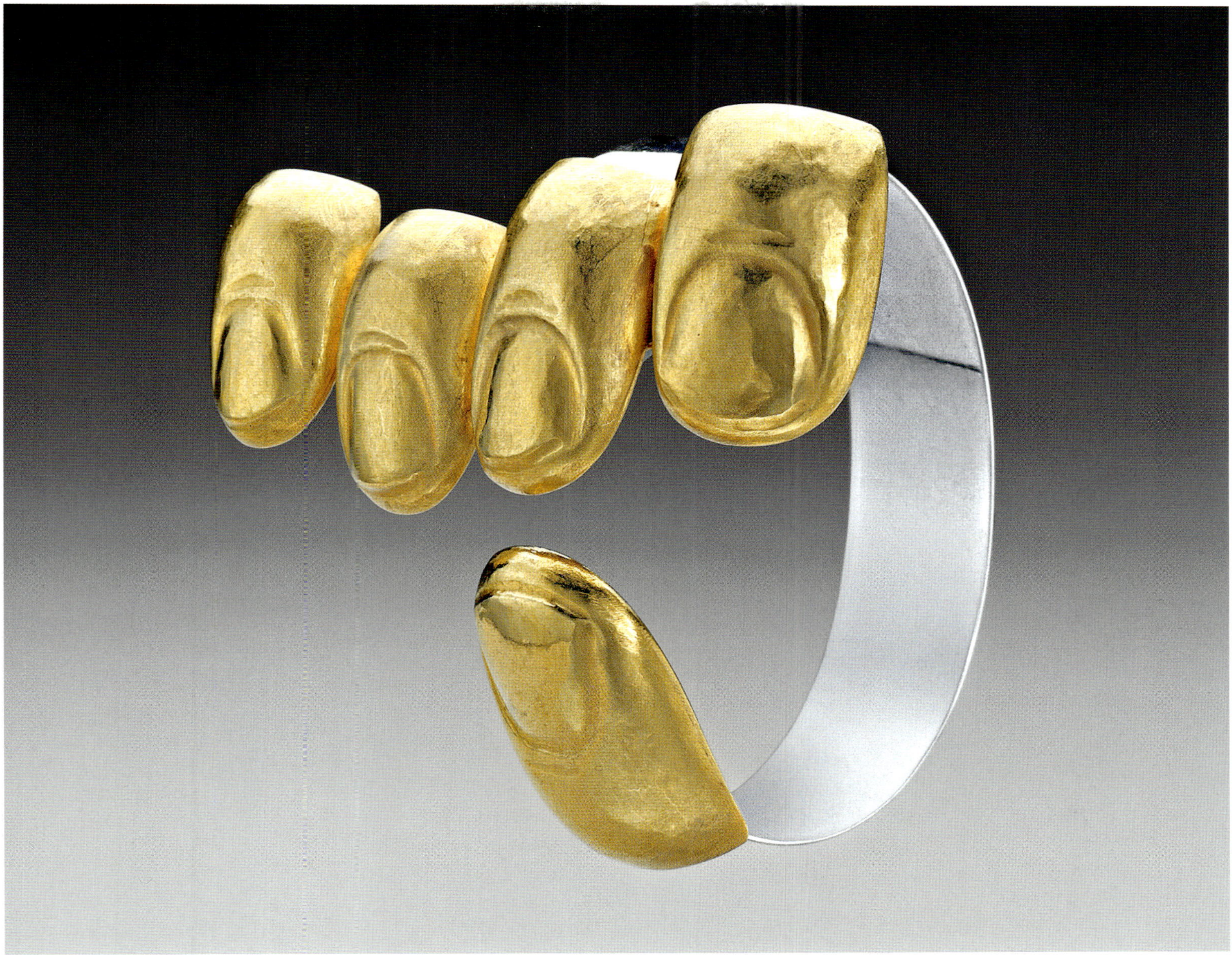

‘Goldfinger’ bracelet
2003
yellow and white gold
The Museum of Fine Arts, Houston,
Helen Williams Drutt Collection,
promised gift of Helen Williams Drutt English,
TR 1068-2006

‘Generation’ brooch
2012
20ct and 18ct gold

Wilhelm Tasso Mattar

Germany / Spain
born 1946

Exhibitions:
1991 20th Anniversary Show
1993 The Magic of the Ring
2002 Amber – Gold of the North
2004 Anti-War Medals

In 1982 there was an exhibition at the Crafts Council in London and it was on this occasion that I first met Barbara. In Düsseldorf there was Galerie Orfèvre run by Peter Hassenpflug and in Cologne there was Map Sauer, however it was well-known to me that Barbara was a pioneer in the field of contemporary jewellery. As jewellery makers we felt we were taken seriously by Barbara and her gallery. Essentially, Electrum was the 'first choice'. In 1987, when Barbara was awarded the Golden David Award in Cologne for her achievements in the field of jewellery, she was described as 'Queen of the Scene' in the speech given by Friedrich Becker.

'Holy Prisoner, Prisoner Saints' brooch
2010
mixed media

'Coca Cola, Nivea, Lift' necklace
1982
mixed media

Alistair McCallum

UK
born 1953

Exhibitions:
1980 Jewellery and Bowls
1981 Electrum – the tenth year
1984 Base + Noble
1991 20th Anniversary Show

I first met Barbara in 1979 shortly after I had graduated from the RCA. I don't remember where, but probably at the gallery as a young silversmith and jeweller trying to find an outlet for my work in the premier UK jewellery gallery. I remember being slightly terrified as Barbara could be slightly intimidating, being very forthright and honestly voicing her opinions.

In my early days as a maker, Barbara was very supportive and occasionally commissioned pieces from me for sale in the gallery. I received a phone call from her in 1980, someone had dropped out of a one-man show at short notice and would I like to take the space. I panicked, as it only left me four months to produce the work but agreed that I would take up the offer if it could be a two-man show. The second person never materialised (was this Barbara's intention all along?!) so I wound up with my first one-man show.

The role that Electrum played for contemporary jewellery has been huge. It must be remembered that contemporary jewellery was new and Electrum was the first gallery in the UK specialising in this field. It provided an outlet for the maker but also a place to see, understand and purchase the best of contemporary jewellery from the UK and abroad. The importance of this in the days before the internet was considerable as it was a way of seeing the work of other jewellers, thus stimulating the growth and interest in contemporary jewellery both as a career and as a customer/collector. From very small beginnings, contemporary jewellery is now a major player in the applied arts, and the influence of Barbara and Electrum played a major role in this.

Bowl
1980–1
copper, gilding metal

Bowls
2015
silver, copper, gilding metal

Jacqueline Mina, OBE

UK
born 1942

Exhibitions:
1971 Opening Exhibition
1991 20th Anniversary Show
1996 Classic and Wild Earrings

I think it must have been in the early '60s when I first met Barbara, after my graduation from the Royal College of Art, when I showed at Ewan Philips Gallery in Maddox Street. I think Barbara was a fellow-student with Ewan's girlfriend/partner at Central School of Art evening classes. Later, she was asking artists to contribute works to a charity art exhibition in Belsize Park Town Hall – *Artists for Vietnam* I think – and my husband, Michael Minas, and I took part annually. Following that, Barbara opened Pace gallery with Ralph Turner in St Christopher's Place where they showed my work.

Initially I was excluded from Electrum as I was at odds with Ralph Turner, then later when I tried to get Barbara's interest in my work, she rejected it as I couldn't agree to give Electrum exclusivity. So really, although we remained on good terms, I never did get close to Barbara and can't say I knew her very well. During the latter years of Electrum I was happy to have my work shown there but I didn't see Barbara very often. As an eclectic showcase, Electrum offered the general public a dedicated place for appreciating contemporary jewellery and, as such, played an important role in educating tastes.

Earrings
2014
18ct gold

Brooches
1996
titanium, 18ct gold

Roger Morris

UK
born 1946

Exhibitions
1973 Aspects of Modern Jewellery
1975 Extra-dimensional Jewellery
1981 Electrum – the tenth year
1985 *Twentieth-Century Jewelry* book launch
1991 20th Anniversary Show
1993 The Magic of the Ring

I first met Barbara at Cameo Corner in 1972 where I was showing my degree show work. She invited me to come along to her gallery with my collection and that was the start of a long working relationship and friendship. Although there were a few galleries that did show a little modern jewellery, Electrum was the first dedicated to showing solely contemporary jewellery. This had enormous significance as there was clearly a movement evolving in Europe, some would say a jewellery renaissance, and Barbara was the catalyst that brought together all the amazing artists.

With her connections she was able to attract the most prestigious international contemporary jewellers and that was truly inspirational. I remember meeting the likes of Hermann Jünger, Claus Bury, Emmy van Leersum, Gijs Bakker, Fritz Maierhofer and Arline Fisch. They would arrive for the private views and Barbara would invite them to her home for dinner and I was lucky to be regularly invited. Barbara and Derrick were great hosts. I remember we were always served a particular brand of rosé wine and of course they were both heavy smokers. Their lovely house in Hampstead was such a welcoming place to visit, I always felt at home there.

I spoke of Barbara's role of course, but mention should also be made of Ralph Turner. Over the years there were differences of opinion and direction between the two, although I am aware that they were originally partners with the same ambitions to promote the emerging jewellery movement. Sadly their differences led to an acrimonious split and Ralph left the gallery. It was interesting to see how different artists were split in their allegiance, but I was devoted to Barbara.

My first collection shown at Electrum was made of hand-carved agate set in precious metals. The neckpieces were, I suppose, quite dramatic and bold and this appealed to Barbara. Sadly the collection was stolen from the gallery by a three-man team of thieves. I was interviewed on the television about the robbery and that was actually followed by Barbara and I being invited onto a chat show to talk about the gallery and its influence on the art world. On graduating from the Royal College of Art in 1975, Barbara gave me my first solo show at Electrum. The success of that event evolved into a design style that has been with me to this day.

Over the years both Barbara and Derrick became close friends – in fact they became surrogate parents in a nice kind of way. I often assisted with photographing work for gallery brochures that I found immensely valuable and she taught me a lot. I became aware that Barbara was developing agoraphobia and that was sad to witness. There was a period when I was struggling to sell enough jewellery to make ends meet and Derrick employed me as a taxi truck driver in his company. Along with deliveries across London I was often asked to run Barbara into town to the gallery and back. I was very aware then that she was struggling with the journey and she was always very relieved when I got her home. By 1980, selling got tougher with a recession and I decided to enter the teaching profession. As this started in Wales and eventually ended in Scotland so my relationship with both the gallery and Barbara began to fade.

Brooch
1978
18ct gold, silver, acrylic

Roger Morris

Pendants
2015
18ct gold aquamarine, tourmaline,
acrylic, resin

Norbert Muerrle

Germany
born 1948

Exhibitions:
1974 Jewellery and Paintings
1981 Electrum – the tenth year
1984 Base + Noble
1985 *Twentieth-Century Jewelry book launch*
1991 20th Anniversary Show
1998 Norbert Muerrle

In 1972–3 I met Ralph Turner from Electrum Gallery when he came to visit me in Pforzheim. One year later I also met Barbara Cartlidge. She was a witty and fun-loving person, an excellent hostess and wonderful cook. I had my first solo exhibition at Electrum Gallery in 1974 when I stayed in London for several weeks. In 1987–8 I introduced Niessing (the German jewellery manufacturer) to Barbara as a way of maximising profits, as she had told me at the time that the gallery was near the point of closing. I had my last exhibition at the gallery in 1998. We had differing opinions on the quality of art in jewellery – her views were much freer and more diverse than mine.

Brooch
1973
18ct gold, ivory, glass,
plastic cow, acrylic

Sculpture
2011
silver, gold

Bernd Munsteiner

Germany
born 1943

Exhibitions:
1991 Bernd Munsteiner
1991 20th Anniversary Show

I first met Barbara in the mid 1970s at Electrum Gallery. On the same day I was invited to visit Barbara and her husband Derrick in their private house and stayed as a guest in their home for three days. I had heard about Barbara before I met her and I believe I had read an article about her in a magazine. She impressed me at our first meeting, as she directly understood the difference of my free stone cutting, in contrast to industrial stonecutting. In my eyes, Electrum was one of the first, and most innovative, contemporary jewellery galleries in all of Europe.

I remember that Barbara and her husband once came to visit my home in Stipshausen, Germany. When they decided to make the trip, Derrick insisted on bringing his own tea pot along. In the two days of their visit, we enjoyed very good English tea together!

'Impressions in Agate' wall panel
2015
natural coloured agates,
wooden frame

'Erotik' brooch
1989
sardonyx relief, 18ct gold,
platinum, diamond

Nele

Germany
born 1932

Exhibitions:
1976 Nele
1981 Electrum – the tenth year
1985 *Twentieth-Century Jewelry* book launch
1991 20th Anniversary Exhibition
1997 E. R. Nele
2006 Midsummer Madness – 35th Anniversary Show

In 1951 I started my studies at the Central School of Art and Design in London where I met Gerda Flöckinger. Our concern was to make new jewellery as had never been seen before. We worked with iron, silver and copper which allowed us to experiment with new ideas. After three years, I had to return to Germany as I was not allowed to work in England even though I had references from Henry Moore and Herbert Read. I studied under Professor Ullmann in Berlin where I began to make sculpture in metals.

I travelled to London quite often – my dream town – and stayed with Gerda. She took me along to see Barbara Cartlidge's new gallery. I was thrilled to finally discover a jewellery gallery with a modern interior design. Each artist exhibited had their own case for display. The gallery was in South Molton Street, one of my favourite streets, in the same street as the sculpture gallery of the Gimpel brothers where I met several renowned British sculptors. I often sat opposite Barbara's gallery in Applebaum's café, eating a pastrami sandwich with a glass of wine and observing who had come to see my exhibition at Electrum.

I believe when Barbara first opened her gallery it was exceedingly difficult to display new jewellery and to draw attention to the extreme and unusual designs, as jewellery had a hard time being recognised by the art scene. The art critics radically rejected the 'all round artist' who dealt with design, metalwork, ceramics, lighting and jewellery, and refused to write about them. Today I know many artists who, alongside painting and sculpture, have been successful as designers.

Barbara was well ahead of her time when choosing artists and their jewellery – for this she should be honoured today. It was extremely brave of Barbara to open a gallery in such an excellent location in central London but she had the courage, imagination and vision. She promoted unknown artists who were often outsiders and made quite unconventional work. Barbara inspired so many young jewellers and from so many countries, and offered them a one man show, which forced them to work for it.

I admired Barbara as, despite caring for her family and running the gallery, she even found time to write books on jewellery, as well as invitation texts to her numerous gallery exhibitions. I loved to stay in her house in Hampstead, where she cooked these wonderful fish dishes. One day she showed me a huge ring, opened it, and there was a stamp with her signature. She told me that she used it on her flights to Vietnam. With this wonderful ring she was able to pass all borders. I admired and loved her very much.

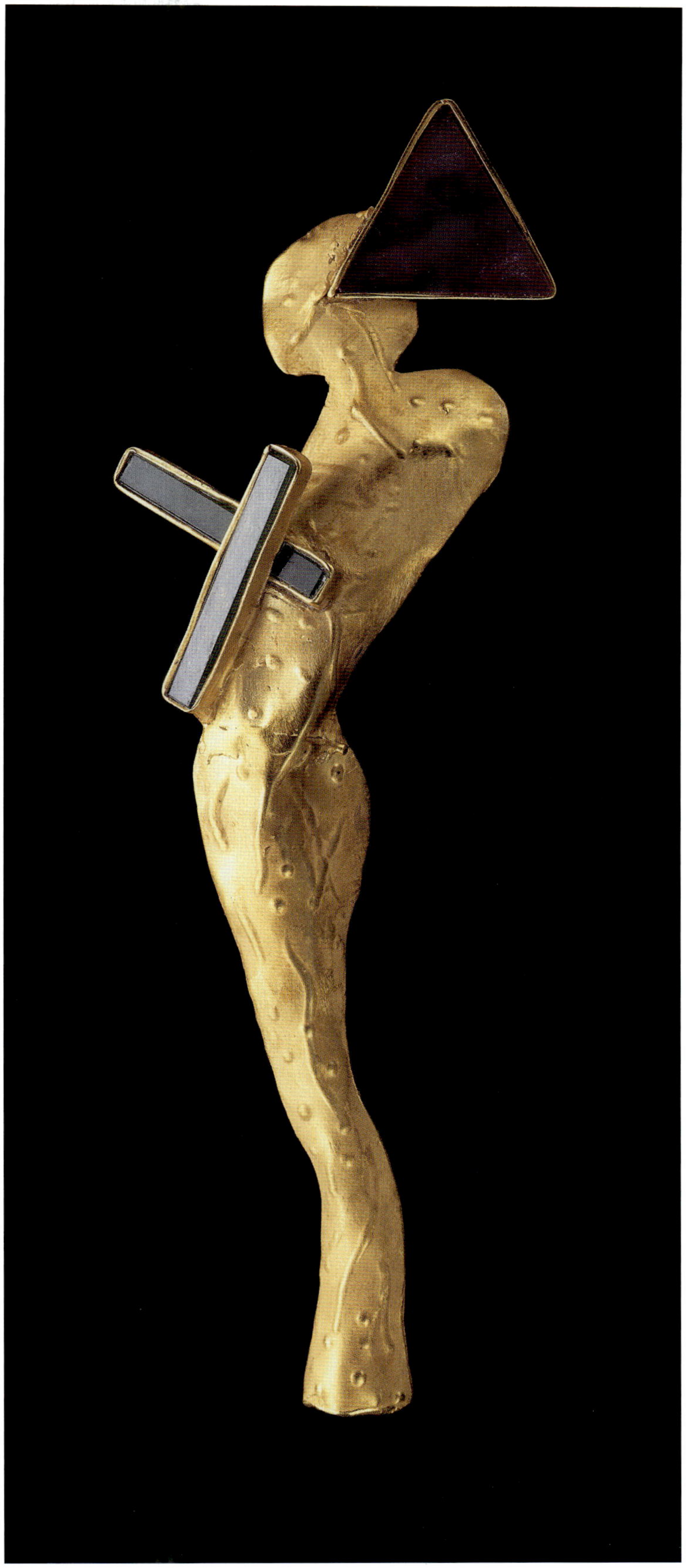

Pendant
1979
18ct gold, silver,
opalised ammonite

Brooch
1997
gold, ruby, haematite

Niessing

Germany
Founded in 1873 by Hermann Niessing

Exhibitions:
1985 The Niessing Collection
1991 20th Anniversary Show
1993 The Magic of the Ring
1994 Niessing – The New Collection
1997 Niessing – The 1997 Collection
1998 The Colour Red

Barbara Cartlidge has accompanied me through my professional life for a good 30 years: for 10 years with my mother Ursula Exner (née Niessing) from the mid 1970s to early 1980s, after which was 'my turn', once I had completed my business studies and was taken into the company's management team. What followed was my training 'on the job' in the field of jewellery creation and design. This included several encounters with the architect Prof. Max von Hausen, and the jewellers Prof. Hermann Jünger, Prof. Friedrich Becker, Peter Hassenpflug, Günter Krauss and Barbara Cartlidge. On these occasions Barbara acted as a guide, outlining to me the different artist-jewellers and their work. She had an extensive historical knowledge of art jewellery on an international scale. As a young man at the time I then could not distinguish between personal and objective evaluations. Through Barbara I learned how to look at a piece of jewellery and describe it without my personal taste coming into play. She never hesitated to share her great knowledge and experience.

As a gallery owner Barbara did not refuse to show jewellery from Niessing at Electrum Gallery, especially if she felt it would be worthwhile and appropriate to show to her customers. Ultimately she secured considerable sales. In the mid-1970s, having recognised the numerous possibilities that the 'Setario' series by Niessing offered, Barbara decided to take on the jewellery at Electrum Gallery, beginning a long-term business relationship with the jewellery manufacturer. It was interesting how Barbara also refused some designs if she had reservations about them. To my disappointment, I could never convince her to show the 'Niessing S' series. She regarded the jewels from this series, with only 0.2 mm thickness, as too sharp and was of the opinion that they could injure the wearer. Of course, I disagreed! Barbara Cartlidge was a likeable and kind 'grande dame' in the field of art jewellery, and in the last quarter of the 20th century played an immense role in its mediation, not only in the UK.

Jochen Exner, Director of Niessing: 1982 to 2008

'Niessing S' bangles
1988
platinum and fine gold

'Setario' rings
1975
18ct gold, platinum,
diamonds, enamel

Martin Page

UK
born 1952

Exhibitions:
1979 In Celebration of Legs
1981 Electrum – the tenth year
1982 New Figurative Jewellery
1982 Love Tokens
1985 *Twentieth-Century Jewelry* book launch
1991 20th Anniversary Show

I first met Barbara when my work returned from an exhibition in Holland, which was organised by Ralph Turner. When the work came back in September 1973 she invited me to leave my graduate work with the gallery – I had just finished three years at the Central School of Art and Design and was about the start at the Royal College of Art. Trying to reconcile my interest in craftsmanship and ideas and my complete contempt for ornate jewelled baubles, my pieces were sculptural repoussé body parts, some of which I had made into Zippo lighter cases. During my time at the Royal College, I worked on commissions which came through Barbara and Electrum as well as continuing to make pieces of work for the gallery. Most of the pieces which I made at the RCA were exhibited and sold through Electrum. Barbara was extremely protective of her clients but she occasionally let out who had bought pieces. I remember her telling me that Tina Turner's manager had bought one of my leg brooches and that Charlie Watts from the Rolling Stones had one of my pieces. I also had a piece back to repair – it was one of my relic pieces – a silver Marilyn Monroe dress encased in a chrome and glass box which I'm sure Barbara said belonged to the guy who owned Aston Martin at the time. I'm sure that no other gallery in London would have been able to sell such pieces of work.

My major exhibition at Electrum was *In Celebration of Legs*, a one-man show in which I exhibited a large number of brooches on tableau plinths, one of which is illustrated in Barbara's *Twentieth-Century Jewelry*. I think it was from this show that the Victoria and Albert Museum purchased a leg brooch and The Goldsmiths' Company purchased a brooch of a pair of dressed legs on a marble and silver plinth which suggested sitting at a bar. Again without this exposure from the gallery I would not be represented in these collections. I have always been reluctant to engage in the business of selling my work, and so the gallery and Barbara's encouragement was so important to my existence as a manufacturing craftsman.

When I moved to my shared workshop in Gospel Oak, it was on Barbara's way home. Her house in Hampstead was also on my way home, so there were many times when she would have pieces of jewellery delivered or given to me to make good which had been purchased from the gallery but needed repairing. Visiting her at home quite often involved a glass of wine with Derrick while Barbara was on the phone. When I moved down to Cornwall I had less contact with the gallery and Barbara, but she did reintroduce me to her daughter Michelle. However, I completed a couple of commissioned pieces for the gallery whilst in Cornwall and once met Barbara at Michelle's house in Mousehole to discuss a modelled Claddagh ring with a large diamond and its delivery.

'Pod' brooch
2011
silver, gold leaf, stainless steel pin

Zippo lighter case (front and back)
1973
silver

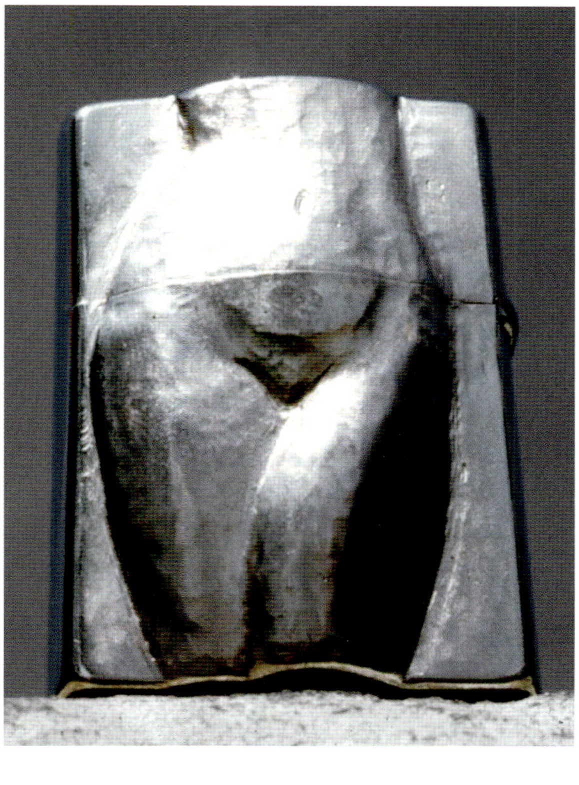

Lina Peterson

Sweden / UK
born 1979

I started working for Electrum when I was studying at the Royal College of Art from 2004 to 2006. Every Saturday I would cycle across Hyde Park to the gallery and later on took on a more permanent position. To work at the gallery was a wonderful eye-opener to the professional and commercial side of contemporary jewellery. Understanding who was interested and who bought what type of jewellery was a real insight. As Electrum had a wide range of jewellery, one of my favourite things was to see how a customer would grow more confident in what they wore, beginning to purchase more contemporary work as well as jewellery made from non-precious materials. The mix of jewellers represented made this possible and was one of the things that made the gallery so special.

When I started work at Electrum, the original shop fittings were still in place, with its interconnected cubes running across the gallery interior. If you bumped into a cube in one room, the entire gallery display would tremble! Barbara was at this time running the gallery remotely from her home and through the gallery manager, Janice Hosegood, but she would make frequent flying visits, driving her car down the lane running behind the gallery, parking up and blocking any traffic that might want to use it. She would pop in, all hair, pick things up, drop things off, and be gone.

Once I had left the Royal College of Art in 2006 I began to show my work through the gallery, which was a great boost as a recent graduate. The unique position of being a jeweller whose work was represented by Electrum, but who was also working for the gallery, gave me an interesting insight into who bought my work and what people's reactions to it were. Working for the gallery also gave me the chance to co-curate the exhibition *Scandinavian Jewellery* in 2008. The curatorial experience allowed me to connect with a group of exciting new Scandinavian jewellers and to extend my own network of jewellers outside of the UK.

The importance of the gallery as a hub for jewellers was great and Electrum's extensive exhibition schedule gave jewellers and audiences access to the best of international jewellery. Hopefully a new generation of 'Barbaras' will come along and continue the promotion of contemporary jewellery, because we need it!

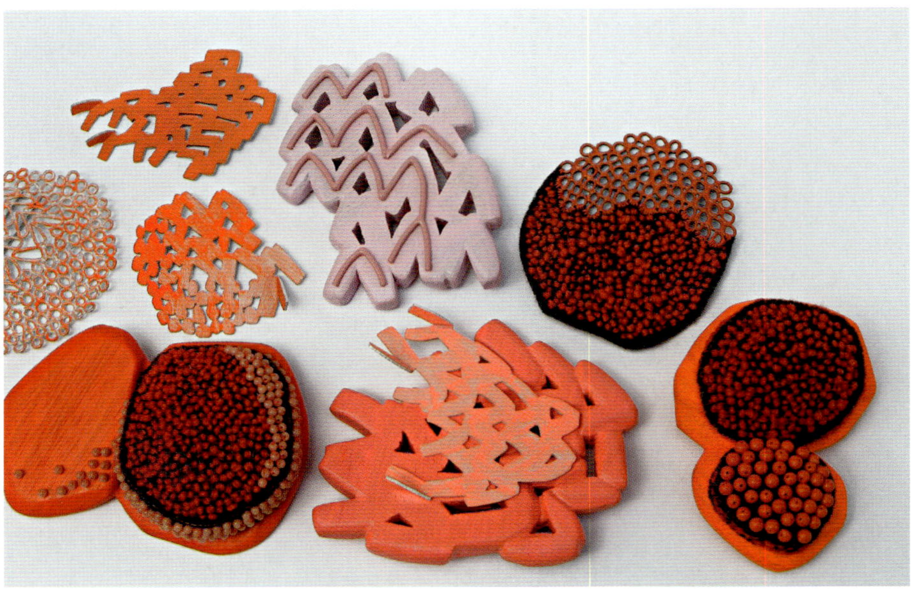

'Shavings' brooch
2013
mixed media

Brooches
2008
mixed media

Michael Petry

USA / UK
born 1960

Exhibitions:
1983 Paper-plus
1991 20th Anniversary Show

I met Barbara by walking in the door of Electrum with some rather poor images of paper performance art jewellery I was making at the time. She put me in touch with Wendy Ramshaw and David Watkins and together we organised a jewellery performance at Goldsmiths' Hall in 1984 with my performance art company. Andy Warhol asked for one of the performance cuffs at a larger guerrilla version of this performance, at the Anthony d'Offay Gallery in 1986 at an exhibition of Warhol's self-portraits. I gave him one and he made me a drawing. Anthony was not pleased! Barbara had such a laugh about it, and she had such a wonderfully wicked laugh!

I became friends with Barbara and she was a mentor to me for contemporary art jewellery. I had not really heard of the ongoing changes to the field and she was a fount of knowledge. The body work I was making featured acrylic paint on cotton rag paper, a form of 'painting to wear'. It crossed quite a few boundaries and when I met Barbara she introduced me to a world of people, many still my friends. All of us seemed to be interested in the art versus craft 'problem' and we got on with making things, whatever they were called. My book, *The Art of Not Making: the New Artist/Artisan Relationship* looks at this division and I am sure I would not have been interested in this topic were it not for the many hours of chatting with Barbara over a coffee at the gallery with her smoking non-stop. I also learnt so much from her about the modern jewellery art movement and how it developed and how it grew under her watchful hand.

I am sure that I will join the chorus of voices singing praises for Electrum. It certainly set the bar for all UK commercial exhibitions of contemporary jewellery and had a huge impact in Europe as well as in America. Each show added to the total impact, and the sum of the whole is greater than its many wonderful parts. It is inconceivable that without Barbara's input and vision that such work would have found its large audience in the UK. During the height of its influence in the 1980s I was often on mainland Europe where there were other jewellery spaces run by equally wonderful people. They were always interested, and wanted to know what was happening at Electrum.

Besides the smoking, the thing I will always remember about Barbara were her fantastic glasses – they were a personal trademark, a piece of jewellery she always wore. If she had walked in wearing contact lenses I am sure I would have not recognised her. I am not sure if she ever changed the large frames over the years but if she did they were all very similar and they complimented the openness of her smile and her warm personality. She was truly a one-off, and she is and will be greatly missed. Otto Künzli may have made personality jewellery well known, but perhaps Barbara got there first.

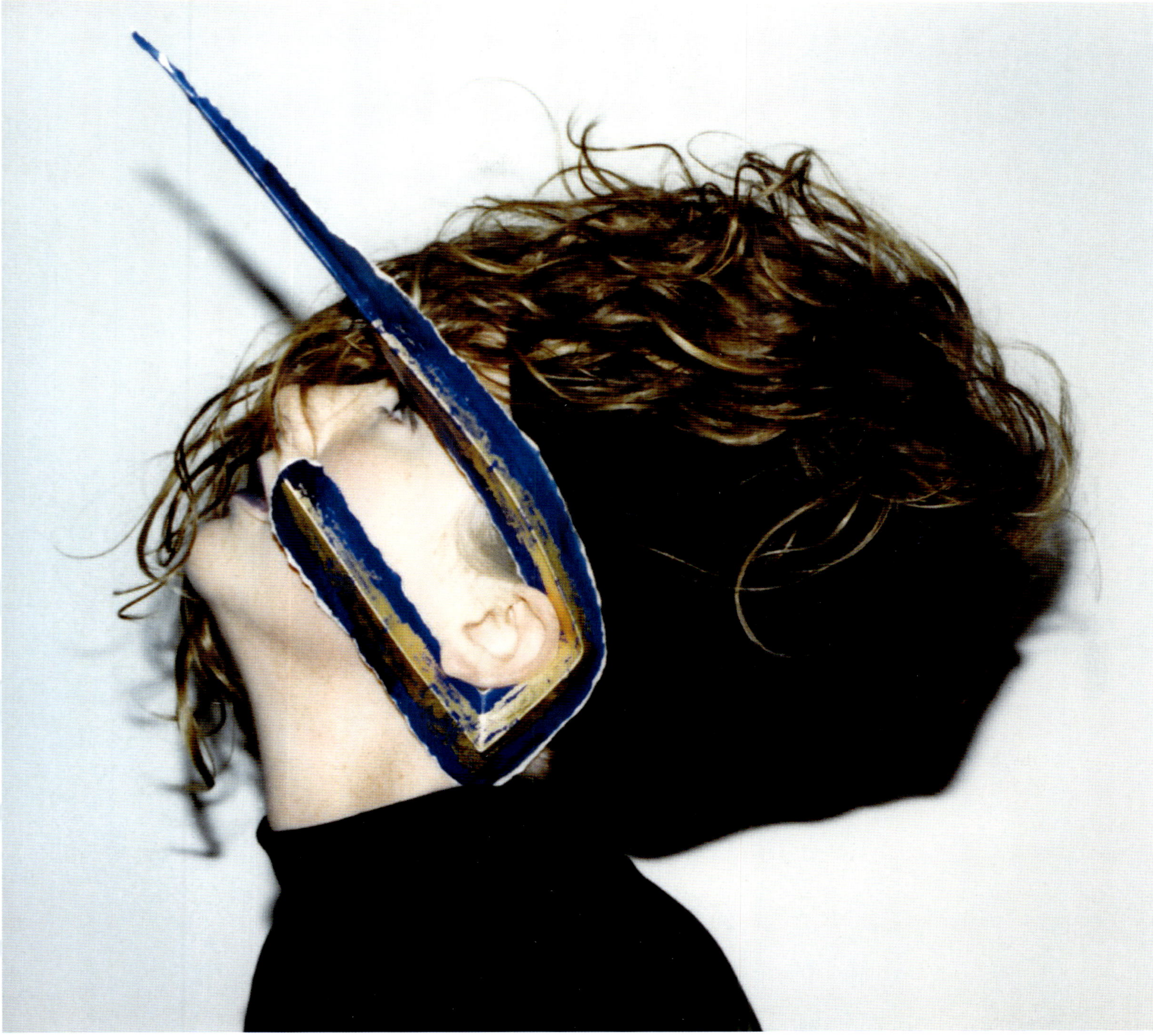

'The Golden Age' solo earring
1985
part of a set of performance art wear,
acrylic, 24ct gold, cotton rag paper

Michael Petry

'The Treasure of Memory' installation
2000
32 glass beads, rope
Glass work by Ian Hankey.
Collection of Museum of Art and Design,
New York

Paul Preston

UK
born 1943

Exhibitions:
1979 Paul Preston
1981 Electrum – the tenth year
1982 Love Tokens
1985 *Twentieth-Century Jewelry book launch*
1991 20th Anniversary Show
1993 The Magic of the Ring
1995 Paul Preston and Alan Ardiff
2006 Midsummer Madness – 35th Anniversary Show

First meeting – 1974: Hi-ho! For South Molton Street and Electrum, there to spread out my silver chains on Barbara Cartlidge's desk. She had big glasses behind which hard, intelligent Jewish eyes dissected you. Then they dissected the work. She told me it was all too like Breon O'Casey. She seemed gratifyingly fierce. The image of the crocodile further vindicated.

Second meeting – 1975: Booty let chains get tarnished in cases. Furious. Up Bond Street and stormed into Electrum, fizzing with indignation. Told a startled Barbara that she had to take his work as he had finished with Booty. The gold chains were really rather good anyway, so she said okay. Whilst in Electrum, I had seen world class work. Not to put too fine a point on it, I was agape. The cases glowed with gold and precious stones, the same as those in the Victoria and Albert Museum that I admired so fervently for so long. My eyes were opened. In later years, working for exhibitions, I would imagine an empty case then, CLICK, I would imagine it filled.

First exhibition – 1979: At that time I wore a donkey jacket that had a long and interesting life. Long hair. During trips involving London I would always drop in on Electrum. I sort of looked like someone sleeping rough and Barbara always asked me to go in the back room, explaining 'she had clients coming'. Ho, ho, shabby rucksack.

Last visit to Barbara was in May 2013. She was losing her grip. We had tea and biscuits in the kitchen and I showed her my latest work. This was difficult, for at times she was more interested in the biscuits and the gripes she had about Royal Mail. I wandered into the carpeted living room – so familiar – and stood. Barbara followed after a minute and I turned towards her, put my hands on her shoulders, and told her that everything of any meaning in my life had come through her and Electrum. Her eyes filled with tears and we hugged for the first and last time.

Brooch
1979
gold

'Mole in Coat of
Many Colours' brooch
2012
gold, gemstones

'Self-Portrait' and
'Mrs Mole' brooches
1990
gold

Wendy Ramshaw, CBE

UK
born 1939

Exhibitions:
1971 Opening Exhibition
1972 Wendy Ramshaw
1973 Aspects of Modern Jewellery
1973 Wendy Ramshaw and David Watkins
1977 Diamond Story
1978 Wendy Ramshaw
1981 Electrum – the tenth year
1982 The Wedgwood Collection
1985 *Twentieth-Century Jewelry* book launch
1986 Wendy Ramshaw – New Rings
1991 20th Anniversary Show
1993 The Magic of the Ring
1996 The Innovators – 25th Anniversary Exhibition
1996 Classic and Wild Earrings
2005 Wendy Ramshaw, CBE, RDI
2006 Midsummer Madness – 35th Anniversary Show

We met while she and Ralph Turner were looking for a gallery to open in central London. Electrum was a great help as artists from Europe also showed and we all benefitted from support of other artists. It was a very positive and a much admired gallery and important to all jewellery artists in the UK – the gallery was a wonderful place to exhibit.

When Barbara developed agoraphobia I accompanied her to events in the UK and Europe to support her while she travelled. Derrick, her husband, operated Taxi-Trucks and was able to sponsor Electrum Gallery. She was a very striking woman with a powerful personality. Her German roots helped her make the gallery international. The original cases were designed by Helga Zahn as was the first, very small, catalogue.

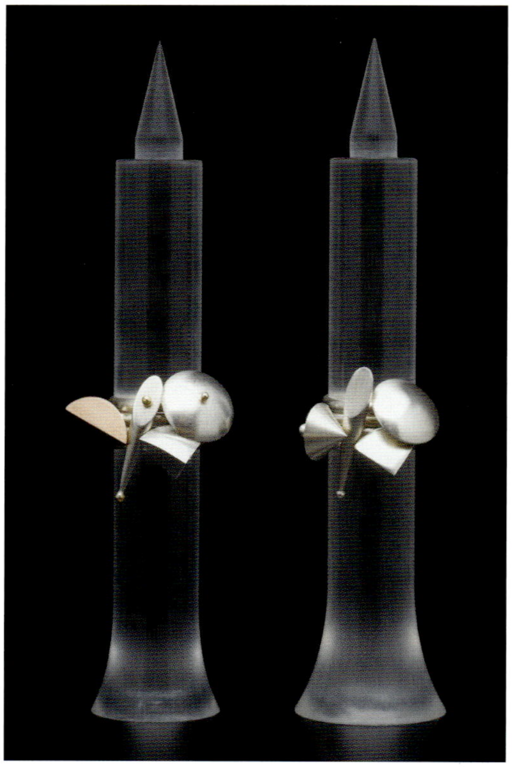

Two ringsets
2009,
silver, gold, acrylic stands

Ringset with 7 rings
1970
silver, surgical mirrors,
acrylic stand

Reinhold Reiling

Germany
1922–83

Exhibitions:
1973 Aspects of Modern Jewellery
1973 Jewellery and the Human Form

Reinhold Reiling came from a metalsmithing background in Pforzheim, for many centuries a major city of jewellery production in Germany. He began his career as an engraver before he turned to jewellery design which he then taught at the avant-garde Fachhochschule für Gestaltung in Pforzheim. His early jewellery had a sculptural quality with distinctive etched gold surfaces.

In 1976, in his book *Contemporary Jewelry: A Critical Assessment 1945–1975,* Ralph Turner praises Reiling as a jeweller of national and international importance and states 'his work in the late fifties and early sixties was two-sided, some of his work showing an almost conservative approach, and the rest being radically creative. Perhaps his strongest period has been from 1966 onwards, when the work becomes less precious and figurative elements began to appear. This he has taken to extreme limits with photoetching'. Reiling developed a special technique of photoetching family photographs onto silver and gold.

By the late 1970s Reiling's jewellery became increasingly geometric and abstract, almost minimalist in approach and incorporating fine inlays. Those who knew Barbara Cartlidge well remember her wearing a bangle by Reiling, which almost became her trademark piece of jewellery.

Beatriz Chadour-Sampson

Ring
c.1980
silver and gold
Alice and Louis Koch Collection,
Swiss National Museum, Zurich

Bangle
c.1970
silver and gold

Gerd Rothmann

Germany
born 1941

Exhibitions:
1971 Opening Exhibition
1972 Twenty Modern Jewellers
1972 Objects and Acrylic Jewellery
1981 Electrum – the tenth year
1982 Body Prints
1985 *Twentieth-Century Jewelry* book launch
1991 20th Anniversary Show
2004 Anti-War Medals

One has to imagine the politically lively times around 1970 in London. In fashion, music, theatre, film, art – all hierarchical and social structures were being questioned. In my work it was the search for new materials and multiple systems with interchangeable components which was vital. From this developed jewellery made of multi-coloured acrylics and prefabricated components made of chromed brass, which Barbara Cartlidge immediately exhibited in her new gallery in South Molton Street. The pieces were inexpensive and at the same time reflected the zeitgeist.

Barbara Cartlidge, who was the personification of energy and had a humourous sense of optimism, was exceptionally stimulating. In 1996 I was invited by David Watkins as a visiting tutor to the Royal College of Art. I asked Bobbi, as she was called by everyone, whether she would join in for an afternoon and she immediately agreed to do so. Our performance was more like a game of ping pong – each of us talked about our experiences. She spoke about the gallery and how she enthused people for the new jewellery, and I about my thoughts and work in the studio. Together we were able to talk about real practical experiences and illustrate existential subtleties. Our successful, spontaneous seminar was much appreciated by the students.

'Pulk Produkte' bangle and pendant
with interchangeable sections
1968
chromium plated brass
plexiglass, paper, film

'Imprint of the Artist' ring
2011
silver, colour pigments

Axel Russmeyer

Germany
born 1964

Exhibitions:
1997 Axel Russmeyer and Joyce Scott
1998 The Colour Red
2003 Axel Russmeyer
2006 Midsummer Madness – 35th Anniversary Show
2007 Vivid Colours

As my career advanced step by step – or should I say bead by bead? – my relationship with Electrum Gallery also evolved as the gallery became the perfect home for my work, providing a window to the world from London. Showcasing my jewellery at Electrum was a vital and integral part of my career.

Necklace
2003
glass, metal, resin, sequins, wood,
pigments, threads, 18ct gold

'Sorbet X' brooches
2008
pigments, lenses, glass, crystal,
metal, steel, lapis lazuli, wood,
steel, threads, 22ct and 18ct gold

Bernhard Schobinger

Switzerland
born 1946

Exhibitions:
1981 Electrum – the tenth year
1982 Bernhard Schobinger
1985 *Twentieth-Century Jewelry* book launch
1991 20th Anniversary Show

My correspondence with Electrum Gallery goes back to the 1970s and relates to my involvement in group exhibitions in London. At the time Barbara was working together with Ralph Turner, however I had not met either of them before. The late '70s was the period when I became interested in music and aesthetics, from Punk to New Wave and I wanted to see and hear these groups live on stage. From 1980 onwards I visited London frequently with Annelie Štrba, my wife, and friends. We had little money and always stayed at the cheapest B&Bs. At the flea markets on Portobello Road and Petticoat Lane we bought clothes and shoes. Unforgettable were the concerts in The Music Machine in Camden, in the Hammersmith Odeon, in Dingwalls and many more.

On one of these occasions I visited Electrum Gallery at South Molton Street, near New Bond Street. Barbara was there and she spontaneously invited me to stay at her house in Hampstead Heath, a quiet area characterised by green hills in the North of London not far from the centre and easy to reach by the Northern Line. I was given a lovely bright room on the second floor. Of course I was astounded by her thoughtfulness and generous hospitality, which I considered as quite unusual. I noticed her accent-free spoken German immediately and, when I asked her about this, she told me about her experiences in Germany before the Second World War – a breath-taking drama of fleeing the Gestapo at the last minute.

When I showed Barbara photographs of my work she offered me a solo exhibition in her gallery on the spot. Apart from my great excitement, I was rather surprised by her courage to host such avant-garde provocations which some people would find disturbing, yet should not be missed as trendsetting in the history of jewellery. Not one piece was sold. Nevertheless it was a great and formative time and Barbara was part of it, for which she deserves my respect and thanks. I can remember she was a heavy smoker, which I found unusual for a lady. Our last contact was when there was a jubilee exhibition at the gallery and I took part, however I cannot remember the year [1991].

Electrum Gallery
exhibition card
1982

Necklace
2015
steel, gold, akoya pearls,
Japanese urushi lacquer

Verena Sieber-Fuchs

Switzerland
born 1943

Exhibitions:
1985 Verena Sieber-Fuchs
1991 20th Anniversary Show

At the time it was the greatest and most exciting thing for me to have the opportunity to exhibit at Electrum Gallery. It had the reputation of being the most avant-garde gallery for jewellery, so it became the dream of many – in my case a solo exhibition in 1985 and a group exhibition in 1991. It meant a lot to me to exhibit at Electrum Gallery. This possibility gave me the courage and drive to continue on the path I had begun.

If I remember rightly, Barbara Cartlidge vividly described her escape from the Nazis and how she left at the last minute, travelled on her own in a train and finally made her way to London. I found Barbara very frank and friendly. For me she was a strong woman who knew what she wanted.

After the opening of my exhibition in 1985, I was with Maya Behn – who had organised the exhibition – and I remember I was invited to dinner together with Wendy Ramshaw and David Watkins. It was a relaxed and jovial evening. From this I have one rather strange flashback: the unusual toilet with an 'antique' blue and white porcelain bowl and dark brown wooden rim!

‘Pilzli mushrooms’ installation
2015
old beads, sequins, yarn, wire

Necklace
1985
firecrackers, wire

Robert Smit

The Netherlands
born 1941

Exhibitions:
1972 Concepts of Modern Jewellery
1972 Twenty Modern Jewellers
1985 *Twentieth-Century Jewelry* book launch

I met Barbara on my first visit for an exhibition in 1972, with other artists like Gerd Rothmann, Otto Künzli and Claus Bury. Barbara appeared to be a very good hostess and a driven gallerist. Not only could we stay in her fantastic house but she also bought us presents. Her husband Derrick enjoyed Barbara's passion and also kept it in perspective with great humour.

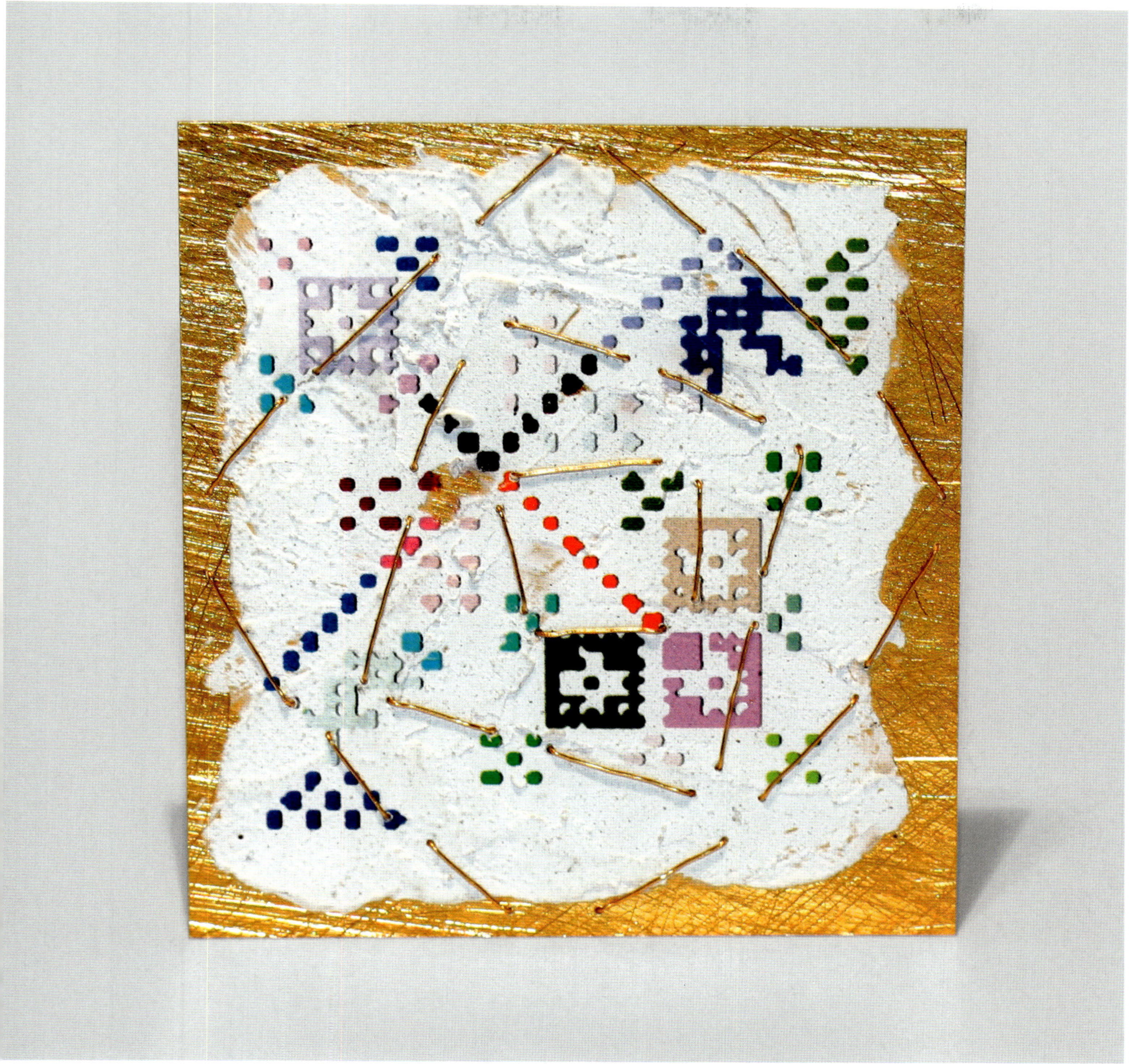

Brooch
2008
gold, silver, paint,
Epson Ultrachrome K3 ink

Brooch
1968
silver, paint

Joachim Sokólski

Poland
1946–2008

Exhibitions:
1977 Diamond Story
1985 *Twentieth-Century Jewelry* book launch

In her book *Twentieth-Century Jewelry,* Barbara Cartlidge honours the work of Joachim Sokólski and illustrates a series of his brooches consisting of heads made from a combination of natural and man-made materials, such as ivory, mother-of-pearl and acrylics. She describes this series as 'anatomical drawings'. Cartlidge recognised the significance of Sokólski in the early phase of his career and showed his work over many years at Electrum Gallery.

Just before his early death in 2007, the Muzeum Miedzi (Museum of Copper) in Legnica hosted a retrospective exhibition *My Tower of Babel* showing Sokólski's work of the past 40 years and documenting his artistic achievements in Poland. In the press, the exhibition was described as a tribute to this 'pioneer of independent Polish artistic goldsmithing'. His jewellery is distinctively Constructivist in style and his choice of materials diverse, from the non-precious to an unconventional use of diamonds. The head theme continued for many years and some pieces include personal or social comments. Sokólski's work is represented in various Polish museums, as well as in the Schmuckmuseum Pforzheim and in the Rose-Asenbaum Collection in the Dallas Museum of Art.

Beatriz Chadour-Sampson

Brooch
1976
silver, acrylic, ebony,
mother-of-pearl

Brooch
1985
silver, ebony,
mother-of-pearl

Torun

Vivianna Torun Bülow-Hübe

Sweden / Indonesia / Denmark
1927–2004

Exhibitions:
1985 *Twentieth-Century Jewelry* book launch
1995 Torun
1996 The Innovators – 25th Anniversary Exhibition

Torun Bülow-Hübe, or simply Torun as she was to be known, became one of the most innovative jewellery designers in the mid 20th century. She introduced a unique style of simplicity and functionalism in her design, forms that followed the human body. Her idea was that women should be able to wear their jewellery while washing up or hanging the laundry. The jewellery should fit a woman like her second skin. The women she had in mind was the 'Parisian Woman' during the1950s. She wanted her jewellery to signal an independent, free-thinking woman and not her husband's status. 'Diamond has a killing effect on a woman's beauty!' Torun established. Her radical theories on jewellery were highly provocative in those days, almost an impossibility - quite simply heretical – in France, where women only had had the right to vote for some years.

Every piece of jewellery that Torun created during whatever period she lived, was from a unique and original idea of form and function. Many jewellery designers around the world have been inspired by Torun's jewellery. Her combination of new thinking, courage, supreme feeling for form and function and technical skill has made her jewellery famous worldwide. Torun is, in many ways, unequalled up to this day.

Torun continued working with her workshop in Indonesia and with Georg Jensen until her death in 2004. Georg Jensen continuously produces her items. She is still their best-selling jewellery designer.
Ann Westin, *Torun: In Conversation with Vivianna Torun Bülow-Hübe* (1993)

Necklace
1955
silver, mother-of-pearl
Gråsilver

Bangle
1955
silver, pebble
Gråsilver

Emmy van Leersum

The Netherlands
1930–84

Exhibitions:
1971 Opening Exhibition
1985 *Twentieth-Century Jewelry* book launch
1972 Objects to Wear

For Emmy, the London public was unfortunately very problematic as her jewellery design was so far away from the more decorative look that the British collectors were used to. She noticed that for them, her pieces were just metal pipes instead of bracelets. However, she encouraged Barbara to allow visitors to the gallery to try on the aluminium cuffs and as a gift, she gave one to Barbara as well. After a while and with Barbara wearing her cuff, her work became more accessible and was better understood.

Gijs Bakker

Emmy in neckpiece
1968
aluminium

Cuff
1971
aluminium

Tone Vigeland

Norway
born 1938

Exhibitions:
1981 Electrum – the tenth year
1981 Tone Vigeland
1985 *Twentieth-Century Jewelry* book launch
1988 Norwegian Jewellery and Textiles
1990 Tone Vigeland
1991 20th Anniversary Exhibition
1996 Classic and Wild Earrings

I am touched to be invited to reminisce about my first contacts with Electrum Gallery and Barbara. Having reached a mature age, it gives me pleasure to remember this important meeting. I visited Electrum the first time in 1978. I had heard about this jewellery gallery, and brought with me some of my pieces from an exhibition just completed. It was early autumn, and I wore a new, much too expensive coat! I entered the premises, feeling most impressed by the beauty of the gallery's design. The pieces exhibited were artists unknown to me at this time. I realized that some represented a new era. My first impulse was to leave, since I did not think my work would fit in. Almost out of the door, the gallery assistant manager asked what material my coat was made of! This broke the ice and initiated many years of close cooperation. The following day I met Barbara and showed her some of my jewellery. This meeting with Barbara, who herself made jewellery, was a great inspiration for me. My works were exhibited, and in May 1981 I was given my first one-person exhibition. For sentimental reasons, I have still kept my expensive coat.

Necklace
1981
steel, silver, 18ct gold
Galerie Riis

Print
1976
ink on paper

Tone Vigeland

Sculpture
2010
steel
National Museum of Art,
Architecture and Design,
Oslo

Manuel Vilhena

Portugal / UK
born 1967

Exhibition:
2001 Solos

I hardly met Barbara as all dealings with the gallery were done through Janice Hosegood. She was the contact and the person who got interested in my work in the first place. I met Barbara fleetingly at the opening of mine and Castello Hansen's show both in 2001 and 2009, but I didn't engage into more than a brief salutation and welcome conversation.

Being able to show at the gallery was, at the time a very big event. It is still now as having been part of a historical venue. For my career, it opened my work to the UK public and consolidated the work done at the RCA. It 'proved' that the work made in school and subsequently had reached a quality level that could be inserted in the contemporary jewellery field. That, naturally, consolidated my professional self-esteem and gave me a CV leverage and worldwide recognition that were unique among Portuguese contemporary jewellers.

The opening of a gallery that showed a new field of the arts was, in itself, a breaking open of a cocoon where contemporary jewellery lived. This was the first opening to the 'outside world' and, as such, a ground-breaking venue. From there things followed in other countries, but perhaps in the wake of, and from the inspiration of, Electrum. I also believe that Ralph Turner had a big impact on the whole thing and, personally, I don't know if there was any association with Barbara, but, in my mind, these two are connected. We do owe that opening to the gallery and it brought contemporary jewellery into the art scene as a field like painting or sculpture. Alas, its full recognition depends totally on heads of important institutions which are only now – some 40 or so years later – accepting this as a fact.

Brooch
2009
fine gold, juniper wood,
rhodochrosite, steel

Rings
2000
oak, steel, citrine

Graziano Visintin

Italy
born 1954

Exhibitions:
1985 *Twentieth-Century Jewelry* book launch
1991 20th Anniversary Show

I met Barbara Cartlidge in 1984 when I first exhibited in her gallery and over the years I have always maintained a working relationship with her. In 1991 I was invited to attend the 20th anniversary exhibition of the gallery and this made me very happy. I was aware that she had been a pioneer for the knowledge of contemporary art jewellery and it was a very important knowledge. Through exhibiting in her gallery I got to know the work of many jewellers including, for example, David Watkins and Wendy Ramshaw who I admired a lot. This especially gave me the urge to believe and continue in my work. I think Barbara has played a fundamental role in the exposure of contemporary jewellery, with all the exhibitions that she put on and through the publication of books, such as *Twentieth-Century Jewelry.*

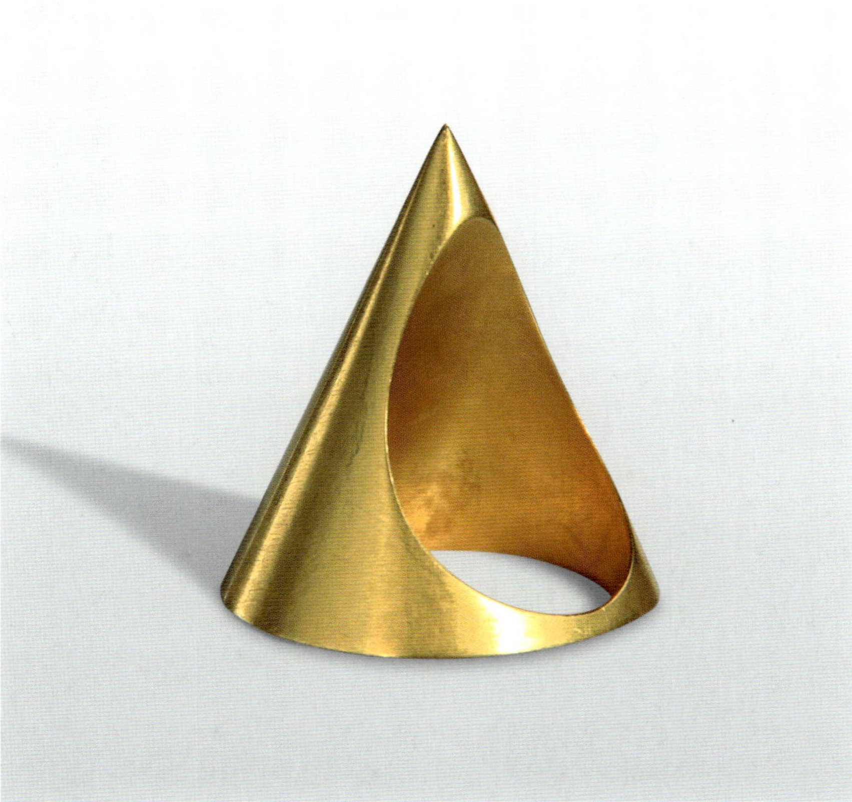

Brooches
2011
silver, enamel, gold leaf, copper

Ring
c.1980
gold

David Watkins

UK
born 1940

Exhibitions:
1971 Opening Exhibition
1973 Wendy Ramshaw and David Watkins
1977 Diamond Story
1979 David Watkins
1981 Improvisations
1981 Electrum – the tenth year
1984 Base + Noble
1985 *Twentieth-Century Jewelry* book launch
1991 20th Anniversary Show
1996 The Innovators – 25th Anniversary Exhibition
2004 David Watkins
2006 Midsummer Madness – 35th Anniversary Show

I think I probably met Barbara earlier, around 1969 or 1970, through her involvement in the Pace Gallery. Pace was, to my understanding, essentially a proto-Electrum. I guess it only functioned between 1968 and 1970 – in St Christopher's Place, Mayfair – but it was an important step.

The opportunity to show new work in an adventurous specialist gallery was encouraging and challenging. It definitely broadened my (otherwise extremely limited) jewellery horizons. It spurred me on at a key moment. It opened up the London/British contemporary jewellery scene by introducing the latest work by leading practitioners from Europe and further afield. In many cases it attracted the practitioners themselves, creating a virtual forum, so that contacts and networks were established. A very important period of greater energy, interchange and expansion was generated in the early years of Electrum.

Necklace
1970
silver

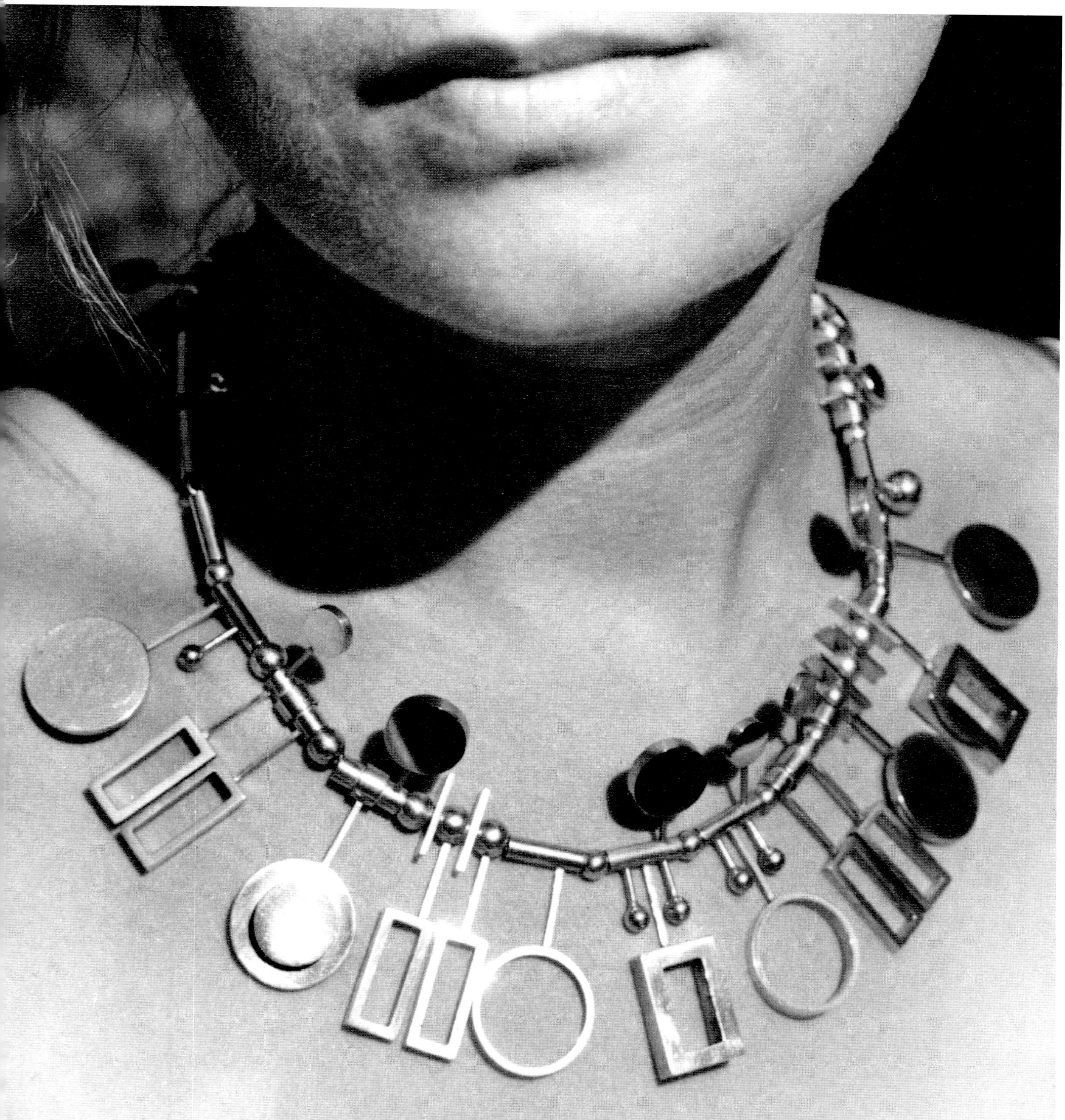

David Watkins

‘Quatrefoil 2A’ necklace
2007
anodised aluminium

Mark Woods

UK
born 1961

Exhibitions:
1999 Mark Woods and Rebecca Scott
2006 Midsummer Madness – 35th Anniversary Show

I was always very proud to show at Electrum – never lost the 'buzz' of finding my way to South Molton Street, checking out the display in the gallery window before going in, usually to present something new to show. Somehow, that place encouraged me to produce work that took chances, one-offs, things that challenged and revealed. I am still working like that to this day. I showed at so few places with my jewellery. I rather shied away from the 'funded outlets', which appeared to favour college graduates over the 'autodidact'. This left only a handful of independent galleries of which, in my opinion, Electrum was the pinnacle. Barbara and me, we had so few conversations, she mainly rather coolly observed me through a haze of cigarette smoke!

‘The Family Jewels’ music box
1999
silver, 22ct gold, plastic,
cellulose acetate veneer, mdf

‘Bead’ ring
2006
silver, plastic, ebony, burrwood,
ebonised plywood, wool

Helga Zahn

Germany / UK
1936–85

Exhibitions:
1971 Opening Exhibition
1973 Aspects of Modern Jewellery
1991 20th Anniversary Show

Helga Zahn was born in Germany but settled in Britain in 1957 where she was trained as a painter and printmaker at the Leeds College of Arts and the Central School of Arts and Crafts in London. She also maintained an artist's studio in New York from 1976 to 1980. It was in 1960s Britain, however, that Zahn became influential and where she developed new radical ideas in jewellery. It was a period of rebellion against traditions and of freedom of artistic expression, a spirit much felt in her work. Zahn challenged the idea of jewellery being associated with wealth, and the concept of investment jewellery. She always questioned the values of jewellery – for her it was solely about the creative process.

Her designs are bold and unconventional. Her imagery, inspired by the natural world, is abstract and her use of precious metals, especially silver, in combination with found objects from nature such as pebbles and stones, was unprecedented. She even experimented with plastics, but was chiefly recognised for her investigations into metal and their surfaces.

Helga Zahn was shown at Electrum's first exhibition when it was founded in 1971. In his book *Jewellery in Europe and America: New Times, New Thinking* (1996), Ralph Turner writes, 'her elegant and sophisticated designs of the 1960s and early 1970s pointed the way forward: unconventional graphic interpretations of natural forms were matched by an uncompromising sense of scale. Her early death robbed her of wider international recognition and public acknowledgment for her unique contribution to British jewellery.'

Beatriz Chadour-Sampson

Necklace
1972–4
silver, nylon, amber
The Crafts Council
Collection, London

Necklace
1965
silver, red moonstone,
arrowhead
The Worshipful Company
of Goldsmiths, London

Ulrike Zehetbauer

Austria
born 1934

Exhibitions:
1985 *Twentieth-Century Jewelry* book launch
1991 20th Anniversary Exhibition

I met Barbara at the exhibition when her *Twentieth-Century Jewelry* book was presented in 1985 – my neckpiece and ring were exhibited. Her friendly and kind way with artists impressed me very much. Unfortunately I had little contact later and although we had several phone calls about a possible exhibition, this never happened. However, I followed her continuous exhibitions from all around the world, which I found of great interest – even if I went my own way.

Necklace
1971
gold, shell, enamel

Brooch
1995
gold, rubies, rutilated quartz

electrum
21
21

Exhibitions at Electrum Gallery 1971–2007

1971

21 June–8 October	*Opening Exhibition* Gijs Bakker, Claus Bury, Hamish Campbell, Barbara Cartlidge, David Courts, Charlotte De Syllas, Joel Degen, Gerda Flöckinger, Peter Gorringe, Rita Greer, Juli Guasch, Peter Hauffe, Bryan Illsley, Fritz Maierhofer, Catherine Mannheim, Jacqueline Mina, Breon O'Casey, Emanuel Raft, Wendy Ramshaw, Gerd Rothmann, Loh Shin-Fen, Rod Smith, Patricia Tormey, Emmy van Leersum, David Watkins, Helga Zahn
13 October–17 November	*Erotic Jewellery* Omar K Bone, Ed Samuels, Patricia Tormey, Hubertus von Skal
November–December	*Christmas at Electrum* All gallery artists, featuring Barbara Cartlidge and Rita Greer

1972

3 January–26 February	*Concepts of Modern Jewellery* Claus Bury, Gerda Flöckinger, Fritz Maierhofer, Robert Smit
24 February–25 March	*Wendy Ramshaw*
15 March–15 April	*Objects to Wear* Gijs Bakker, Emmy van Leersum
17 April–24 June	*Twenty Modern Jewellers* Including Gerda Flöckinger, Robert Smit, Gerd Rothmann, Otto Künzli, Claus Bury
28 June–29 July	*Objects and Acrylic Jewellery* Claus Bury, Fritz Maierhofer, Gerd Rothmann
1 August–21 October	*Jewellery and Objects by Gallery Artists*
25 October–25 November	*Susanna Heron*
November–January	*Christmas Exhibition* All gallery artists

1973

15 January–31 March	*Aspects of Modern Jewellery* Malcolm Appleby, Gijs Bakker, Karel Bartosik, Onno Boekhoudt, Caroline Broadhead, Claus Bury, Barbara Cartlidge, Pierre Degen, Gerda Flöckinger, Brian Glassar, Rita Greer, Susanna Heron, Hermann Jünger, Helfried Kodré, Elisabeth Kodré-Defner, Karen Lawrence, Jens-Rüdiger Lorenzen, Roger Morris, Celia Over, David Poston, Lutz Quambusch, Emanuel Raft, Wendy Ramshaw, Reinhold Reiling, Jeremy Ross, Gerd Rothmann, Hubertus von Skal, David Taylor, Patricia Tormey, Gunilla Treen, Helga Zahn
7 March–7 April	*Dutch Art in Jewellery*
4 April–5 May	*Figurative Jewellery* Rita Greer, Geli Lukin Johnstone, Barbara Cartlidge
9 May–9 June	*Things Remembered* Barbara Cartlidge
19 September–20 October	*Jewellery and the Human Form* Eberhard Burgel, Bruno Martinazzi, Reinhold Reiling, Hubertus von Skal
22 October–10 November	*Wendy Ramshaw and David Watkins*
November–January	*Christmas Exhibition* All gallery artists

1974

6–30 March	*Jewellery from the Silver Screen* Rodolfo Azaro
3 April–11 May	*Revolt in Jewellery* Onno Boekhoudt, Francoise van der Bosch, Marion Herbst, Peter Berend, Karel Niehorster
13–18 May	*Diamonds Today* – competition with DeBeers
22 May–22 June	*Jewellery and Paintings* Norbert Muerrle
18 September–12 October	*5 New Jewellers* Ellen Chapman, Paul John Gay, Michael Kane, Ann Oxley, Julia Whitman
16 October–16 November	*Susanna Heron*
November–January	*Christmas at Electrum featuring Rita Greer*

1975

4–22 February	*Gold and Acrylic Jewellery* Fritz Maierhofer
3–26 April	*Kinetic Jewellery* Brian Glassar, Jeremy Ross
29 April–24 May	*A Tactile Approach to Jewellery* David Poston
26 May–21 June	*Hermann Jünger and Students / Jens-Rüdiger Lorenzen and Students* Hermann Jünger, Jens-Rüdiger Lorenzen, Daniel Kruger, Hilla Dirks, Otto Künzli, Therese Künzli, Rita Mazouat, Gabi von Pechmann, Julia Reidel, Bettina Sauerbruch, Margrit Schneeweiss, Heidi Schneider, Jan Wehrens, Wolfgang Schneider, Erhard Niedenhoff, Egon Reautschnig, Cornelia Sattler, Wolfgang Zoeller, Manfred Schaefer
12 September–11 October	*The Complete Erté*
14 October–15 November	*Extra-Dimensional Jewellery* Roger Morris
November–January	*Christmas Exhibition* All gallery artists

1976

4–28 February	*The Amazing Miniatures of Karel Bartosik*
4–29 May	*Giampaolo Babetto*
2–26 June	*6 Contemporary American Jewellers* Eleanor Moty, Arline Fisch, Hiroko Sato Pijanowski, Richard Mawdsley, Mary Lee Hu
6–23 October	*Titanium Jewellery* Kevin Coates, Edward de Large, James Ward
27 October–20 November	*Nele*
November–January	*Christmas Exhibition* All gallery artists

1977

2–26 February	*Jewellery and Sculptures* Harry Abend
2–26 March	*Emanuel Raft*

4–28 May	*Tom Saddington*
1–25 June	*Kazuhiro Itoh and Takao Mitsuyasu*
21 September–15 October	*David Hensel and Rod Edwards*
1–19 November	*Diamond Story* Sieglinde Brennan, Roger Doyle, Victor Ely, Gerda Flöckinger, Gillian Packard, Wendy Ramshaw, Joachim Sokólski, David Thomas, Geoffrey Turk, David Watkins
November–January	*Christmas Exhibition* All gallery artists

1978

15 February–11 March	*Jewellery Grows on Trees* Giampaolo Babetto, Michael Burton, Peter Chatwin, David Hensel, David Goodship, Julia Manheim
12 April–6 May	*Wally Gilbert and Sue Carney*
9 May–3 June	*Victor Salinger*
11–23 September	*Jewellery and Silversmithing of Bezalel, Jerusalem*
21 September–7 October	*Joby Baker*
11 October–4 November	*Wendy Ramshaw*
November–January	*Christmas Exhibition* All gallery artists

1979

7 February–3 March	*In Celebration of Legs* Martin Page
6–31 March	*Five Danish Goldsmiths* Jytte Kløve, Birte Stenbak, K. Holst Andersen, Thor Selzer, Ole Bent Petersen
8 May–2 June	*David Watkins*
18 June–7 July	*Kumihimo Jewellery* Aya Nakayama
2–20 October	*Hermann Schafran*
23 October–10 November	*William Harper*
12 November–1 December	*Paul Preston*
November–January	*Christmas Exhibition* All gallery artists

1980

5–23 February	*Richard Fishman*
22 April–10 May	*Elisabeth Kodré-Defner*
4–21 June	*Arline M. Fisch*
25 June–19 July	*Erté–A Retrospective*
15 October–2 November	*Frank Bauer*
5–22 November	*Jewellery and Bowls* Alistair McCallum
November–January	*Christmas Exhibition* All gallery artists

1981

4–28 February	*Onno Boekhoudt and Jan Tempelman*
28 April–16 May	*Improvisations* David Watkins
19 May–6 June	*Tone Vigeland*
9–27 June	*Electrum Gallery–The Tenth Year* Harry Abend, Vicki Ambery-Smith, Karel Bartosik, Frank Bauer, Onno Boekhoudt, Sieglinde Brennan, Ros Conway, Pierre Degen, Arline Fisch, Gerda Flöckinger, Elizabeth Gage, Wally Gilbert, Jan Goodey, David Hensel, Marion Herbst, Elisabeth Holder, Kazuhiro Itoh, Nuala Jamison, Elisabeth Kodré-Defner, Gabriele Kutschera, Edward de Large, Mary Lee Hu, Alistair McCallum, Fritz Maierhofer, Julia Manheim, Catherine Mannheim, Bruno Martinazzi, Takao Mitsuyasu, Roger Morris, Norbert Muerrle, Aya Nakayama, E. R. Nele, Martin Page, Paul Preston, Wendy Ramshaw, Gerd Rothmann, Tom Saddington, Hermann Schafran, Bernhard Schobinger, Miriam Sharlin, Ann Marie Shillito, Helen Shirk, Jan Tempelman, James Ward, David Watkins, Tone Vigeland, Rosemary Zeeman
7–24 October	*Miriam Sharlin and Elisabeth Holder*
27 October–28 November	*The Ring from Antiquity to the Twentieth Century* book launch
November–January	*Christmas Exhibition* All gallery artists

1982

9 February–6 March	*James Ward Brent and His Titanium*
8–27 March	*Body Prints* Gerd Rothmann
4–22 May	*Bernhard Schobinger*
12–30 October	*New Figurative Jewellery* Vicki Ambery-Smith, Sophie Chell, Martin Page
2–20 November	*Love Tokens* Ian Falcon Hammond, David Hensel, John Hull, Bryan Illsley, Martin Page, Paul Preston, Geraldine Serpa, Nick Stevens
November–January	*The Wedgwood Collection* and *Christmas Exhibition* Wendy Ramshaw and all gallery artists

1983

8–26 February	*Paper-plus* Clarissa Mitchell, Michael Petry
1–19 March	*Grup Nou* Marta Breis, Lluis Gilberga, Angeles Lopez-Antei, Núria Matabosch, Ramón Puig Cuyàs
31 May–18 June	*Arline Fisch*
11–29 October	*Hephaistos–Association Française des Createurs de Bijoux* Therese Sudre, Catherine Noll, Goudji, Francine Sixou, Joel Faivre-Chalon, Henri Boltz, Dominique Favey, Gerard Chacun, Jiri Ledecky, Françoise and Claude Chavent
1 December–29 January	*Mouse Gallery* Rita Greer
November–January	*Christmas Exhibition* All gallery artists

1984

21 February–10 March	*Base + Noble* Fritz Maierhofer, Alistair McCallum, Norbert Muerrle, David Watkins
March	*Patricia Meyerowitz*
8–26 May	*Jewellery from Hungary* Andras Banfalvi, Akos Sajo, Maria Lugossy, Márton Horváth, István Schuszter, Vladimir Péter
1–13 October	*Double Gold for Waterman* Waterman Pens Centenary
16 October–3 November	*Contemporary Japanese Jewellery* Kazuhiro Itoh, Aya Nakayama, Yasuki Hiramatsu
November–January	*Christmas Exhibition* All gallery artists

1985

5–23 March	*Verena Sieber-Fuchs*
23 April–11 May	*Chan, Evans and Tortell* Kei Chan, James Evans, Louis Tortell
18 June–6 July	*The Niessing Collection*
6–26 October	*Ulrike Bahrs*
29 October–16 November	*Twentieth-Century Jewelry* book launch Renata Ahrens, Helen Aitken-Kuhnen, Gilbert Albert, K. Holst Andersen, Malcolm Appleby, Giampaolo Babetto, Ulrike Bahrs, Gijs Bakker, Karel Bartosik, Frank Bauer, Friedrich Becker, Onno Boekhoudt, Christina Brade, Caroline Broadhead, Susan Cohn, Noma Copley, Paul Derrez, Charlotte De Syllas, Lam de Wolf, Robert Ebendorf, James Evans, Dominique Favey, Arline Fisch, Gerda Flöckinger, Ana Font, Ute Feiler, Max Fröhlich, Goudji, Rowena Gough, Andrew Grima, Marie Hassenpflug, Peter Hassenpflug, Susanna Heron, Therese Hilbert, Yasuki Hiramatsu, Elisabeth Holder, Mary Lee Hu, Wahei Ikezawa, Bryan Illsley, Kazuhiro Itoh, Hermann Jünger, Svatopluk Kasalý, Jeanne Keefer, Hajime Kimata, Helfried Kodré, Lisa Kodré-Defner, Daniel Kruger, Johannes Kuhnen, Otto Künzli, Okinari Kurokawa, Edward de Large, Helge Larsen, Stanley Lechtzin, Emmy van Leersum, Darani Lewers, Rolf Lindner, Randy Long, Maria Lugossy, Fritz Maierhofer, Carlier Makigawa, Bruno Martinazzi, Takeo Mitsuyasu, Edith Mostböck-Huber, Eleanor Moty, Norbert Muerrle, Aya Nakayama, E. R. Nele, Manfred Nisslmüller, Louis Osman, Martin Page, Sigurd Persson, Vladimir Péter, Eugene Pijanowski, Hiroko Sato Pijanowski, Paul Preston, Grete Prytz-Kittelsen, Ramón Puig Cuyàs, Robin Quigley, Emanuel Raft, Börje Rajalin, Wendy Ramshaw, Antoinette Riklin-Schelbert, Ivy Ross, Gerd Rothmann, Tom Saddington, Hermann Schafran, Bernd Schobinger, István Schuszter, Hubertus von Skal, Peter Skubic, Christina Smith, Joachim Sokólski, Birte Stenbak, Jan Tempelman, Barbara Tipple, David Tisdale, Louis Tortell, Torun, Jenny Toynbee-Wilson, Waltraud Viehböck, Tone Vigeland, Graziano Visintin, David Watkins, Björn Weckström, Walter Wittek, Margaret West, Ulrike Zehetbauer
November–January	*Christmas Exhibition* All gallery artists

1986

11 February–1 March	*Peter De Wit*
15 May–7 June	*New Rings* Wendy Ramshaw
26 August–9 September	*Australian Impressions* Sieglinde Karl
November–January	*Christmas Exhibition* All gallery artists

1987

23 March–11 April	*Perspectives–New Ideas in Platinum* Hans Ulrich-Baus, Franz Berger, Paul Binder, Peter Birkenmeier, Michael Bischoff, Michael Bondanza, Caprice, Citizen Trading, Bob Chrzanowski, Les Createurs de Carlos de Milo, Simon Peter Eiber, Juerg Eggenberg, Arline Fisch, Ron Hartgrove, Ursula Haupenthal, Hirai Necklace Industry, Kingei Kogyo Kawaguchi, Michaela Kirchner, Brane Kosec, Christina Kube, Norbert Mack, Jacqueline Mina, Murao, Nagahori, Kurt P. Neukomm, Thomas Niederreuther, Niessing, Erhard Nolte, Renzo Pasquale, Max Pollinger, Rudolf Michael Scheffold, Ursula Scholz, Tiffany Sun, Tokyo Casting Club, Uchida Gold, Hans Bernd Ufer, Urban Gold, Patricia von Weichs, Ingrid Wriedt, Yamazaki, Alberto Zorzi
6–23 May	*British Society of Enamellers* Phil Barnes, Maureen Carswell, Aliette de Lacombe, Keryn Evely, Georgina Follett, Amal Ghosh, Edward Heath, Sue Hennings, Anny Hooton, Pat Johnson, Terry Jones, Sarah Letts, Evangeline Long, Joan MacKarell, Sheila MacDonald, Alexandra Placzek, Fred Rich, Ian Robertson, Ruth Rushby, Jane Short, Catherine Swann, Elizabeth Turrell, Jeanne Werge-Hartley, Rosemary Zeeman
26 May–13 June	*Carl F. Dau*
27 October–14 November	*Ian Frew, Jonathon Greenwell, Tracy Hopkirk*
November–January	*Christmas Exhibition* All gallery artists

1988

1–19 March	*Elisabeth Holder*
10–28 May	*Norwegian Jewellery and Textiles* Tove Becken, Millie Behrens, Inger Marie Berg, Toril Bjorg, Liv Blavårp, Sigurd Bronger, Gry Eide, Toril Glenne, Marit Gulbrandsen, Ingjerd Hanevold, Kjell Hommerstad, Gro Jessen, Morten Kleppan, Synnøve Korssjøen, Konrad Mehus, Marit Norheim, Laila Irene Olsen, Anna Sophie Rodin, Bente Saetrang, Heidi Sand, Lise Schønberg, Åse-Marit Thorbjørnsrud, Tone Vigeland, Ann-Rita Wold
11–29 October	*Canadian Jewellery* Beth Alber, Ellen Fraser, Andrew Goss, Sandra Nobel Goss, Akira Ikegami, Michel Letki, Paula Letki, David McAleese and Alison Wiggins, Judge Ortiz, Sue Parke, Wendy Shingler, Mimi Shulman, Kim Snyder, Donald A. Stuart, Ken Vickerson, Betty M. Walton, Lynn Wiggins
1–19 November	*British Society of Enamellers* Sally Ann Alpin, Ruth Ball, Phil Barnes, K. Hali Baykov, Maureen Carswell, Aliette de Lacombe, Keryn Evely, Amal Ghosh, Edward Heath, Sue Hennings, Endre Hevezi, Anny Hooton, Valerie Isherwood, Terry Jones, Sarah Letts, Evangeline Long, Sheila MacDonald, Alexandra Raphael, Fred Rich, Ian Robertson, Ruth Rushby, Catherine Swann, Elizabeth Turrell, Jeanne Werge-Hartley, Tamar Winter, Rosemary Zeeman
November–January	*Christmas Exhibition* All gallery artists

1989

25 April–13 May	*Danish Metal* Claus Bjerring, Kim Buck, Agnete Dinesen, Louise Grønlykke, Jan Lohmann, Peder Musse, Annemarie Serritslev
17 October–4 November	*Jewellery from Cuba* Carlos Raúl de la Torre Oliva, Julio Enrique Hernández Figueredo, Jorge Omar González Cata, José Carlos Rafart Pérez, Luis Alberto Franqui Martinez, Osvaldo Castilla Romero, Rafael Angel Bello Rodriguez, Xerxes Jorge Carruana Pérez
November–January	*Christmas Exhibition* All gallery artists

1990

15–31 May	*New Brooches and Rings from Holland* Jan Tempelman
19 June–7 July	*Wilhelm Buchert*
11–29 September	*Jivan and Katie Gayle*
9–27 October	*Tone Vigeland*
13–24 November	*Yasuki Hiramatsu*
November–January	*Christmas Exhibition* All gallery artists

1991

5–23 March	*Bernd Munsteiner*
14 - 31 May	*Lina Fanourakis*
18 June–6 July	*Electrum–20th Anniversary Show* Mike Abbott, Renate Ahrens, Vicki Ambery-Smith, Malcolm Appleby, Giampaolo Babetto, Karen Bachmann, Ulrike Bahrs, Gijs Bakker, K. Hali Baykov, Friedrich Becker, Toril Bjorg, David Blass, Onno Boekhoudt, Christina Brade, Heinz Brummel, Wilhelm Buchert, Peter Chang, Ros Conway, Cynthia Cousens, Alan Craxford, Susan Cross, Rae Duncan, Kim Ellwood, Keryn Evely, Lina Fanourakis, Dominique Favey, Arline Fisch, Gerda Flöckinger, Ian Frew, Margot Gardiner, Katie Gayle, Wally Gilbert, Barbara Gronus, Cathy Harris, Sue Hennings, Jean Hilger, Elisabeth Holder, Annie Hooton, Tracy Hopkirk, Ulla Hornfeldt, Sarah Fitzalan-Howard, Katzie Hughes, Philip Hughes, Bryan Illsley, Kazuhiro Itoh, Kay Ivanovic, Steve Jamieson, Jivan, Hermann Jünger, Osnat Kermisch, Jytte Kløve, Elisabeth Kodré-Defner, Helfried Kodré, Daphne Krinos, Helen Aitken-Kuhnen, Johannes Kuhnen, Gabriele Kutschera, Hilde Leiss, Anna-Rütta Lord, Donna Lynas, Carlier Makigawa, Catherine Mannheim, Anne Carroll Marshall, Bruno Martinazzi, Wilhelm Tasso Mattar, Tomasz Mayzel, Alistair McCallum, Rainer Milewski, Jacqueline Mina, Takeo Mitsuyasu, Isgard Moje-Wohlgemuth, Roger Morris, Norbert Muerrle, Bernd Munsteiner, Aya Nakayama, E. R. Nele, Jill Newbrook, Niessing, Mitch Nugent, Johannes Oppermann, Emma Paolozzi, Sarah Parker-Eaton, Brett Payne, Michael Petry, Diego Piazza, Paul Preston, Wendy Ramshaw, Quona Rankin, Alexandra Raphael, André Ribeiro, Ruth Robinson, Gerd Rothmann, Ruth Rushby, Ute Sanne, Bernhard Schobinger, Deganit Schocken, Dagmar Stühler, Jan Tempelman, Liz Tyler, Dina Varano, Tone Vigeland, Graziano Visintin, Esther Ward, David Watkins, Tamar Winter, Annette Wohlleber, Alan Wright, Rosemary Zeeman, Ulrike Zehetbauer, Tomasz Żylka
17 September–5 October	*Jewellery and Vessels* Yukie Osumi
29 October–16 November	*Ahead Of Time* Marianne Forrest, Kim Ellwood, Mike Abbott, Wilhelm Buchert, Kurt Riedl
November–January	*Christmas Exhibition* All gallery artists

1992

17 March–4 April	*Of Crystals And Magnets (1)* Jesus Elisabeth Gu. Defner
30 April–21 May	*Contemporary Japanese Jewellery* Kazuhiro Itoh, Kimiaki Kageyama
6–15 October	*De Beer's European Diamond Jewellery Collection*
20 October–7 November	*Susan Cross, Barbara Tipple and Wally Gilbert*

10–27 November	*Contemporary Scandinavian Jewellery from Denmark, Finland, Iceland, Norway, Sweden* Millie Behrens, Ófeigur Björnsson, Karen Ihle, Jens Eliasen, Wolfgang Gessl, B. Malin Gunnarsson, Thorbergur Halldórsson, Ingjerd Hanevold, Juhani Heikkilä, Ulrik Jungersen, Jytte Kløve, Anders Olsson, Marita Carlborg Olsson, Heidi Sand, Sebastian Schildt, Sigrídur Anna Sigurdardóttir, Janna Syvänoja, Olli Tamminen
November–January	*Christmas Exhibition* All gallery artists

1993

2–20 March	*The Magic Of The Ring* Nurit Agur, Vicki Ambery-Smith, Malcolm Appleby, Malcolm Betts, Christoph Blum, Susan Cross, J. E. G. Defner, Peter de Wit, Lina Fanourakis, Gaby Felgenträger, Gerda Flöckinger, Dorothee Freese, Jivan, Helfried Kodré, Wilhelm Tasso Mattar, Roger Morris, Niessing, Johannes Oppermann, Paul Preston, Wendy Ramshaw, André Ribeiro, Gisela Seibert-Philippen, Richard Roney-Dougal, Uli Rossner, Sabine Strobel
27 April–15 May	*Toril Bjorg*
25 May–12 June	*Jean Hilger*
6 – 23 October	*Friedrich Becker, Hermann Jünger and Bruno Martinazzi*
November – January	*Christmas Exhibition* All gallery artists

1994

26 April – 14 May	*Niessing – The New Collection*
17 May – 4 June	*Wolfgang Skoluda*
7 – 25 June	*Alan Craxford*
4 – 22 October	*Elisabeth Holder, Helen Aitken-Kuhnen and Johannes Kuhnen*
November – January	*Christmas Exhibition* All gallery artists

1995

21 February – 11 March	*Architectural Gems* Vicki Ambery-Smith, Michael Becker, John Fuller, Hans Härtel
11 May – 3 June	*Torun*
6 – 24 June	*New Japanese Jewellery* Kazuhiro Itoh, Yasuki Hiramatsu, Aya Nakayama
3 – 21 October	*Paul Preston and Alan Ardiff*
24 October – 11 November	*J. E. G. Defner and Helfried Kodré*
November – January	*Christmas Exhibition* All gallery artists

1996

6 – 24 February	*Straight from the Heart – Valentine's Show* Pat Flynn, Daniela Mundt, Catherine Currell, Gerda Flöckinger, Catherine Mannheim, Jivan, Ute Münchinger, Thomas Schunk, Des Doyle
30 April – 18 May	*Six from Sweden* Lars Åsling, Cecilia Johansson, Margareta Selander, Charlotte Skalegard, Tore Svensson, Mona Wallström

20 June – 13 July	*The Innovators – Electrum's 25th Anniversary* Friedrich Becker, Hermann Jünger, Arline Fisch, Stanley Lechtzin, Giampaolo Babetto, Torun, Gerda Flöckinger, Wendy Ramshaw, David Watkins
17 October – 9 November	*Classic and Wild Earrings* K. Hali Baykov, Malcolm Betts, Emma Farquharson, Gerda Flöckinger, Bettina Hahn, Bryan Illsley, Petra Käser, Hilde Leiss, Catherine Mannheim, Alistair McCallum, Jacqueline Mina, Robert Pfrogner, Wendy Ramshaw, André Ribeiro, Marjorie Schick, Verena Sieber-Fuchs, Marc Tafler, Brigitte Turba, Tone Vigeland, Tamar Winter
November – January	*Christmas Exhibition* All gallery artists

1997

27 February – 21 March	*E.R. Nele*
29 April – 17 May	*Niessing – The 1997 Collection*
27 May – 14 June	*Nada Le Cavelier and Wolfgang Skoluda*
8 – 25 October	*Axel Russmeyer and Joyce Scott*
29 Oct – 15 November	*Arline Fisch*
November – January	*Christmas Exhibition* All gallery artists

1998

5 – 21 February	*The Colour Red* Jane Adam, Poppy Dandiya, J.E.G. Defner, Corinna Heller, Jivan, Carol Mather, Daniela Mundt, Niessing, Alexandra Raphael, Claire Robinson, Ruth Robinson, Axel Russmeyer, Brigitte Turba, Reiko Wanibuchi, Karen Whiterod
21 May – 13 June	*Norbert Muerrle*
4 – 26 September	*Inger Blix Kvammen*
30 October – 21 November	*Hilde Leiss and Jan Adam*
November – January	*Christmas Exhibition* All gallery artists

1999

29 January – 13 February	*Mark Woods and Rebecca Scott*
15 October – 6 November	*Noma Copley*
November – January	*Christmas Exhibition* All gallery artists

2000

15 March – 8 April	*The Spirit and The Context* Helge Berger, Marlies Braun, Silvia Bunke, Firma Catena, Galerie D'Or, Herbert Fischer, Snorre Flatheim, Petra Georg-Achenbach, Aninka Harms, Roland Grändorf, Batho Gündra, Ingrid Holtman, Claudia Horstmann-Kaiser, Langes and Ufer, Rolf Müller, Tom Munsteiner, Kurt Neukomm, Wolfgang Otterpohl, Torsten Reissmann, Barbara Schnöckel, Dietmar Sebastian, Janus Turek, Firma Wiehmeyer, Michael Zobel
26 May – 17 June	*Ulrike Bahrs*
8 – 30 September	*Gold – Contemporary Irish Jewellery Design* Siliena Coyle, Kevin Emanuel, Breda Haugh, Inga Reed, Celine Traynor

7 – 28 October	*Diverse Routes* Jane Adam, Jivan Astfalck, Norman Cherry, Maria Hanson, Terry Hunt
November – January	*Christmas Exhibition* All gallery artists

2001

23 February – 17 March	*Solos* Castello Hansen and Manuel Vilhena
27 April – 19 May	*Contemporary Jewellery from Austria* Alois Bauer, J. E. G. Defner, Andrea Maxa Halmschlager, Susanne Hammer, Margit Hart, Anna Heindl, Gabriele Kutschera, Fritz Maierhofer, Gertrud Pölzl, Martina Riegler, Katja Seitner
12 October – 3 November	*Inger Blix Kvammen and Lilian Busch*
November – January	*Christmas Exhibition* All gallery artists

2002

12 April – 4 May	*Metals and Method* Disa Allsopp, Nina Bukvic, Michael Carberry
10 – 31 May	*Amber – Gold of the North* Wilhelm Tasso Mattar, Michael Zobel, Giedymin Jabłoński
November – January	*Christmas Exhibition* All gallery artists

2003

11 July – 2 August	*Tom and Jutta Munsteiner*
3 – 25 October	*Axel Russmeyer*
November – January	*Christmas Exhibition* All gallery artists

2004

5 – 27 March	*Contemporary Jewellery from Japan* Noriko Asano, Masako Hamaguchi, Nagi Nakajima, Kazuko Nishibayashi, Michihiro Sato
7 – 29 May	*Anti-War Medals* Mike Abbott and Kim Ellwood, Alison Antelman, Hratch Babikian, Boris Baily, Brad Bartlett, Rosa Batalia, Brooke Battles, Jesse Bert, Heidi Bigknife, Nancy Blair, Rebecca Blankley, Richard Blue, Susan Brooks, Douglas Bucci, Emily Bullock, Helen Carnac, Tina Cartledge, Pierre Cavalan, Ellen Cheek, William Clark, Tracey Clement, Lori Colina-Lee, Deborah Corsini, Jennifer Cross-Gans, Paula Cunningham, Scott and Lisa Cylinder, Ann Davis, Sylvia de Murias, Kristin Diener, Jan Donaldson, Diana Dudek, Liisa Eckersberg, Glenna Fleiner, Autumn Dawn Griffiths, Joan Hammond, Amy Haskins, Anne Heinz, Tom Hill, Leonor Hipolito, Mike Holmes, Joyce Hulbert, Alison Hunt, Xavier Ines Monclus, Elaine Jek, Mary Frisbee Johnson, Masumi Kataoka, Linda Kaye-Moses, Guigui Kohon, Olga Kosica, Francisca Kweitel, Florian Ladstätter, Timothy Lazure, Marie Lechat, Kim Eric Lilot, Theresa Lovering-Brown, Susan Lowell, Deborah Lozier, Marcia MacDonald, Rita Marcangelo, Kelly Mann, Samuel Martinez Saavedra, Ashi Marwaha, Susanne Matsché, Agata Max, Jo McAllister, Judy McCaig, Anne Michie, Mike and Maaike, Christina Miller, Charlene Modena, Taweesak Moisawat, Wilhelm Tasso Mattar, Lucia Moure, Dawn Nakanishi, Suzanne Nayduch, Patty Nelson, Rita de Oliveira Ruivo, Olle Olls, Susanne Osborne, Kathryn Osgood, Monterrat Pascual Salat, Leslie Perrino, Jane Petrie, Hilary Pfeifer, Ingrid Psuty, Ramón Puig Cuyàs, Bruce Raper, Todd Reed, Susanne Remnant, Camille Rizzo, Diana Maria Rossi, Gerd Rothmann, Diana Serakos,

	Silvia Serra Albaladejo, Carla Shanks, Kristin Mitsu Shiga, Alison Shiboski, Jan Smith, Cathy Stafford, Sandi Stankov, Raif Stautner, Sherry Tesarik, Paula Morris Thomford, Timothy, Jen Townsend, Sarah Troper, Clara Vichi, Jeremy Waak, Maciek Walentowicz, Polly Wales, Silvia Walz, Heike Wanner, Jane Wells-Harrison, Donovan Widmer, Greg Wilbur, Jennifer Wolfe, Natasha Wozniak, Sally Wright, Yuko Yagisawa, Sayumi Yokouchi, Noel Yovovich, Diana Zeiler, Laura Zell
15 October – 6 November	*David Watkins*
November – January	*Christmas Exhibition* All gallery artists

2005

7 – 29 October	*Wendy Ramshaw, CBE, RDI*
November – January	*Christmas Exhibition* All gallery artists

2006

22 June – 15 July	*Midsummer Madness* – 35th Anniversary Show Jane Adam, Disa Allsopp, Hidemi Asano, Gijs Bakker, Malcolm Betts, Eylem Binboga, Inger Blix Kvammen, Flora Book, Angie Boothroyd, Nina Bukvic, Lilian Busch, Michael Carberry, Joanna Cave, Amanda Coleman, Emily Collins, Cynthia Cousens, Alan Craxford, Charlotte De Syllas, Joel Degen, Romy Derman, Mykala Djørup, Alison Evans, Emma Farquharson, Arline Fisch, Gerda Flöckinger, Gill Galloway-Whitehead, Grace Girvan, David Goodwin, Monica Guevara, Loekie Heintzberger, Sarah Herriot, Ulla Hornfeldt, Bryan Illsley, Katerina Ioannidis, Živa Jelnikar, Tanvi Kant, Sieglinde Karl-Spence, Sarah King, Josef Koppmann, Daphne Krinos, Hilde Leiss, Sarah Lyndsay, Edgar Maag, Catherine Mannheim, Sarah May Marshall, Carol Mather, Susan May, Irene Metaxatos, Noon Mitchelhill, Isgard Moje-Wohlgemuth, Malcolm Morris, Tom and Jutta Munsteiner, Lynne Kirstin Murray, Jo McAllister, E.R. Nele, Mark Nuell, Carla Nuis, Angela O'Kelly, Hiroko Okuzawa, Louise O'Neill, Felicity Peters, Robert Pfrogner, Paul Preston, Wendy Ramshaw, Alexandra Raphael, Ghita Ring, Zoe Robertson, Ruth Robinson, Kamilla Ruberg, Axel Russmeyer, Kayo Saito, Olivia Schlevogt, Lise Schønberg, Simone Selaib-Salandini, Christina Soubli, Lesley Strickland, Ruth Tomlinson, Clara Vichi, Elena Votsi, Polly Wales, Reiko Wanibuchi, David Watkins, Georgia Wiseman, Mark Woods, Michiyo Yoshida
November – January	*Christmas Exhibition* All gallery artists

2007

9 February – 3 March	*Vivid Colours* Katerina Ioannidis, Angela O'Kelly, Axel Russmeyer, Jennifer Trask
20 April – 12 May	*Gerda Flöckinger, CBE*
November – December	*Christmas Exhibition* All gallery artists

Electrum Gallery continued an exhibition programme under the new ownership of Contemporary Applied Arts, London, until finally closing its doors at the end of June 2012.

Biography
Bibliography

Biographical Timeline

1922	2 September: born Emma Feistmann in Berlin, Germany
1929–33	Attended Volksschule, Berlin
1933–6	Attended Waldschule Grunewald, Berlin
1936–8	Attended Landschulheim Caputh, near Potsdam in Brandenburg
1938	3 September: fled Berlin and travelled to Copenhagen
1938	6 December: arrived in England as a Jewish refugee, settled in London
1939	Studied life and fashion drawing at St Martin's School of Art, London; studied shorthand and typing at Pitman's College, London
1940–4	Worked as personal assistant to film maker, Alexander Korda and as administrator to home appliance manufacturer, Kelvinator
1944	9 September: married Derrick Cartlidge at St Pancras Town Hall, London
1944–56	Self-employed with Derrick Cartlidge for Homecord and Taxi-Trucks
1957–60	Studied jewellery making at Central School of Arts and Crafts, London
1960	Began as a freelance jewellery designer and maker
1971	Founded Electrum Gallery
1978	Appointed Freeman of the Worshipful Company of Goldsmiths and the City of London
2007	Retired as owner of Electrum Gallery; sold gallery to Contemporary Applied Arts, London

Exhibitions as Jeweller

1960	*Handmade Silver Jewellery by Barbara Cartlidge*, Heal's, London
1965	*Jewellery 65,* Ewan Phillips Gallery, Maddox Street, London
1966–70	Regular exhibitor, Design Centre, London
1969	*Development of Modern Jewellery*, Pace Gallery, London
1971	*Contemporary Jewellery,* Durham Light Infantry Museum and Art Centre
1971	*British Design,* Musée des Arts Décoratifs, Paris, France
1972	*Handwerksmesse,* Munich, Germany
1972	*Sierrad 1900–1972,* Museum De Zonnehof Museum, Amersfoort, The Netherlands
1973	*British Jewellery,* Deutsches Goldschmiedehaus, Hanau, Germany
1973	*Aspects of Jewellery,* Aberdeen Art Gallery
1973	*Things Remembered*, Electrum Gallery, London
1974	*Schmuckmesse Basle*, Basle, Switzerland
1975	Breede Gallery, Kiel, Germany
1977	*Doors*, Arkwright Arts Trust, London
1992–4	*Les Grandes Époques de la Bague,* Festival de L'Or (organised by the World Gold Council), Musée des Arts Décoratifs, Paris, France

Professional Activities

1971	Craft Advisory Committee, Goldsmiths' Hall, London
1977	External assessor and guest lecturer at Bezalel College, Jerusalem, Israel
1987	External assessor, Royal College of Art, London
1987	Jury member, international competition *Jewellery in Movement – Movement in Jewellery,* Hanau, Germany
1988	External assessor, Royal College of Art, London
1989	Jury member for award by the Bundesverband der Edelstein- und Diamantenindustrie e.V., Idar-Oberstein, Germany
1989	Panel member for symposium *Ornamentale Geschäfte,* Forum für Schmuck und Design, Schmuckmuseum, Pforzheim, Germany
1989–2001	Lecturer at Sotheby's, London
1990	Film commentary, *Zygosis*: *John Heartfield and the Political Image* (by Gavin Hodge and Tim Morrison)
1990	Jury member, *Jewellery as Sculpture – Sculpture as Jewellery*, National Gallery of Ireland, Dublin, Ireland
1990	Lecturer, National Gallery of Ireland, Dublin, Ireland
1990	Panel member for symposium at *Schmuck Europa 90,* Frankfurt, Germany
1991	Lecturer at Christie's, New York, for the Society of American Jewelry Historians, USA
1991	Lecturer on *Contemporary Japanese Jewellery* at Crafts Council, London
1992	Lecturer on *Electrum Gallery* at Central St Martin's School of Art, London
1993	Jury member for *Precious Metal Jewellery* at Irish Crafts Council, Dublin, Ireland
1993	Lecturer on *Contemporary Jewellery in Britain Today* for students of Mizuno College, Tokyo, Japan, held in London

Select Bibliography

Family correspondence and memoirs from the Cartlidge family archive, and unrecorded interviews with family, friends, colleagues and artist-jewellers are not listed individually but have been used extensively throughout the book.

Recorded Interviews with Barbara Cartlidge

Aston, Judith. Interview with Barbara Cartlidge: Director of Electrum Gallery, Royal College of Art, London, 20 November 1990.

Interview with Barbara Cartlidge about her amateur films in the IWM Film and Video Archive, Imperial War Museum, London, 2001 (21620).

Interview with Barbara Cartlidge about German Jewish Civilians in Germany and Denmark 1922–1938, Imperial War Museum, London, 2001 (21621).

Hughes, Hawksmoor. Interview with Barbara Cartlidge, British Library Sound Archive, London. October 2007–April 2008 (Ref. C 960/78).

Works by Barbara Cartlidge

Published works:

Cartlidge, Barbara. 'Posters from Poland', in *Design Journal*, 1968, pp. 35–7.

Cartlidge, Barbara. *Twentieth Century Jewelry*, Harry N. Abrams, New York, 1985.

Cartlidge, Barbara. 'Flying visit to Hanoi', in *News Bulletin of The Medical Aid Committee for Vietnam*, May 1985.

Cartlidge, Barbara. 'Contemporary Jewellery', in *British Arts & Antiques Yearbook 1986*, pp. 49–52.

Ward, Anne, John Cherry, Charlotte Gere and Barbara Cartlidge. *The Ring from Antiquity to the Twentieth Century,* Thames and Hudson, London, 1981.

Films:

Berlin Artists. Film made by Barbara Cartlidge, 1963. Imperial War Museum, London (MGH 4895).

Hampstead Artists. Film made by Barbara Cartlidge, 1963. Imperial War Museum, London (4896).

Vietnam-Medical Aid Committee for Vietnam: Visit at End of War. Film made by Barbara Cartlidge, May 1975, Imperial War Museum, London (4894).

Berlin in the 1920s

Friedrich, Otto. *Before the Deluge: A Portrait of Berlin in the 1920s*, Harper Perennial, 1995 (first published 1972).

Metzger, Rainer. *Berlin in the 1920s*, Harry N. Abrams, London, 2007 (first published 2006).

Peters, Olaf (ed.). *Berlin Metropolis: 1918–1933*, exhibition catalogue, 1 October 2015–4 January 2016, Neue Galerie, New York, 2015.

Pfeiffer, Ingrid. and Max Hollein (eds.). *Sturm-Frauen. Künstlerinnen der Avantgarde in Berlin 1910–1932*, Wienan Verlag, Frankfurt, 2015.

Roth, Joseph, translated by Michael Hofmann. *What I Saw: Reports from Berlin 1920-33*, Granta, London, 2013 (first published 1996 in German).

Willett, John. *The Weimar Years: A Culture Cut Short*, Thames and Hudson, London, 2011 (first published 1987).

A Liberal Jewish family

Adam, Ursula. *Helene Feistmann, Ich blieb eine Deutsche* (Jüdische Miniaturen, vol. 179), Hentrich & Hentrich, Berlin, 2016.

Berger, Manfred. 'Elisabeth Kitzinger (1881–1966) und die jüdische Wohlfahrtsarbeit in München (1904–1943)', in Angelika Baumann and Landeshauptstadt München (eds.), *Jüdisches Leben in München*, Buchendorfer Verlag, Munich, 1995, pp. 57–60.

Szkolny, Eugen. 'An Oberndoerffer Family History', digitized memoir from Leo Baeck Institute for Jewish History Memoir Collection, New York (www.lbi.org/collections/archives).

A Family in Exile

Badia, Gilbert. *Les bannis de Hitler: Accueil et luttes des exilés allemands en France 1933–1939,* Études et documentation internationals, Paris, 1984.

Bessel, Richard. *Life in the Third Reich*, Oxford University Press, Oxford, 2001 (first published 1987).

Herf, Jeffrey. *Divided Memory: The Nazi Past in the Two Germanys*, Harvard University Press, Cambridge MA and London, 1997.

Kießling, Wolfgang. *Exil in Lateinamerika*, Philipp Reclam Verlag, Leipzig, 1980.

Kießling, Wolfgang. *Partner im Narrenparadies: Der Freundeskreis um Noel Field und Paul Merker*, Dietz Verlag, Berlin, 1994.

Killough McClafferty, Carla. *In Defiance of Hitler: The Secret Mission of Varian Fry*, Farrar Straus Giroux, New York, 2008.

Miles, Jonathan. *The Dangerous Otto Katz: The Many Lives of a Soviet Spy*, Bloomsbury USA, New York, 2010.

Noack, Bernd. *Spurensuche: Eine Entdeckungsreise durch Fürth*, ars vivendi Verlag, Cadolzburg, 2013.

Stern, Guy. *Arno Reinfrank (1934–2001): Dichter aus der Pfalz im Exil – Autor der 'Poesie der Fakten'* (Jüdische Miniaturen, vol. 84), Hentrich & Hentrich, Potsdam, 2009.

Early Creativity at the Landschulheim Caputh

Berger, Manfred. *Gertrud Feiertag: Eine Wegbereiterin der modernen Erlebnispädagogik? Das Jüdische Kinder- und Landschulheim Caputh als Beispiel jüdischer Erziehung im Dritten Reich*, Verlag Ed. Erlebnispädagogik, Lüneburg, 2003.

Feidel-Mertz, Hildegard and Andreas Paetz. *Das Jüdische Kinder- und Landschulheim Caputh (1931–1938): Ein verlorenes Paradies*, Klinkhart, Bad Heilbrunn, 2009.

Friedländer, Sophie. Personal Papers and Interviews 1935–2006 (Document Collection 1733), The Wiener Library for the Study of the Holocaust and Genocide, London.

Friedländer, Sophie and Hilde Jarecki. *Sophie & Hilde: Ein gemeinsames Leben in Freundschaft und*

Beruf, Ein Zwillingsbuch, Edition Hentrich Druck, Berlin, 1996.

Rosenthal, Elizabeth. 'Sophie Friedländer', obituary in *The Guardian*, 20 April 2006.

Fleeing Germany

Benz, Wolfgang. *Flucht aus Deutschland. Zum Exil im 20. Jahrhundert*, dtv, Munich, 2001.

Wildt, Michael and Christoph Kreutzmüller (eds.). *Berlin 1933–1945*, Siedler Verlag, Munich, 2013.

Alone in Copenhagen

Unpublished letters between Barbara Cartlidge (then Emma Feistmann) and Luise Feistmann from the Cartlidge family archive.

Interview with Barbara Cartlidge about German Jewish Civilians in Germany and Denmark 1922–1938, Imperial War Museum, London, 2001 (21621).

Life as a Refugee in London

Benz, Wolfgang. *Flucht aus Deutschland. Zum Exil im 20. Jahrhundert*, dtv, Munich, 2001.

Berghahn, Marion. *Continental Britons: German-Jewish Refugees from Nazi-Germany*, Berghahn Books, New York and Oxford, 2011 (first published 2007).

Brinson, Charmian and Richard Dove. *Politics by other Means: The Free German League of Culture in London 1939–1945*, Vallentine Mitchell, London, 2010.

Brinson, Charmian and Richard Dove. *A Matter of Intelligence: MI5 and the Surveillance of Anti-Nazi Refugees 1933–1950*, Manchester University Press, Manchester, 2014.

Brinson, Charmian, Richard Dove, Marian Malet and Jennifer Taylor (eds.). *'England? Aber wo liegt es?': Deutsche und österreichische Emigranten in Grossbritannien 1933–1945*, Iudicium, Munich, 1996.

Brinson, Charmian and William Kaczynski. *Fleeing from the Führer. A Postal History of Refugees from the Nazis*, History Press, Stroud, 2011.

Dove, Richard. *Journey of No Return. Five German Speaking Literary Exiles in Britain, 1933–1945*, Libris, London, 2000.

Ebert, Hans. *René Graetz: Grafik und Plastik 1908–1974*, exhibition catalogue, August - October 1978, Staatliche Museen zu Berlin, Berlin, 1978.

Fleischhacker, Alfred with Stoecker, Holger. *Das war unser Leben: Erinnerungen und Dokumente zur Geschichte der Freien Deutschen Jugend in Großbritannien 1939–1946*, Verlag Neues Leben, Berlin, 1996.

Grenville, Anthony. *Jewish Refugees from Germany and Austria in Britain 1933–1970; Their Image in AJR Information*, Vallentine Mitchell, London and Portland Oregon, 2010.

Grenville, Anthony (ed.). *Refugees from the Third Reich in Britain* (The Yearbook of the Research Centre for German and Austrian Exile Studies, vol. 4), Rodopi, Amsterdam and New York, 2002.

Grenville, Anthony and Andrea Reiter (eds.). *'I didn't want to float; I wanted to belong to something': Refugee Organisations in Britain 1933–1945.* (The Yearbook of the Research Centre for German and Austrian Exile Studies, vol. 10), Rodopi, London, 2008.

Hitzer, Friedrich. *Aus alten Schulheften 1941–51*, Röderberg, Frankfurt am Main, 1985.

Krejsa, Michael. *Bildende Künstler im Exil: der Freie Deutsche Kulturbund (FDKB) in London und seine Maler-Sektion (1938–1946)*, in: *Aus Exil. Forschung, Erkenntnisse und Ergebnisse*, 30, 1, Frankfurt am Main, 2010.

Kriebel, Sabine T. *Revolutionary Beauty: The Radical Photomontages of John Heartfield*, University of California Press, Berkeley and Los Angeles, 2014.

Laqueur, Walter. *Generation Exodus. The Fate of Young Jewish Refugees from Nazi Germany*, I.B. Tauris, London, 2004.

London, Louise. *Whitehall and the Jews 1933–1948: British Immigration Policy, Jewish Refugees and the Holocaust*, Cambridge University Press, Cambridge, 2000.

Malet, Marian and Anthony Grenville. *Changing Countries: The Experience and Achievement of German-speaking Exiles from Hitler in Britain from 1933 to Today*, Libris, London, 2002.

McDougall, Alan. *Youth Politics in East Germany: The Free German Youth Movement 1946–1968* (Oxford Historical Monographs), Oxford University Press, Oxford, 2004.

Meyer, Beate, Hermann Simon and Chana Schütz (eds.). *Jews in Nazi Berlin. From Kristallnacht to Liberation*, University of Chicago Press, Chicago and London, 2009.

Pachnicke, Peter and Klaus Honnef. *John Heartfield*, Harry N. Abrams, New York 1992.

Prager, Peter. *From Berlin to England and Back: Experiences of a Jewish Berliner* (The Library of Holocaust Testimonies), Vallentine Mitchell, London and Portland, 2002.

Schleifstein, Joseph and Hans Fladung. *Erfahrungen: Vom Kaiserreich zur Bundesrepublik*, Röderberg, Frankfurt am Main, 1986.

Shaw, Elizabeth. *Wie ich nach Berlin kam: Eine Irin in der geteilten Stadt*, Verlag für Berlin-Brandenburg, Berlin-Brandenburg, 2013.

Willett, John. *Heartfield versus Hitler*, Hazan Editeur, Paris, 1997.

Winder, Robert. *Bloody Foreigners. The Story of Immigration to Britain*, Abacus, London, 2013 (first published 2004).

An Unusual Love Affair

Cartlidge, Derrick. *Wild Oats and the Wooden Pillow*, The Twenty Two Press, London, 2004.

Cartlidge, Derrick. 'Best of Times, Worst of Times: Derrick Cartlidge', in *The Sunday Times*, 6 March 2005.

Hutton, Mike. *The Story of Soho: The Windmill Years 1932–1964*, Amberley Publishing, Stroud, 2012.

Making a Living

Unpublished letters between Barbara Cartlidge and Luise Feistmann from the Cartlidge family archive.

A Political Conscience

Brie, Horst. *Erinnerungen eines linken Weltbürgers*, Dietz Verlag, Berlin, 2006.

Kuczynski, Jürgen. *'Ein linientreuer Dissident': Memoiren 1945–1989*, Aufbau, Berlin, 1994.

Lidgard, Peter. 'Our Work in 1985', in *Vietnam Laos Cambodia, Medical and Scientific News Bulletin*, no. 185, February 2016, p. 3.

Shellard, E. J. 'Medical & Scientific Aid for Vietnam Laos & Cambodia: Twenty Five Years of Devoted Support 1965–1990', in *Vietnam Laos Cambodia, Medical and Scientific News Bulletin*, 1990.

A Jeweller Emerges

Davenport, Tarby. 'Craftsmen in modern jewellery', in *Design Journal*, 1967, pp. 33–7.

'Do-it-Yourself Silverware: Mrs. Cartlidge', in *The Hampstead News*, 12 August 1960.

Lesley, Tamsin. 'Striking it rich', in *Harper's Bazaar*, June 1968, p. 32.

Pace Gallery exhibition booklet, November 1969.

Electrum Gallery

Adler, Claire. 'Barbara Cartlidge: The Electrum Gallery', in *j-dex, The Jewellery Trade Directory*, March 2004, p. 46.

Aston, Judith. Interview with Barbara Cartlidge: Director of Electrum Gallery, Royal College of Art, London, 20 November 1990.

Broadhead, Caroline. 'Ralph Turner: Upstart from the Valleys, Living National Treasure – an occasional series', in *The Association of Contemporary Jewellery's Quarterly Newsletter*, December 2005, p. 3.

Callaghan, Sarah. 'Electrum', in *Goldsmiths Review*, 1991/2, pp. 32–4.

'Electrum Gallery', in *Goldschmiedezeitung*, 2, 1992, pp. 106–8.

Evans, James B. 'Silver and Electrum', in *Metalsmith*, Spring 1997, no. 2, pp. 22–8.

Gray, Ilse. 'Precious Plastics at the Electrum', in *Design Journal*, 1971, pp. 36–7.

Jammers, Judith. 'Eine schreckliche Optimistin. Über Leben und Werk der Schmuckdesignerin und Galeristin Barbara Cartlidge', in *Die Süddeutsche Zeitung*, no. 256, 6 November 1998.

Lakin, D. Malcolm. 'Profile. An interview with Barbara Cartlidge, the director and founder of London's Electrum Gallery', in *Aurum* (English edition), 7, 1981, pp. 23–9.

'New Outlet for Artists', in *Country Life*, July 8, 1971.

Pinto, José. Forum for the Avant-Garde of Jewelry, 35 Years of the Electrum Gallery in London, in: Goldschmiedezeitung Art + Design, 2, 2006, pp. 18–9.

Sanders, Beverly. 'Electrum Gallery', in *American Craft*, 1981, pp. 26–8.

Turner, Ralph. 'Schmuck-Stiefkind der Kunst', in *Goldschmiedezeitung*, 5, 1973, pp. 32–5.

Turner, Ralph. 'Electrum Gallery – London', in *Gem Craft*, May 1974, pp. 68–71.

Wilson, Muriel. 'Living National Treasures – 1: Barbara Cartlidge', in *The Association of Contemporary Jewellery's Quarterly Newsletter*, Issue 6, Winter 1999, pp. 3–4.

Epilogue: The Cartlidge Family

Donnelley, Paul. *Fade to Black: A Book of Movie Obituaries*, Omnibus Press, 2005 (first published 2000).

Katrin Cartlidge Collection, British Film Institute, London.

Leigh, Mike. 'We have lost a great actor', obituary in *The Guardian*, 13 September 2002.

www.cartlidgeandbrowne.com

www.dancingcrow.com

www.katrincartlidgefoundation.org.uk

www.michellecartlidge.com

Books on Contemporary Jewellery

Astfalck, Jivan, Caroline Broadhead and Paul Derrez. *New Directions in Jewellery*, Black Dog Publishing, London, 2005.

Besten, Liesbeth den. *On Jewellery: A Compendium of International Contemporary Art Jewellery*, Arnoldsche, Stuttgart, 2012.

Cheung, Lin, Beccy Clarke and Indigo Clarke. *New Directions in Jewellery II*, Black Dog Publishing, London, 2006.

Dormer, Peter and Ralph Turner. *The New Jewelry: Trends + Traditions*, London, 1994 (first published 1985).

Drutt English, Helen W. and Peter Dormer, *Jewelry of Our Time: Art, Ornament and Obsession*, Thames and Hudson, London, 1995.

Falk, Fritz and Cornelie Holzach, translated by Barbara Cartlidge. *Schmuck der Moderne / Modern Jewellery 1960–1998*, Arnoldsche, Stuttgart, 1999.

Heigl, Kurt. *Gold+Silber Schmuck + Gerät von Albrecht Dürer bis zur Gegenwart*, exhibition catalogue, 19 March–22 August 1971, Verlag Karl M. Lipp, Nuremberg, 1971.

Erlhoff, Michael, Fritz Falk, Jens-Rüdiger Lorenzen, Wilhelm Mattar and Sabine Strobel (eds.). *Ornamenta 1*, exhibition catalogue, Schmuckmuseum Pforzheim, Munich, 1989.

Ransome Wallace, Rosemary. *Treasures of the 20th Century: Silver, jewellery and art medals from the 20th Century Collection of the Worshipful Company of Goldsmiths*, exhibition catalogue, The Goldsmiths' Company, London, 2000.

Schollmayer, Karl. *Neuer Schmuck: Ornamentum Humanum*, Wasmuth, Tübingen, 1974.

Strauss, Cindi. *Ornament as Art. Avant-garde Jewelry from the Helen Williams Drutt Collection*. The Museum of Fine Arts, Houston, Arnoldsche, Stuttgart, 2007.

Turner, Ralph. *Contemporary Jewelry. A Critical Assessment 1945–1975*, Studio Vista, London 1976.

Turner, Ralph. *Jewelry in Europe and America: New Times, New Thinking*, Thames and Hudson, London 1996.

Walgrave, Jan. *The Ego Adorned: 20th Century Artists' Jewellery*, exhibition catalogue, Koningin Fabiolazaal Antwerp, Antwerp, 2000.

Authors' Biographies

Beatriz Chadour-Sampson is an international and established jewellery historian, scholarly author and lecturer. Her extensive publications range from Antiquity to the present day. These include her doctoral thesis on the Italian goldsmith Antonio Gentili da Faenza (1980) and works about the jewellery collection of the Museum für Angewandte Kunst, Cologne (1985), the gold treasure from the Nuestra Señora de la Concepción (1991) and 2000 finger rings from the Alice and Louis Koch Collection, Switzerland (1994). She continues to be curator of this ring collection and consultant to the Swiss National Museum, Zurich, where it is on loan. Her publications reflect a particular interest in contemporary jewellery including a retrospective of the artist in jewellery David Watkins. She was the consultant curator in the re-designing of the William and Judith Bollinger Jewellery Gallery at the Victoria and Albert Museum, London and also guest curator of the *Pearls* exhibition (2013/4). Associate member of The Goldsmiths' Company, London.

Janice Hosegood is a passionate authority in contemporary jewellery. She worked with Barbara Cartlidge as her Manager at Electrum Gallery from 1987 to 2009. Involved with the very best of British and international jewellery designers, she built up her expertise in curating exhibitions, managing special commissions and overseeing one of the most important platforms for showcasing talented craftsmen and women. Since 2007, Janice has developed her own consultancy and applied her experience to many varied projects. She has made significant contributions to various companies and organisations including The Goldsmiths' Company, Crafts Council, Victoria and Albert Museum and Ruthin Crafts Centre. She has taught at The Royal College of Art, City Lit and been a guest speaker for Jerwood and Hidden Art Cornwall.

Picture Credits

All images from *Barbara Cartlidge: Life and Work* are from the Cartlidge family archive unless otherwise stated.

All images from *Barbara Cartlidge and Electrum Gallery* have been provided by the contributing artist-jewellers, who are responsible for copyright unless otherwise stated.

Terje Agnalt: p. 109

Alice and Louis Koch Collection, Swiss National Museum, Zurich: pp. 57 bottom, 120, 158, 170, 232

AntFarm Photography, NYC: p. 143

Simon B. Armitt: pp. 119 top, 123

Gijs Bakker: p. 249

Rien Bazen: p. 104

Lazlo Becket: p. 149

Elke Bock: pp. 55–6, 61, 65 top and bottom right, 72 centre, bottom left and right, 73, 173, 244–5

Peter Boyce: p. 79

bpk, Berlin: p. 13

Breede Collection, Kiel: p. 210–1

Ray Carpenter: p. 67

Barbara Cartlidge: pp. 151, 226, 270

Cartlidge Collection / Courtesy of LACMA, Los Angeles: p. 248

Giustino Chemello VI: p. 103

Christopher Christodoulou: p. 136

Chris Connors: p. 169

Helen Craig: pp. 2, 10, 49, 51, 284

Bob Cramp: p. 231

Guri Dahl / The National Museum of Art, Architecture and Design, Oslo: pp. 252–3

Joel Degen: pp. 120, 180–1, 230

Didier Ltd, London: pp. 155, 157, 233

David Ellis: p. 119 bottom

Liv Engholm: p. 185

Dan Fox: p. 167

Sylvain Georget and Federico Pazienza: p. 105

William Gullette: p. 129 top

Jacqui Gray / Gråsilver: pp. 246–7

Lars Gundersen: p. 138

Heal & Son Ltd, London: p. 52

Matthias Hoffmann: pp. 100, 107, 121 top, 146–7, 159, 228–9

Rob Jewell: p. 96

Jeremy Johns: p. 148

Daniella Kerner: pp. 186–7

Tony Latham: p. 177

A. Laurenzo: p. 115

Lichtblick / Cullmann: p. 212

Neil Mason: pp. 204–5

The Museum of Fine Arts, Houston: p. 199

Sophie Mutevelian / Contemporary Applied Arts, London: p. 168

Andra Nelki: pp. 202–3

Geoff Onyett: pp. 236–7

Jörg Rodighiero: p. 213

RSV Collection: p. 106

Lene Stavå: p. 183

Franco Storti: p. 257

Studio Miko: pp. 188–9

Philippa Swann: p. 101 top

Jean Thomas: p. 227

Todd-White / Crafts Council, London: pp. 145, 265

Lorenzo Trento: p. 102

Paul Tucker: pp. 262–3.

The Victoria and Albert Museum, London: pp. 64, 65 bottom left

Jay Watson: p. 135

Peter White / FXP: p. 197

Michael Wolchover: p. 121 bottom

Zoltan Wegner: p. 37

The Worshipful Company of Goldsmiths, London: p. 267

Doug Yaple: p. 165

Authors
Beatriz Chadour-Sampson
Janice Hosegood

Editor
Sophie Lee

Project coordinator
Matthias Becher

Graphic designer
Petra Lüer, Munich

Offset reproductions
Repromayer, Reutlingen

Printed by
Gorenjski tisk, Kranj

Paper
170 gsm Core Silk

Bibliographic information published by the Deutsche Nationalbibliothek
The Deutsche Nationalbibliothek lists this publication in the Deutsche Nationalbibliografie; detailed bibliographic data are available on the Internet at www.dnb.de.

ISBN 978-3-89790-470-5

Made in Europe, 2016

Cover illustrations
front: Barbara Cartlidge, pendant, c.1967, silver, agate. Photo copyright: © Victoria and Albert Museum, London.
back, from top to bottom:
Wendy Ramshaw, ringset with 7 rings, see pp. 230–1
Lina Peterson, 'Shavings' brooch, see p. 221
Claus Bury, brooch, see p. 115
Paul Preston, 'Mole in Coat of Many Colours' brooch, see pp. 226–7

Introductory illustrations
p. 2, Barbara Cartlidge, c.1960
p. 10, Barbara Cartlidge, c.1960
p. 270, Electrum Gallery, 1996
p. 284, Barbara Cartlidge, c.1980

This book has been produced with the generous support of The Goldsmiths' Company.

The
GOLDSMITHS'
Company